Atonement

Atonement

God's Means of Effecting Man's Reconciliation

Chris Woodall

WIPF & STOCK · Eugene, Oregon

ATONEMENT
God's Means of Effecting Man's Reconciliation

Copyright © 2015 Chris Woodall. All rights reserved. Except for brief quotations in critical publications or reviews, no part of this book may be reproduced in any manner without prior written permission from the publisher. Write: Permissions, Wipf and Stock Publishers, 199 W. 8th Ave., Suite 3, Eugene, OR 97401.

Wipf and Stock
An Imprint of Wipf and Stock Publishers
199 W. 8th Ave., Suite 3
Eugene, OR 97401

www.wipfandstock.com

ISBN 13: 978-1-4982-0795-9

Manufactured in the U.S.A. 01/21/2015

All Scripture quotations, unless otherwise indicated, are taken from the Holy Bible, New International Version, NIV, copyright © 1973, 1978, 1984 by Biblica, Inc. Used by permission of Zondervan. All rights reserved worldwide.

Scripture quotations marked Amplified are taken from the Amplified Bible, copyright © 1954, 1958, 1962, 1964, 1965, 1987 by the Lockman Foundation, La Habra, CA 90631. Used by permission.

Scripture quotations marked ASV are taken from the American Standard Version, copyright expired.

Scripture quotations marked Darby are taken from The Holy Scriptures: A New Translation from the Original Languages by John Nelson Darby, copyright expired.

Scripture quotations marked ERV are taken from the English Revised Version, copyright expired.

Scripture quotations marked KJV are taken from the King James (Authorized) Version (crown copyright).

Scripture quotations marked (The) Message are taken from Eugene H. Peterson's translation of the same name, copyright © 1993, 1994, 1995, 1996, 2000, 2001, 2002. Used by permission of NavPress Publishing Group.

Scripture quotations marked NASB are taken from the New American Standard Bible, copyright © 1960, 1962, 1963, 1968, 1971, 1972 by the Lockman Foundation, La Habra, CA 90631. Used by permission.

Scripture quotations marked NLT are taken from the New Living Translation, copyright © 1996, 2004, 2007. Used by permission of Tyndale House Publishers Inc., Carol Stream, IL 60188. All rights reserved.

Scripture quotations marked RSV are taken from the Revised Standard Version, copyright © 1946, 1952, 1971, 1973 by the Division of Christian Education of the National Council of Churches of Christ in the USA. Used by permission.

Scripture quotations marked Weymouth are taken from the Weymouth New Testament, copyright expired.

Contents

Acknowledgment | vii
Introduction | ix

1 The Necessity of the Atonement | 1

2 The Reality of the Atonement | 60

3 The Benefits of the Atonement | 123

Conclusion | 203
Bibliography | 207

Acknowledgment

Thank God for Jesus!

Introduction

Theology and history, though vastly different disciplines, also share some remarkable similarities. Quite apart from the fact that each may provide the potential basis for studying the other, so that it is possible to speak both of the theology of history and the history of theology, they are equally prone to subjectivism, depending upon the bias of the interpreter. The study of Scripture, even by eminent theologians of the same general persuasion, has almost invariably produced excessively wide-ranging results. We need only to examine the works of Bavinck[1] and Barth,[2] on the one hand, or Schleiermacher[3] and Strong,[4] on the other, for evidence of this.

In terms of theology, the Christian church has generally struggled to maintain a proper balance between its role inwardly and that externally. Consequently, its history has displayed evidence of two extremes, neither of which have managed to do full justice to the biblical presentation of its function in society. It has been laudable in many ways, especially in times such as our own, for an emphasis toward mission, evangelism, and social interaction in an environment that is largely hostile, dominated by unbelief, and reliant upon so many forms of false ideologies, to be perceived as the more pressing need. The very nature of that urgency, however, surely demands that in the midst of such a turbulent infrastructure, the church—more than at any other time in history—must itself be thoroughly cognizant and absolutely coherent in the message it seeks to proclaim.

The constant danger in embarking upon a work such as this is that we allow ourselves to elevate the intellect to such a position of authority that we effectively thereby subject God, his nature, and his dealings with us to its perceived supremacy. That our comprehension is itself conditioned

1. Bavinck, *Doctrine of God*.
2. Barth, *Church Dogmatics*.
3. Schleiermacher, *Christian Faith*.
4. Strong, *Systematic Theology*.

by the time/space continuum in which it exists is but one example of the potential folly of such an approach. But God has made some things plain to us, primarily—though not exclusively—through the revelation of his Word.

Scripture's presentation of the gospel message is intrinsically disagreeable. It does not initially soothe man or comfort him or reassure him in his path, but violently opposes the anthropocentric conditioning of his mind, which is universally bound in slavery to the sinful nature. Where divine truth grapples with human deceit, the natural instinct of conservation within man causes him to hide behind his misconception of self-sufficiency, self-congratulatory achievement, and pseudo-religiosity in order to protect and preserve against the divine charge. The Word of God and the mind of man are diametrically opposed and only the Spirit of God can unite them by imparting faith. In much the same way, God's holiness and man's unrighteousness can only be bridged by the central theme of this work: the atonement of God's Son, Christ Jesus.

The enigma faced by anyone who tackles a subject like this is that the same question can be asked from within either an anthropological or a theological framework, with not necessarily comparable results. The approach I have tried to sustain has tended more toward anthropology, but from a particularly theocentric position. I readily acknowledge the difficulties this may present to some, even those of my closest friends and from backgrounds not dissimilar to my own, but—in this case—I believe the means are justified by the end. The message of the Bible is such that God is the center, root, foundation, and cause of all things. To Christians, this is not an oracle to which we are encouraged to proffer mere mental assent, but we are required to demonstrate the truth of such a doctrine in the practicalities of how we conduct our lives.

One has only to pick up any work bearing the title *Systematic Theology* to discover the vast array of theories surrounding the different aspects of the atonement, each purporting to rely on the testimony of the Bible in support of its analysis. Although the very idea of theology allows for a certain degree of mystery to be maintained, I would nevertheless claim that not everyone has made the best application of that which God has sovereignly and graciously chosen to reveal to us through his Word.

That notwithstanding, however, it has been both satisfying and rewarding to find my conclusions generally confirmed by such scholarly masters as Berkhof,[5] Brunner,[6] Hammond,[7] Lloyd-Jones,[8] and Grudem,[9] for all of whom I have the utmost respect. But I have also been surprisingly challenged by the provocation of men like Pannenberg,[10] Dabney,[11] Hodge,[12] Smith,[13] and Bonhoeffer,[14] whose approach to the role of the atonement lays less stress on its necessity than that of God's means of fulfilling his purpose for creation.

Because of the stimulation to search extensively beyond the parameters of my normal reading circle, I have discovered that each differing view is substantially preconditioned by a partiality that often owes more to constitutional allegiance than to an entirely unprejudiced desire to explore the Scriptures. What I mean is this: those who feel most comfortable with the general observations of someone like John Calvin will usually have their intellect predetermined to read the Bible and interpret it from a purely Calvinistic tradition, as will those who slavishly follow Luther, Arminius, the Council of Trent, or the Heidelberg Confession. It is precisely this kind of bias that I propose to address and correct by presenting an appropriate understanding of the centrality of the atonement, which must begin and end with what Scripture actually says.

Of course, this same argument could be employed in the defense of any doctrine, not just the atonement. I do feel, however, that the implications are so far-reaching, the dangers of neglect so perilous, and the advantages of getting it right so bountiful that the primacy of the atonement to Christianity—and, indeed, to humanity—deserves our foremost attention. The reality of the atonement as a fact in history can only properly be grasped in the light of its absolute necessity and the subsequent benefits arising from it, which will be dealt with as separate chapters of this work.

---

5. Berkhof, *Systematic Theology*.
6. Brunner, *The Mediator*.
7. Hammond, *In Understanding*.
8. Lloyd-Jones, *Atonement and Justification*.
9. Grudem, *Systematic Theology*.
10. Pannenberg, *What is Man?*
11. Dabney, *Systematic Theology*.
12. Hodge, *The Atonement*.
13. Smith, *The Atonement*.
14. Bonhoeffer, *Creation and Temptation*.

1

The Necessity of the Atonement

Although the necessity of the atonement is not the crux of the matter before us—that accolade belongs wholly and unreservedly to its reality—why the atonement became necessary is vital to our, albeit limited, understanding. Otherwise, the death of Jesus was simply a gross miscarriage of justice, not unlike so many others before and since. The biblical evidence and the testimony of millions of Christians over the past couple of millennia are such that it was clearly much more than that. The atonement was, in fact, the unfolding of a divinely initiated plan of redemption for humanity and beyond.

Here, it becomes necessary for us to grasp something of the difference between plan and purpose, for they are not synonymous terms. Perhaps it would help if we thought of purpose as destination and regarded the plan as the designated journey to be taken toward that destination. Thus, God's purpose for creation is his pre-determined arrival point for us. This is fixed and beyond being disturbed, changed, or otherwise affected. His plan, on the other hand, is merely his preferred choice of the means by which we should come to that unalterable objective. To suggest or imply that God's original plan was thwarted, however, is to misapply our finite understanding to matters of an ultimately incomprehensible nature. What we may say with some degree of certainty is that the entrance of sin into man's domain necessitated a course of action that would not have been otherwise required had Adam not rendered it so.

But it is equally important that we recognize this not so much in that the atonement was as good an idea as any to resolve an awkward problem. Nor was God systematically working through a whole catalogue of potential solutions until he stumbled across one that actually worked or seemed to be the pick of the crop. The atonement effected by the substitutionary sacrifice of God's Son could not have been attained in any other way. Thus, not only was the atonement itself necessary, but the means chosen to bring it about was exclusively so.

In this section, we shall begin by looking at man—in its generic sense—as the pinnacle of God's creation and in a state of original righteousness, as created. We will then turn our attention to the fall of Adam and the effects that had upon, not only himself, but also in relation to his race and his environment. It is in many ways a tragic story, but it must readily be conceded that the darkness of such tragedy makes the glory of the atonement necessitated by it shine all the more brightly, as we shall see in due course.

MAN—THE PINNACLE OF GOD'S CREATION

The subject of anthropology is one that naturally lends itself to being considered from a biblical perspective. Although humanity has often been viewed from an entirely philosophical vantage point, the scriptural data referring to human nature ideally must be acknowledged as taking place within the larger framework of man's role in creation. Of course, any dogma is ultimately dependent upon and governed by the particular bias of those who propose such a conviction. In this respect, biblical anthropology makes no claim to be any different, for the fundamental catalyst of Christian doctrine is its dogged determination to hold firmly to the authority of the Bible in matters of faith. Thus, the unveiling of the mysteries of creation—and, for that matter, restoration—are not, in the final analysis, subject to the enquiring mind so much as to the believing heart. The key is not a scientific approach, but a faithful attitude.

The Creation of Mankind

Although it is true that creation accounts are not unique to Scripture, it must also be pointed out that concepts with a mutual theme need not necessarily be produced from a kindred source. Many of the ancient peoples believed in a pre-existent divine being who brought about the creation of the cosmos by a verbal command. That man is regarded as the pinnacle of such an effect and that he bears in some measure the reflected personality of his Master is similarly widespread. When we isolate the Genesis representation from other contemporary narratives, however, many of them share comparatively little else in common. One apparent exception is that of the *Babylonian Chronicles*. Such is the similarity between the two that a number of learned scholars have seen them as the potential source for their Hebrew counterpart, though more recent discoveries have demonstrated this idea to be totally without foundation.

The *Atrakhasis Epic*, again from early Babylonian literature, shares some features with the Genesis account concerning the origin of man, his stewardship role over the created order, and the destruction of all but one family by universal deluge. However, the differences between the two are, again, far more significant than their apparent similarities. *Atrakhasis* is devoid of any specific moral instruction, it presents man as having been designed for toil from the onset, it distances itself from the idea of a distinct act of creating womanhood, makes no mention of either Eden or the fall, and generally seems to suggest that man is but a plaything in the hands of an impersonal deity.

In an age where there is an almost unprecedented desire for—or, at least, the capacity to acquire—knowledge, a longing for enlightenment, and a yearning for some modicum of stability and permanence, only to find that quest impeded by the inherent falseness of human nature, disillusionment, change, and decay, it is good to remind ourselves that the Bible presents man as created in the image of God. (It goes without saying that our concept of that image is often conditioned by our perception of God.) Without this assurance, any enquiry into the destiny and purpose of humanity appears to be futile in the extreme. This *imago Dei* consists primarily in the fact that man was created with the original intention of reflecting the personality and spirituality of God in the earth. As such, he had the capability to become active in deliberate spiritual, intellectual, and moral pursuits. He was also in a position to represent the glory of God's communicable attributes. Flawless intellect, equitable probity, and an as yet untarnished relationship with his Maker set man aside as clearly unique from all other creatures.

The late David Watson beautifully and concisely alludes to this distinctiveness of man in contrast to the rest of the created order. He speaks of man's exclusive creation in the image of God in terms of him:

> . . . [having] at least five characteristics which are not shared by the rest of the animal creation. Man can reason, with the powers of reflection; choose, as a free agent; love, consciously preferring one before another; and, above all, worship God and know God; and he is personally responsible to his Creator. He is meant to live in complete dependence upon God. Indeed, the whole point of the Genesis 1 account of creation is that man is seen, not as the ape, but as the apex of creation . . . Further, God has made

man with a large spiritual appetite, which cannot be satisfied with anything less than himself.[1]

It is also perhaps worthy of mention that the tonal content of God's deliberation to create man differs considerably from that of the rest of creation. Where previously the mere word of command was both sufficient and appropriate to effect the bringing into being of water, sky, stars, and living creatures, the dignity afforded one created in his image required divine consultation (Gen 1:26). Many commentators have alluded to this verse in support of the argument for the doctrine of the Trinity, and rightly so. It is not just the "Let *us* . . ." but also "in *our* image." Of course, it could be reasoned that this would have been necessarily redundant elsewhere, because of nothing else is it said to have been created in God's image. But neither is there the same intimation of consultation. The Father decided and spoke the word, which effected the desired objective. It may well have been that the spoken command was but the enacting of a decision already agreed upon in the predetermined counsel of the Godhead. But surely that was true of the creation of man; it could hardly have been a whim on the spur of the eternal moment: "Do you know what would be a good idea now, guys, and I'm surprised we didn't think of it before?" No, there is honor attached to the creation of man, reinforced by the idea of him being the subject of divine counsel.

It is clear from the biblical revelation, then, that man is the zenith of God's creation. In the Genesis account, the Hebrew verb *bara* (that is, "to create") is employed. On the six occasions where we find this, three of them relate to man as created in the image of God, the climax to all that had preceded this momentous act. Although there is an acknowledged difficulty in being able to comprehend the very idea of One who is essentially Spirit being represented in such a tangible form, I am particularly indebted to the literary expertise of Alec Motyer for his clarifying matters thus:

> At all events, the emphasis in the creative act rests on the novelty that now for the first time the divine image is seen in the creature. The words used, *image* (*selem*) and *likeness* (*demuth*), have an undoubted reference to outward form, (eg 1 Sam 6:5; 2 Kgs 16:10), and we must not resist the implication that while God is Spirit (Isa 21:3) and outward appearance does not belong to his essence, yet there is an outward appearance which is suitable to the glory of God, (eg Num 12:8), and in this likeness man was

---

1. Watson, *In Search of God*, 45.

created. This affords a basis for the dignity which Scripture ever accords to the human body.[2]

The early church fathers drew a distinction between "image" and "likeness" as referring to bodily characteristics and spirituality respectively. The biblical evidence, however, is such that the two words seem to be used almost interchangeably. Moreover, their employment appears to suggest that not only does man *bear* God's image (1 Cor 15:49), but also that he actually *is* his image (11:7). The image of God in man includes original righteousness—renewable in Christ as true knowledge (Col 3:10)—and holiness (Eph 4:24). This is often spoken of as the moral image of God.

The image of God in man also possesses elements that belong equally to the unregenerate as part of his natural constitution. Although tainted with sin in both their effect and efficiency, there are yet traces of intellectual capacity, natural affections, and moral freedom in all of mankind. Man would cease to be man, for instance, if he were to lose his power of reason, so essential is it to his being. Indeed, Scripture is apt to discuss humanity, even after the fall, as maintaining its representation of God's image (see Gen 9:6; Jas 3:9). The existence of spirituality within man, though often finding expression in idolatrous pursuits and pagan worship, is further evidence that eternity has been set within our hearts (Eccl 3:11). Even our—albeit limited—ability to relate to others, the inclination to create objects of beauty, and a disposition to rule over the created order, though all subject to abuse and ill motives, are nonetheless remnants of the fact that in some small measure, at least, the image of God can yet be traced in the fallen nature of mankind.

I have repeatedly cautioned against the temptation to speculate on matters where Scripture is generally silent. This is not to say, however, that the reasoned deduction of issues by applying known principles is entirely unavailable to us. In the case before us, it is possible to arrive at a reasonable conclusion of what Scripture might mean by the image of God in man by eliminating those definitions that it cannot mean. As we have seen, because God is essentially and necessarily Spirit, it cannot refer to likeness of bodily form *per se*. Nor does it relate exclusively to man's invested authority as vice-regent over the rest of the created order. Similarly, the idea that God's proclamation of man as "very good" can only be regarded as such in view of his design being of divine origin. Man—even in the state of original righteousness—possessed no inherent goodness outside of that relationship.

---

2. J. A. Motyer, "Old Testament Theology," in Guthrie and Moyer, *New Bible Commentary*, 27.

Any goodness in pre-fallen Adam was derived; it was not a product of any perceived self-sufficiency.

Although there exists an obviously exclusive relationship between God and man, this must not be allowed to overshadow the fact of man's inherent creatureliness. A noteworthy consideration in the biblical account of the creation of Adam, for instance, is that in stark contrast to the universe, he was not strictly *creatio ex nihilo*. Whereas the implication of Genesis is that "God created the heavens and the earth" (1:1) out of nothing (that is, from no other pre-existent material), man is clearly recorded in Scripture as having been "formed . . . from the dust of the ground" (2:7). Ronald Gregor Smith offers a balanced analysis when he says that:

> The Christian doctrine of creation is rather obscure, at least in its positive implications. But what makes it quite clear is the negative—the negation of sameness: the Creator and the creatures are not the same. The link connecting them is the grace of the Creator. Creatures are what they are not by virtue of a sameness of being with the Creator, but in virtue of the grace of the Creator. Nevertheless, it is unnecessary to conclude from this that there is no analogy between the Creator and the creatures. If there were no analogy . . . there could not even be an understanding of grace. Grace is paramount in the creaturely situation . . . [but] the paramountcy of grace does not mean the exclusion of a sufficient participation by way of an analogy of being. Grace, to be understood, requires an analogy of being. It is hardly necessary to add that an analogy is always a link indicating difference as well as likeness.[3]

In his excellent treatment on the subject, Emil Brunner has the following to say:

> The original biblical word "creation" means first of all that there is an impassable gulf between the Creator and the creature, that for ever they stand over against one another in a relation which can never be altered. There is no greater sense of distance than that which lies in the words Creator—creation. Now this is the first and the fundamental thing which can be said about man: He is a creature, and as such he is separated by an abyss from the divine manner of being. The greatest dissimilarity between two things which we can express at all . . . is that between the Creator and that which is created. For all other dissimilarities . . . are related to that which has been created, and thus they

---

3. Smith, *Doctrine of God*, 103.

are included in the fundamental similarity which they possess as that which has been created. God, however, is the Uncreate, the Creator. Man, whatever may distinguish him from all other creatures, has this in common with them, which distinguishes him from God: *like them, he has been created.*[4]

And so we have this apparent dichotomy: man is the image of God and yet he is so essentially unlike God. Thus, we must decide precisely what we mean by *imago Dei*. Or, rather, we should determine what we understand Scripture to mean by using the term. This is not easy, as the Bible offers no conclusive definition. For whatever reason, the Holy Spirit considered it unnecessary to illuminate us further. In some ways, of course, it is beyond our comprehension. Any attempt to paint a picture would inevitably fail to do justice to the subject matter and, therefore, be ultimately devoid of value. However, one of the widely acknowledged principles of hermeneutics is that Scripture is its own interpreter. Another is that we should never seek to interpret the obvious in the light of the obscure, but *vice versa*. It is also a bizarre statement of fact that, all too often, the obvious can be obscured by overfamiliarity in such a way as to transform it into the non-obvious. The question we must set ourselves, therefore, is this: is there a sufficient body of information at our disposal to arrive at a satisfactorily true understanding, however short of completeness that might be? I believe there is.

The same phrase is used of Adam's first son in connection with his father (see Gen 5:3). Did this image and likeness consist in Seth being a more recent clone of Adam? Of course not. Again, Scripture does not specify in what ways the son replicated his father, nor would it be any more fruitful to hazard a guess in this matter than in Adam's own "imageness" of God. I am grateful to Wayne Grudem for many things, of which the following is a worthy example: "It is evident that *every* way in which Seth was like Adam would be a part of his likeness to Adam and thus part of his being 'in the image' of Adam. Similarly, *every* way in which man is like God is part of his being in the likeness and image of God."[5]

To my mind, on the evidence of what we know from Scripture concerning God, this leaves us—in summary terms—with consciousness and conscience. Man is aware of himself, his surroundings, that he has a purpose of existence, and that he has a moral responsibility to behave in accordance with his better instincts. Again, I must stress that the ultimate reflection of these qualities can only truly be perceived in man's state of original

---

4. Brunner, *Man in Revolt*, 90.
5. Grudem, *Systematic Theology*, 444.

righteousness, though the effect of sin has not removed them altogether, as we shall discover.

By way of review, then, the beginning of the human race as a creative act of Creator God is explicitly taught in the Bible (see Gen 1:26–27; 2:7). The origin of Adam as the acme of that creation is also implied by the vastness of the gulf that exists between him and his earthly cohabitants. In terms of intellect, wisdom, and understanding man's dominion is rightly an expression of him having been created in the image of the Father. Man is no mere product of nature; he is a son of God. The revelation of Scripture and the unfolding of history, despite the atrocities of sin and the abuse of authority, furnish ample testimony that man is in possession of a dimension not known to bird or beast: religious awareness; for it is in the heart of man alone that God has set eternity.

The Constitution of Man

The constitution of man rightly falls within the domain of anthropology. Although it is feasible to study anthropology completely outside of a theological milieu and with little or no reference to faith, I remain convinced that it is impossible to arrive at legitimate conclusions concerning man without divine revelation, irrespective of whether that may or may not be acknowledged by the pursuant of such information. Indeed, it would seem far less arduous a task to understand something of the human frame than it would be to grasp the image of God in us given that we are, after all, human.

If only it was that easy. Any serious attempt to discover more about any topic is immediately flawed by just that fact: that we are human. As such, we can never guarantee absolute objectivity. In other words, however pure we may claim our motives to be, they will always be subject to predetermined methodological criteria. Even this work is so conditioned: my perception of the authority of Scripture. Many of those with whom I most fervently disagree on certain theological issues could make the same claim. If the recording of history is truly subject to the bias of the historian, then are not doctrinal matters equally subject to the theologian's preconceptions and, similarly, humanitarian issues governed by the anthropologist's partiality?

I say this not to alarm the reader, but merely to alert you to the perils of making hasty and unfounded assumptions. One of my roles is as a supervisor for a high school leavers' examination awards body in Religious Studies. A regular type of question is to pose a potentially controversial statement and ask the candidate to discuss it from a religious perspective. Such a statement might be something along the lines of: "The law on euthanasia/abortion/

gay rights should be changed." Whenever I get the opportunity, I advise students to refrain from making general comments that begin: "Christians believe . . ." It is always a far safer option to qualify with "Some/Most/Many . . ." Why? Quite simply because it is a dangerous thing to imagine that all believers share the same understanding, even on matters that others might consider fundamental to the Christian faith.

Historically and traditionally, Christianity has generally perceived man's constitution to be either trichotomic (that is, body, soul, and spirit) or dichotomic (where the spirit is either synonymous with the soul or else a faculty of it). Because Scripture does not speak with distinct clarity on the subject, both dichotomists and trichotomists can lay claim to alleged proof texts with equal conviction. There is also a minority who prefer to regard man as essentially one element, his body. Their particular theory is often referred to as "monism." The fact that the Bible makes specific reference to the conscious existence of the spirit after the physical death of the natural body, however, renders monism to be almost completely lacking in any serious theological appeal.

The tripartite viewpoint found particular approval originally with those Christians who were culturally influenced by Hellenistic thought. Amongst its most persuasive advocates—though in identifiably different degrees—were Clement of Alexandria, Origen, and Gregory of Nyssa. It became generally disparaged, however, after it had been used as the basis for Apollinaris's attempts to discredit the doctrine of Christ's true humanity. Athanasius and Theodoret categorically renounced such an idea as preposterous, their position being formally ratified by the Council of Constantinople in AD 381, though the tripartite view of man's composition persisted in popularity amongst the ranks of the Greek Fathers.

The general consensus of opinion tended to commend the dichotomy of man until the nineteenth century, when a few prominent theologians began to speak once more of the possibility of man as a three-element being. The so-called proof texts cited as "evidence" may well sound legitimate, but they are by no means iron clad. The apparent distinction alluded to by the New Testament writers feature prominently amongst such arguments. For example, Paul's prayer for the Thessalonian believers that God would sanctify them wholly and protect them in "spirit and soul and body" until Christ's return (1 Thess 5:23) might seem to close the case altogether, until one realizes that the layering of synonyms for idiomatic effect was a common Hebrew literary device (see also Matt 22:37; Luke 10:27).

Similarly, the writer to the Hebrews, when speaking of the penetrative power of the Word of God, employs a number of terms that would have been commonly understood in a variety of settings for the innermost part of man (see Heb 4:12). Again, the conclusion that they are separate identifiable parts is not necessarily invalid so much as far from conclusive. Other arguments claiming personal feelings or experience are not worthy of comment in a work that values the authority of Scripture as the primary basis for credibility.

And so, there was widespread disharmony and confusion amongst the proponents of the trichotomy controversy, augmented in no small measure by futile attempts to reconcile either science and religion, by way of materialism, or theology and philosophy, in the guise of idealism. Louis Berkhof seems to allude to the truth of the matter, though his framework of reference restrains him from going the whole way:

> The prevailing representation of the nature of man in Scripture is clearly dichotomic. On the one hand the Bible teaches us to view the nature of man as a unity, and not as a duality, consisting of two different elements, each of which move along parallel lines but do not really unite to form a single organism. The idea of a mere parallelism between the elements of human nature . . . is foreign to Scripture. While recognizing the complex nature of man, it never represents this as resulting in a two-fold subject in man. Every act of man is seen as an act of the whole man. It is not the soul, but man that sins; it is not the body, but man that dies; and it is not merely the soul, but man, body and soul, that is redeemed in Christ.[6]

For analytical purposes, it can be helpful to consider the whole of man as the sum of his parts, just as it is beneficial for a student doctor to learn the physiological relationship of the bodily parts. Biblical anthropology, however, perceives man to be an amalgamate being, comprising parts both anatomical and intangible, which correlate with such complexity as to be virtually indistinguishable. Herwant Volländer interestingly points out that:

> The [Old Testament] is not acquainted with anything corresponding to the Greek division of man into two or three parts, consisting of *nous*, *psuche* and *soma* (mind, soul, and body). The following concepts indicate, in rough outline comparison, different aspects of man, always seen as a whole:
>
> (a) Flesh (Heb *basar*)—often indicating man's transitoriness (Psm 78:39).

---

6. Berkhof, *Systematic Theology*, 192.

(b) Spirit (Heb *ruah*)—man is a living being (Psm 146:4), as a person (Ezk 11:19; spirit and heart are mentioned in reference to man in relation to God).

(c) Soul (Heb *nepes*)—man as life bound up with his body (1 Sam 19:11b), as an individual (Dt 24:7a; Ezk 13:8ff). The soul is neither pre-existent nor immortal, for it is the whole man (Gen 2:7).

(d) Heart (Heb *leb*, *lebab*)—the essential inner man, as opposed to his outward appearance (Job 12:3; 1 Sam 16:7b).[7]

Volländer further reminds us that it was largely because of the translation of the Hebrew Scriptures into the Septuagint that such Greek philosophies began to influence the biblical concept of anthropology in Jewish thought, as may also frequently be observed in the New Testament.

As created beings, mankind shares something in common with the animal kingdom, though is admittedly of a superior order, as we have seen. This is expressed in the oft-used phrase "living soul," employed both of Adam (Gen 2:7) and of animals (throughout Gen 1). Where they differ is especially highlighted in another transcription, "breath" (or "life"), particularly in relation to man's uniqueness in that his life is directly sourced in the breath of God. The covenant equation of "blood" with "life" (Deut 12:23) would also appear to make "blood" an alternative translation for "soul" (see Lev 17:11). Although it would clearly be inappropriate and potentially misleading to speak of "blood" and "soul" as synonymous terms, their relationship is surely so obvious as to be incontrovertible.

Our English word "soul" is the rendering we use for the Hebrew *nephesh* and Greek *psuche*. In the Old Testament in particular, its usage can be clearly associated with the seat of physical appetite (Num 21:5; Eccl 2:24; Mic 7:1), the source of emotion (Job 30:25; Ps 86:4; Isa 1:14), individual personality (Lev 7:21; Judg 16:16; Ezek 18:4), or even a dead body (Lev 19:28; Num 6:6; Hag 2:13). Perhaps the easiest way to understand the word "soul," however, is through the prevalent translations of the same Hebrew word *nephesh* and the root from which it derives.

Just as "soul" is used to translate *nephesh* with more than one possible application, so the Hebrew *ruach* (Greek—*pneuma*) conveys our English word "spirit" with a similar diversity of meanings. It too can refer to "breath" or "vitality," especially as a life principle of divine origin (see Gen 6:17; Ezek 11:19; Jas 2:26); is commonly used for "wind" as a manifestation of God's sovereign power (Exod 14:21); and human attitude, whether of permanent disposition (Num 14:24; 1 Cor 14:21) or a temporary impulse (see John

---

7. H. Volländer, "Man," in Brown, *Dictionary of New Testament Theology*, 2:565.

11:33). Whilst there is a close relationship between soul and spirit (as, indeed, there is between both body and soul, and spirit and body), the doctrine that regards them as equivalent terms for the same aspect within man must be subject to considerable question on the basis of the vast divergence of biblical usage of the two words.

It is also of great importance to note that man's body did not become his as a prison in which to house Adam's fallen spirit, nor merely a vehicle through which the soul could find legitimate expression, but belonged to his essential being from the point of creation. He no more *has* a body than he *has* a spirit; man *is* body and spirit. And yet, for man to know anything of life, he is so utterly dependent upon the breath of his Creator, God's Spirit invigorating, quickening, and energizing man's spirit.

Thus, there is no biblical warrant for the idea that the soul of man is either separate or separable from his being. Quite the reverse, in fact. The difficulty does not necessarily arise as a direct consequence of the apparent limitations of the English language to fully convey the manifold nuances inherent in the original Hebrew tongue, but such frailties do not help. This is similarly true of the Greek, though that too is not without its own inadequacies. Remove the idea that man's living existence in the created realm is dependent upon the will of God to effect it and all manner of ultimately inconsistent theories become suddenly acceptable. The constitution of man belonged to the creation of man and, therefore, relied just as much upon the will of the Creator for its composition. What we need to know of both has been made plain to us in the revelation of Scripture; what we do not need to know must remain a mystery.

On that basis, it cannot be denied that the soul/spirit is capable of existing without the body, for the Bible hints at a period of time between the physical death of the believer and their receipt of a glorious resurrection body when this is the likeliest state of affairs. What seems equally clear, however, is that such a condition is both presented and perceived to be most unnatural. Of course, this in itself does not negate the arguments in favor of either a dichotomic or a trichotomic approach. That man is made up of two or maybe even three essential elements remains plausible enough (though, personally, I believe the references usually cited in support of the latter are sufficiently inconclusive upon which to form any unchallengeable dogma). In response to the question: "What is man?" it appears to me unwise to answer any more definitively than that he is a human being, made both male and female by the Creator God in his own image, and comprising those parts which together are essential to him expressing his manhood and fulfilling the obligations of the divine decree toward him.

Where clues may be sought to that which is otherwise at best only implicit, one need only look again to man's creation in the image of God. If we are to allow either position to hold sway, then does this suggest that God, too, is body, soul, and/or spirit? Well, Scripture clearly records him as being essentially spirit and it might not be quite so unreasonable to assume that this is also true of man. It cannot be denied that the Bible speaks of some of God's acts as lending themselves more specifically to those normally associated with the physiological (though allowing for the acknowledged use of anthropomorphism), the psychological, or the spiritual. However, this does not mean that any are suspended while the other(s) take precedence, any more than a deed of God can be said to be more loving than it is just, or *vice versa*. To my mind, God cannot be compartmentalized thus; as a reflection of the divine image that he bears within himself, neither can man.

God's favorable comment upon the pinnacle of his creative work in Adam was that he considered him to be "*very* good" (Gen 1:31) in his whole being. Indeed, the weight of biblical evidence, though admitting the diverse functions of humanity in his various relations, consistently emphasizes the unity of man. Man, then, is a living being. The life he enjoys is only possible because of and insofar as it is derived from the one true life-giving source, Creator God. When—or, perhaps, if it were possible that—man should cease to be a living being, in the sense of his continuing existence, then he would also cease to be man in the fullest understanding of that term.

Original Righteousness

With reference to the Greek word *dikaiosune*, Vine defines righteousness as "the character or quality of being right or just; it was formerly spelled 'rightwiseness,' which clearly expresses the meaning."[8] Tom Wright speaks of the biblical use of the word "righteousness" in both Testaments thus: "It . . . denotes not so much the abstract idea of justice or virtue, as right standing and consequent right behaviour."[9] A laudable definition from a worthy commentator.

However, we must not be tempted to divorce the quotation from the context in which Wright places it, that is, the biblical use of the word "righteousness." This is always presented in relation to a divinely approved moral standard. In current practice—even modern-day Christian practice—right behavior is sometimes dictated by subjective notions about the governing

---

8. Vine, *Expository Dictionary*, 970.

9. N. T. Wright, "Righteousness," in Ferguson and Wright, *New Dictionary of Theology*, 590–92.

principles. This is perhaps no more evident than in the ethical maxim of mid-twentieth century Episcopal priest, Joseph Fletcher (1905–1991), whereby he encourages us to always seek to "do the most loving thing" in any given situation. It is often—though not exclusively—cited as an argument in favor of allowing euthanasia, abortion, or divorce to take place, or as a premise upon which supporters of the so-called "just war" theory build their defense.

The difficulty lies in placing one's trust in human conscience and/or the wholly impartial appraisal of known factors to make that decision. Attempts to align such a philosophy with Scripture on the basis of the apostle John's declaration that "God is love" (1 John 4:8) have failed to uphold one of the key principles of hermeneutics regarding contextual interpretation, for just a little further along John reminds his readers: "This is how we know that we love the children of God: by loving God and carrying out his commands. This is love for God: to obey his commands. And his commands are not burdensome..."[10] Righteousness that is not annexed to obedience is not the righteousness of which Scripture speaks. Adam became unrighteous when he failed to continue to walk in obedience to the revealed will of his Creator God, in loving fellowship. In the period of time prior to him making that decision, we can only assume that he did walk in what theologians describe as a condition of "original righteousness" (see Gen 1:31; Eccl 7:29). When tempted, the most loving thing for Adam to have done would have been to continue to obey, thereby prolonging his state of original righteousness.

In order for us more fully to grasp the effects of Adam's original sin, we must first of all enlarge our understanding of the consequence of it upon this condition of original righteousness. Far from being an exclusively Roman theological position, the doctrine of original righteousness lies at the heart of what Scripture suggests Adam fell from. Moreover, the believer's standing in Christ's righteousness can only properly be gauged in relation to a restored original righteousness. There is, of course, the added bonus that it can never again be subject to loss, quite simply because it is built upon a more sure foundation of one who has fulfilled the covenantal obligations where Adam failed.

The narrative concerning Adam before the incident in the garden, limited though it might be, does not suggest a nature that is yet predisposed to be red in tooth and claw. Also, at the root of the etymological understanding of the word "righteousness" is the sense of behaving justly, usually within the context of recognized familial obligations. Although this may not necessarily be at the forefront of any formal definition of either *sedeq* or *dikaiosune*,

---

10. 1 John 5:2–3.

it is certainly not absent. Indeed, those who derive the root noun from the Greek mythological daughter of Zeus would insist that it is related to behavior in accordance with parental instruction. Certainly, Adam's original sin was an abrogation of such conduct. Is it therefore unreasonable to assume that his actions prior to this first instance of betrayal were fully in keeping with his Father's instruction?

The *Concise Oxford Dictionary of the Christian Church* defines original righteousness as: "God's gratuitous impartation to man of perfect rectitude in his condition before the fall. The state of Original Righteousness in which man was created is held to have included freedom from concupiscence, bodily immortality and happiness."[11] Whilst this may be an accurate description according to the Roman Catholic tradition, I am not entirely convinced that its qualifying inclusions would meet with broader appeal.

Although there may be minor points of discussion that give cause for a distinction to be retained, to all intents and purposes the original righteousness we have in mind here may also be spoken of as Adam's state of Edenic sinlessness. Far from being conveyed as a position of tepid indifference or detachment, the idea is always presented as one of being like God in "true knowledge," "true righteousness and holiness" (Eph 4:24). In the words of Louis Berkhof: "These three elements constitute the original righteousness, which was lost by sin, but is regained in Christ. It may be called the moral image of God, or the image of God in the more restricted sense of the word. Man's creation in this moral image implies that the original condition of man was one of positive holiness, and not a state of innocence or moral neutrality."[12]

It is here that we see the true significance of—and, indeed, the subtle difference between—the image of God and the likeness of God in man. Adam was created in God's image and was, thus, righteous in himself and, therefore, also in his dispensations toward his Maker, toward others, and toward the rest of the created order. Although not essential to his being in the strictest sense of the word, it was essential to his task of reflecting God's image by becoming like him in the features that were consistent with the divine decree concerning him. Once this was lost, though echoes of the image remained, the potential for likeness in those areas became irretrievably lost. John Calvin expressed his understanding of the image of God thus:

> . . . by this term . . . is denoted the integrity with which Adam was endued when his intellect was clear, his affections subordinate to reason, all his senses duly regulated, and when he truly

---

11. Livingstone, "Original Righteousness."
12. Berkhof, *Systematic Theology*, 204.

ascribed all his excellence to the admirable gifts of his Maker. And though the primary seat of the divine image was in the mind and the heart, or in the soul and its powers, there was no part even of the body in which some rays of glory did not shine.[13]

According to Hammond, when speaking of Adam expressing the image and likeness of God:

> Though he was righteous in his unfallen state, that righteousness was obviously not inherent, for God told him His will. He required tuition in righteousness and, having received it, he disobeyed. On the other hand, the Fall was not a necessity. By maintaining his communion with the upholding Creator, he need not have sinned. At his Fall, the image was retained (although permanently defaced and debased), but the righteousness was lost.[14]

The original condition in which Adam was created enabled him to adhere perfectly to the law of God as a natural proclivity of his moral understanding. The affections of his will were subject to the breath of God in him, that is, his Spirit. Man's nature continues to assert that he is a morally responsible agent, conscience itself bearing witness to the fact. Having concluded the creative process, God declared man to be abundantly adequate to fulfill his role in God's purpose (Gen 1:31). This extreme probity, that he was "very good," can only properly be understood in relation to his conformity of will to the moral law.

The image of God as represented in Adam ensured that man was originally like his Maker in regard to knowledge (Col 3:10), righteousness (Eph 4:24), and authority (Gen 1:28). This is not to imply, however, that he was essentially good, any more than that he was omniscient or supreme. But there was built in to man's blueprint the seed of potential that, left to germinate unhindered by sin, may well have seen him attain to a more perfect knowledge, sinless perfection, and overwhelming dominion, as is befitting God's proper agent of glory in the earth.

Adam's state of original righteousness is but a reflection of him having been created in God's image in that respect. As I have mentioned elsewhere, however, though man was perfectly created, he was not created perfect.[15] For something to be perfect negates the idea of anything more perfect

---

13. Calvin, *Institutes*, I. 15:3.
14. Hammond, *In Understanding*, 72.
15. See Woodall, *Kingdom*, 10.

being possible. This is the folly of the Anselmian idea that the perfection of God remains valid even if it exists only in the mind of the one who holds to that belief. Clearly, a more perfect example is possible: the God who is similarly perfect in reality. Man's imperfection lay in his capacity to become imperfect, which was not only possible, but ultimately proved to be a well-founded cause for concern.

Objections to the idea of man being created in a state of original righteousness have generally been based on a misconception of righteousness as a virtue. For it to be so, then righteousness would have to be conditional upon appropriate choices having been made, they argue. Thus, righteousness is not perceived as an element of the image of God in man, but as a potential fruit of him exercising that image in God's likeness. While admitting that man was created in innocence, neither sinful nor righteous, what he would become was dependent upon making the correct choice when tested. Such a position cannot be arrived at by cool intellects, for it fails to do justice to both the revelation of Scripture and the reason of the mind on a number of counts.

First of all, the proponents of original righteousness usually speak of it in terms of relative perfection, thus conceding that it should not be understood to mean that man had already attained the highest possible state of righteousness within his means. Its loss, therefore, was not only the relinquishing of positive holiness, but also the potential for what it might have developed into. Secondly, the objection seems to suggest that only the fruit of good choices determine their virtue, whereas the reverse seems to be the case: they are virtuous because they emanate from a pure source. God does not become good because of tangibly righteous acts, but we recognize his goodness because of and through them (though even if his goodness was undetectable by us, this would not negate his inherent goodness). Finally, the divine declaration concerning man at his creation was not that he was neutral, but that he was very good, and this before he had committed any act other than that of simply being.

Similarly, man had original knowledge, that is, an understanding and perception of himself and his surroundings that transcended his capacity to acquire such knowledge. Thus, from the very beginning he was both self-aware and world-conscious. There are subtle clues to this throughout Scripture (e.g., Col 3:10; Eph 4:24), but arguably the most overt evidence is to be found in the creation narrative itself. Whilst it is impossible to determine the extent of Adam's knowledge beyond the albeit limited revelation of God's Word on the matter—though that fact has not stemmed the attempt of some—we do know, for example, that he was sufficiently sentient to adequately name the animals in perfect accordance with their characteristic traits (Gen 2:19–20). We also know that Adam's knowledge was restricted insofar that it did not yet include cognition of good and evil (v. 17). Moreover, he was still subject to divine instruction which, it might be argued, would have been unnecessary for one endowed with perfect knowledge. But it was neither dormant nor neutral. And we have no reason to believe that his state of original righteousness was any different in this regard.

A distinction must also be made between righteousness and holiness, delicate though it may be. They are commonly—and erroneously—used interchangeably. Although their annexing together in Scripture does not in itself guarantee a dissimilarity of definition, their separate use elsewhere does go some way toward doing so. We have seen that righteousness as a condition is what produces righteous acts. Similarly, the state of holiness is the source of holy deeds. Whilst neither is dependent upon their respective products for validity, it would be strange indeed to imagine righteousness or holiness that was not fruitful in this regard. Whereas righteousness is the quality of being right or just, holiness signifies separation unto God. As Christian believers, the condition of both of them in us is at the same time a crisis and a process: we are righteous and holy, and yet we are becoming increasingly more so. As far as pre-fallen Adam is concerned, he simply was.

The concept that lies behind the Hebrew idea of righteousness still prevails amongst many orthodox Jews. Justice for the poor, appropriate conduct and behavior toward dependants, looking after the needy, the underprivileged, the downtrodden, and the disenfranchised all remain part of what modern Judaism acknowledges as its "righteous" responsibilities. From a Christian perspective, of course, we might argue that true righteousness is unattainable outside of Christ, which we will come to later. But, that being so, in terms of the practical expression of obedience toward God, should we be any less "righteous" than those who claim to be so under an old covenant sense of duty in this regard? Surely not!

Just one final cautionary note before I press on. I always try to consider all the evidence at my disposal before arriving at a conclusion that may or may not sit comfortably with the reader. Sometimes, the weight of proof forces me toward a resolution that I find less than appealing to my natural sensitivities. I also make a concerted effort to avoid couching my findings in dogmatic terminology unless I am absolutely convinced of what I propose (which isn't necessarily the same thing as being correct; it's just that at the time of writing I believe myself to be so). Because of this, I purposefully evade unnecessary and ultimately unhelpful conjecture. In relation to the subject matter before us, my research has led me to consider the arguments of those who wonder what might the state of Adam's children have been had they been born prior to his fall in Eden. In other words, would original righteousness have been transferrable in the same way that we claim original sin to be? I'm afraid I did not consider it for long, for I soon saw the folly. Quite frankly, I regard my time as being much better spent pondering those things of which we can have some assurance, which have been made known to us, rather than those that have not, let alone those that never even materialized.

Promises of Blessing

It may come as somewhat of a surprise for the reader to learn that, linguistically speaking, there is no such thing as a promise in the whole of the Bible. Now that I have your attention, allow me to explain. Our English word "promise" derives directly from the Latin, with no alteration in meaning, which according to the *Oxford English Dictionary* is "a declaration or assurance made to another person with respect to the future stating that one will do or refrain from some specified act, or that one will give or bestow some specified thing, usually in a good sense, implying something to the advantage or pleasure of the person concerned." There is no corresponding word in the Scriptures with exactly this definition.

In the Old Testament, the Hebrew word translated "promise" is *dabar*, literally meaning to "speak," "say," "utter," or "pronounce." Its Greek counterpart in the Septuagint and the New Testament is *epangelia*, the root of which means "something announced." The lack of precision in the ancient languages to affirm the seriousness of one's declaration is possibly what gave rise to the practice of sworn statements in the form of oaths. These were usually made in the context of some religious connection and were singularly denounced by Jesus as of evil origin, his advice being to "simply let your 'Yes' be 'Yes,' and your 'No,' 'No'" (Matt 5:37). It goes without saying, of course, that the fundamental integrity of God's nature was the automatic guarantee of his promissory statements.

In Scripture, the idea of divine blessings is always presented in the context of covenant. More specifically, such blessings are seen as the reward for faithfulness on the part of the recipient to the duties and responsibilities to that covenant. I have written extensively on this elsewhere.[16] Suffice to say here, however, that covenant treaties were a common feature of the ancient peoples of the Middle East. They were, in effect, an agreement between two (or more) parties of not necessarily equal standing, the key features of which include obligations, benefits, and sanctions. These were negotiated in advance so that each contributor was fully aware of its (or

---

16. See Woodall, *Covenant*.

their) responsibilities toward the other(s), the rewards that such compliance might generate, and the penalties that may be induced should such loyalty be disregarded.

Once these were agreed, then a final feature came into play that bound both parties to the terms and conditions of the covenant, by which they effectively became joint signatories, the biblical expression of which was commonly sealed by the shedding of blood.[17] The essential nature of the divine covenants is such that they are established solely by the prerogative of God, their conditions being offered only for receipt or rejection; they were never a subject for consultation. Such is God's covenant with Adam.

The covenant agreements of the Old Testament, and those of which we know of the period from extrabiblical sources, often included a sign of the covenant having been established. A cairn of stones as a witness heap was a common feature; for the people under Abraham, it was circumcision; for New Testament believers in Christ, it is the sacraments of baptism and the covenant meal; the practice of cutting across the palm of the right hand and allowing the blood of the participants to mingle will be familiar to many even today. I was brought up by my maternal grandparents, both of whom were born in the second decade of the twentieth century. For those of that generation, their word really was their bond, a vigorous handshake being as concrete to the agreement as any signed document under legal auspices. We live in very different times. But was there any such sign in Adam's case? Wayne Grudem observes the following:

> No "sign" for the covenant of works is clearly designated as such in Genesis, but if we were to name one, it would probably be the tree of life in the midst of the garden. By partaking of that tree Adam and Eve would be partaking of the promise of eternal life that God would give. The fruit itself did not have magical properties but would be a sign by which God outwardly guaranteed that the inward reality would occur.[18]

As well as addressing the issue in question concerning the apparent presence of a sign to accompany the covenant agreement having taken place, Grudem also—albeit unwittingly—resolves the matter I raised at the beginning of this section. Although the concept of "promise" as it is properly understood is entirely absent in both the Hebrew and Greek vocabulary of the Old and New Testaments respectively, if we accept the guaranteed outcome of compliance to certain conditions as a valid definition, then the idea is most certainly present throughout the pages of Scripture.

17. See Robertson, *Christ of the Covenants*, 11.
18. Grudem, *Systematic Theology*, 517.

In Adam's case, such "promises" consisted of a number of elements, all derived from the "blessedness" of a deepening of fellowship, as the progressive expression of relationship, with his Maker. These included Adam's mandate to rule as God's vice-regent over the created order, the continuation of tranquility and concord throughout that creation, and life in its fullest sense; so rich, in fact, that its extent is most probably beyond our sin-tainted comprehension. We will look at these in turn:

Dominion and Stewardship

Consider the following:

> God blessed them and said to them, "Be fruitful and increase in number; fill the earth and subdue it. Rule over the fish of the sea and the birds of the air and over every living creature that moves on the ground."[19]

> The LORD God took the man and put him in the Garden of Eden to work it and take care of it.[20]

It is often said that with privilege comes responsibility, as if these are but two sides of the same coin. In many respects, this is a valid assessment. In Adam's case, however, the responsibility was itself a privilege. Once again, his endowment with vice-regency on God's behalf was a reflection of the image of the Creator in the pinnacle of his creation.

Although it would not be unproductive to separate man's dominion over the earth from his stewardship of it for the purpose of analysis, it is perhaps even more beneficial to keep them together, lest we otherwise equate dominion with domination. The likelihood of doing so is indubitably further compounded by the fact that the original Hebrew verb carries with it the idea of ruling by treading upon, a thought not lost on the psalmist:

> ... what is man that you are mindful of him, the son of man that you care for him? You made him a little lower than the heavenly beings and crowned him with glory and honor. You made him ruler of the works of your hands; you put everything under his feet; all flocks and herds, and the beasts of the field, and the fish of the sea, all that swim the paths of the seas.[21]

---

19. Gen 1:28.
20. Gen 2:15.
21. Ps 8:4–8.

Indeed, the writer to the Hebrews cites this very verse in connection with Christ having wrought not only the restoration of the image of God in man, but also the recapturing of man's lost destiny through him by virtue of his death and subsequent resurrection (see Heb 2:6–9). What is perhaps the most startling revelation of all is that the writer to the Hebrews followed the Septuagint rendering of what was to become the Old Testament, with which most English translations also identify. In the original, however, the Hebrew has *elohim* (literally "gods," but usually acknowledged as relating to plurality of "persons" within the one Being of God in monotheism). Nowhere else in the whole of the Old Testament is this translated "heavenly beings/angels."

At the root of the idea conveyed by the Hebrew word translated "dominion" (that is, *hdr*) is the subjection to one's will, but with the hidden implication that to do so is in the best interests of the one or those who are being asked to submit to that will. Because Adam was effectively representing another, it was not his own will that he was being required to bring everything under subjection to, though in his pre-fallen state it might reasonably be argued that his will and that of the Creator were virtually one and the same.

Extend this thought process just a little further and we can see that Adam did not need to eat from the tree of the knowledge of good and evil in order to distinguish right from wrong in his role as God's appointed servant. For him, he simply had to act in accordance with the revealed divine will to know that by so doing he was doing right. Similarly, to have failed to do so would have been to do wrong. Thus, dominion without stewardship is as authority without responsibility. Looking after the environment is not the exclusive domain of the new ageist, nor is it a topic solely of interest to the politically correct. It was intrinsic to God's creational mandate for Adam and, therefore, also to us all. Moreover, godly dominion exercised through faithful stewardship is both a blessing in itself and the harbinger of still further blessings, as anyone remotely curious about household gardening will testify.

Tranquility and Concord

The level of tranquility and concord enjoyed by our first parents prior to the fall is unimaginable. If that was only a token of what might have become theirs as a product of prolonged faithfulness, then we cannot even begin to understand the concept. Perhaps the only clue that might aid us in our quest is to consider our own experience of the exact opposite and try to imagine an existence utterly devoid of those things that presently bring only dispeace and disharmony.

Of course, the chief evidence of this was the fact that the source of their stillness was as yet untainted, that is, the intimacy of fellowship they took pleasure in with their Creator. It was only when this became subject to despoilment that they knew anything of shame and guilt. Until that time, Adam and Eve's consciences were as unadulterated as was their relationship with God, with each other, and with their environment. Their reciprocal love for each other was unrestricted with no suggestion of quarreling, rift, or dissatisfaction. Unlike the current *zeitgeist*, any functional differences of their roles and responsibilities were not perceived as a threat to their creational equality, but rather embraced as hallmarks of their mutual recognition of need in and for each other.

We may also surmise that their efforts as stewards did not bring with them the sense of futility and wearisomeness that we might experience in similar circumstances. Work was not a product of the fall, though the now all too familiar sweat and toil associated with it most certainly was (Gen 3:17). Imagine the possibilities: gardening without unwelcome obstructions, crops and trees that willingly gave up their produce without being subject to decay and decomposition, being able to delight in the beauty of the landscape without having to turn a blind eye to unsightly intrusions, and under no compulsion to apportion blame if things failed to work out as intended, because they always would go precisely according to plan. We cannot be certain that this is how it was, but there is surely more than a hint in what the curse wrought to suggest that it alone ushered in those things that countered it.

What we do know is that whatever peace and harmony Adam and Eve experienced in their relationship with God, with each other, and with the created order, they sacrificed it all on the altar of vanity and rebellion. Thereafter, the human experience would never quite be the same again.

Life, But Not As We Know It

Again, we must concede the lack of conclusive evidence to support the idea of Adam's conditional immortality, though the introduction of death—in all its aspects—as a direct consequence of the fall certainly seems to point unfalteringly in this direction. The wording of the divine pronouncement serves only to lend further credence to the argument: "for dust you are and to dust you will return" (Gen 3:19b). But does this necessarily mean that Adam would have continued to live on had he not sinned? And does not the asking of that question without sure testimony from Scripture alone suggest that it belongs to the realm of speculation and mystery? If so, then surely the relentless pursuit of an answer is ultimately a fruitless exercise, not to mention folly in the extreme.

Everlasting life was certainly not essential to man's unfallen nature. Had it been, he would have ceased to be man once the principle of death was allowed to intrude his being. In this sense, immortality may only properly be applied to God himself (1 Tim 6:15–16). This notwithstanding, however, it does not seem unreasonable to posit that continued existence belongs also to others of God's created order, such as angelic beings, so we must conclude that qualified immortality might be used in a sense other than that restricted only to what Berkhof calls "an original, eternal, and necessary endowment."[22]

It was clearly possible for man to become subject to death, because that is exactly what happened when Adam sinned; it is equally possible for him to become the recipient of "immortality" in this restricted sense, because that is precisely what will happen to those who are found to be in Christ and he in them at the end of the age. Are we, therefore, to understand this bestowal as a part of the restoration of what once belonged to him or what would have become his had Adam not fallen? I believe there is much weightier biblical evidence to support the latter proposition.

The promises of blessing toward Adam—allowing for them to be described as such—are inextricably linked to the covenant of works, and can be summed up in but one word: life. If the penalty for disobedience was death, then the reward for obedience can be no other than life (see Lev 18:5; Neh 9:29; Rom 10:5; Gal 3:12). This being the case, it must be assumed that we have in mind far more than a mere continued existence, for surely that belonged to man already by virtue of him having been brought into being. There was to be an unspecified period of probation, the successful conclusion of such moral excellence resulting in mortal endurance.

Earlier, you will remember, I noted that there was a uniqueness attached to the creation of man, which has been signposted for us in Scripture by the idea of that alone being the subject of divine counsel (Gen 1:26). We get exactly the same thing again on the occasion of that honor having been besmirched: "And the LORD God said, 'The man has now become like one of us, knowing good and evil. He must not be allowed to reach out his hand and take also from the tree of life and eat, and live forever'" (3:22). It would seem, then, that not only was the possibility of Adam's everlastingness contingent upon him partaking of another fruit—which, presumably, was

---

22. Berkhof, *Systematic Theology*, 672.

not excluded from his grasp until this point in the narrative—but that his expulsion from the garden was primarily to prevent him from now availing himself of that opportunity. I would even go so far as to suggest that God's eviction of Adam and Eve from Eden was an act of grace, lest they take also of the fruit of the tree of life and be eternally confirmed in their newly acquired sinful nature without hope.

Although it is quite true that there is no definitive statement of promise with regards to the possibility of eternal life, it is surely implied by the fact that disobedience wrought death. It is also widely acknowledged that the covenantal relationship that existed between God and Adam demanded that this be so. Whether the negation of death—or, more strictly speaking, the continuation of life—as the fruit of Adam's compliance could have meant life eternal has been the subject of many a theological objection. Where Scripture is silent, it is usually advisable not to speculate. What can be upheld is that the very ethos of the biblical presentation of eternal life is that in the presence of and continuing communion with God. There is no legitimate reason to assume that this would not have continued to be the case had Adam persisted in honoring his covenant obligations.

All of these features—dominion and stewardship, tranquility and concord, and life of a quality presently unknown to us—were effectively dealt a death blow by the introduction of the death principle.

The Purpose of Creation

Before we embark upon a journey to discover what God's purpose in creation might be, we must first of all determine whether it is altogether necessary—or even possible—for us to come to know that purpose. Consider the thoughts of the nineteenth-century theologian, A. A. Hodge:

> This is not a question of vain curiosity. It is evident, since God is eternal, immutable, and of absolutely perfect intelligence, that the great end or ultimate purpose for which he at the beginning created all things must have been kept in view unchangeably in all his works, and so all his works must be more directly or remotely a means to that end . . . And although God has hid from us many of his subordinate purposes . . . he has revealed to us that great ultimate design, without a glimpse of which the true character of his general administration never could be in any degree comprehended. None can deny that if he has revealed his

ultimate purpose in creation, that it must be a matter of the very highest importance.[23]

Ask any six of your Christian friends what they think God's purpose in creation is and it is likely that you will attract half a dozen different responses. Ask twice as many and you could probably double the entries on your list. Why is this so? Is it because of generally poor teaching on the subject? Might it be because there is a relative dearth of interest across the churches in such matters? Could it conceivably be that we, as believers, are so constantly reminded to look to the future hope and relinquish the ghosts of the past that we are often blinkered in our approach to applying lessons of what has gone that it might benefit our understanding of what is to come? All of these—and many other alternatives besides—are both plausible and possible. What cannot be held as a viable excuse is the absence of biblical data concerning God's purpose in creation.

One of the questions on last year's G.C.S.E. Religious Studies paper in the U.K. asked why some non-religious people have a belief in life after death. Some of the stock answers given included an affinity with the paranormal, a personal near-death experience, occultist proclivities, comfort at times of bereavement, and the belief that it gives meaning or purpose to our existence. I have encountered many who profess to be Christians and yet fail to recognize any purpose in their lives, being quite content to adopt an almost *che sarà, sarà* approach to life, which usually consists of little more than reacting to circumstances as they are unveiled. If they had been one of the friends you had asked to reflect upon God's purpose in creation, they would probably have thought that he had decided to do so for no loftier reason than to relieve the boredom of nothingness. This is the fundamental flaw of the teleological argument for God's existence, which tends toward believing him to be wholly uninvolved in his creation from the point of it being brought into being. Just like William Paley's watch theory, it goes some way to proving a designer, but should we thereby assume God to be as detached thereafter as a jeweler might be subsequent to selling on his *pièce de résistance*?

Clues as to the purpose of God in creation are to be gleaned from the interpersonal relationships of God within his own Being. It is also implied by the relational name by which we are instructed to address him in prayer (Matt 6:9). Although it would be erroneous to suggest that the Fatherhood of God is dependent upon a family of sons and daughters through which to express that fatherhood, it remains true that he has chosen to extend his creative powers in that direction and for that purpose. This is possibly why

---

23. Hodge, *Outlines*, 243.

THE NECESSITY OF THE ATONEMENT

man was created in his image: to replicate his characteristics in facsimile form and then to further reproduce that throughout the earth. It is said only of Adam and Eve that they were created in the Father's image, but surely the directive to be "fruitful and increase in number" (Gen 1:28a) indicates a desire for more than just the two of them to represent him as the family of God on earth.

We might also deduce further evidence from Paul's insight into the pre-creational counsel of the Godhead. As if to bring out my ever so mildly Calvinistic tendencies, I did not choose God; he chose me. When? On a wet autumn Saturday evening in September 1976? No! Did he decide to include me in his family when I was old enough to display signs of being a half-decent acquisition? If that were so, many would argue that he would still be waiting patiently. What about at the moment I was born, or even at the point of conception? Further back still. According to the apostle's letter to the Ephesians, God's choosing of me did not take place in time at all, but in eternity: "Praise be to the God and Father of our Lord Jesus Christ . . . For he chose us in him before the creation of the world to be holy and blameless in his sight . . . in accordance with his pleasure and will" (Eph 1:3–5).

This very small portion, which in its original context forms little more than an introduction of Paul's main treatise to the believers at Ephesus, is itself a mine of information. Concerning the question before us, it tells us the who, the what, the when, and the why:

who	–	God the Father;
what	–	chose us in Christ Jesus;
when	–	before creation;
why	–	because it was in accordance with his pleasure and will.

This is not to imply, of course, that the "to be what" (that is, "holy and blameless in his sight") is unimportant; it is just not altogether relevant to the main objective of this particular study at this specific juncture.

The arguments relating to predestination belong to later centuries. For Paul, there is no controversy, no apology, and no explanation. He simply makes the statement, offering no hint of what objections might subsequently follow. Somehow, for some reason, those who find themselves in Christ do so because of a decision made by God outside of the time/space continuum, simply because it was his will to do so and it gave/gives him pleasure. What about those not so chosen? Well, reason would seek to insist that they are chosen to be excluded from God's family. However, all that we may reasonably deduce from the evidence before us is that they are not chosen to be included, which is not necessarily the same thing at all. Am I being pedantic over semantics? Quite possibly so. Allow me to put it another way. Scripture informs us that there is "a time for everything . . . a time for every activity, a time for every deed" (Eccl 3:1, 17). All I am saying is that the time to know such things, that is, the hidden or unrevealed things, is not yet. Chasing after them will serve only to compound our frustration.

Although he strains every last ounce of Reformed self-gratification out of the text, William Hendriksen manages to compose himself sufficiently to offer a more balanced insight into the qualifying clause "in accordance with his pleasure and will":

> When the Father chose a people for himself, deciding to adopt them as his own children, he was motivated by love alone. Hence, what he did was a result not of sheer determination, but of supreme delight. A person may be fully determined to submit to a very serious operation. Again, he may be just as fully determined to plant a beautiful rose garden. Both are matters of the will. However, the latter alone is a matter of delight, that is, of his will's good pleasure.[24]

Apart from his unrivalled capacity to expound truth, convey doctrine, and communicate the practical application of Christian living, the Apostle Paul was also particularly adept at literary structure. An oft-used template of his was to introduce the themes he wishes to transmit, outline the theological premise behind his arguments, identify specific areas in which these can sensibly become operational, and conclude with a brief but poignant summary. A prime example of this is to be seen in his epistle to the Ephesian believers. Having touched upon God's purpose in election in chapter one, he then goes on to provide more details of what this actually means in practice in chapter three:

> Although I am less than the least of all God's people, this grace was given to me: to . . . make plain to everyone the administration of this mystery, which for ages past was kept hidden in God, who created all things. His intent was that now, through the church, the manifold wisdom of God should be made known to the rulers and authorities in the heavenly realms, according to his eternal purpose, which he accomplished in Christ Jesus our Lord.[25]

Because of its New Testament context, it would be easy to catalogue these verses solely under the category of "the purpose of the church." In

---

24. Hendriksen, *Ephesians*, 79.
25. Eph 3:8–11.

many ways, however, the purpose of the church—as an agent of God's kingdom—is to effect God's purpose in creation. Over the past almost forty years of my Christian experience, I have seen the emphasis of interest shift dramatically within the kind of church circles with which I am most familiar. In most recent times, this has tended toward attempting to discover how best to "do" church. Business models drawn from professional management courses have all laid the same claim, usually presented in terminology seeking to arrest the attention of the casual onlooker. "How to live in the bullseye of God's will for your life," "A hundred steps to successful Christian living," "Hang up your hang-ups and go for God," and "Twelve keys to biblical worship" are the most memorable, if not the least productive in the long term.

The emphasis of the New Testament, however, is not so much on "doing" church as it is on "being" it. Consider the structure of Revelation 22:11:

> Let him who does "x" continue to do "x";
> Let him who is "y" continue to be "y" . . .
> . . . where "x" is behavioral and "y" is dispositional.

This is not to say that what we do is unimportant or irrelevant, but it can only be either insofar that it is a valid expression of who we are. The point here, however, is that the word "church," like the word "witness," is not a verb but a noun. As such, it does not describe what a Christian group can or must be expected to do, but that which we simply are. This is certainly true of Paul's instruction on the matter to those early Christians at Ephesus and is no less so in the wider milieu of God's purpose in creation: it is to be a legitimate expression of his wisdom as sons and daughters of the living God, to his eternal glory.

Scripture provides us with an explicit answer to the question: "Why did God create?" Through the prophet Isaiah, God speaks of "my sons . . . and my daughters . . . whom I created for my glory" (Isa 43:6–7). The context shows that the use of plurality does not imply the creation of a whole race, but it does help us to better understand God's purpose in creation. The natural elements of the universe also owe their origin to the creative handiwork of Almighty God, for "[t]he heavens declare the glory of God; the skies proclaim the work of his hands" (Ps 19:1). John's eyewitness account of heaven's worship also associates creation with divine glory and purpose:

> You are worthy, our Lord and God, to receive glory and honor
> and power, for you created all things, and by your will they were
> created and have their being.[26]

---

26. Rev 4:11.

The King James Version translates this same verse:

> Thou art worthy, O Lord, to receive glory and honour and power: for thou hast created all things, and for thy pleasure they are and were created.

Not only are both legitimate translations, but both are necessary to complete our understanding of what was being conveyed in the original, for the Greek noun *thelema* when used subjectively retains the sense of "the will being spoken of as the emotion of being desirous, rather than as the thing willed."[27] However, to speak of a dual purpose in creation, viz., God's glory and man's sanctification, is not only to miss the point, but it also demonstrates a remarkable failure to distinguish between purpose and desire. Of course, man's holiness is essential to him fulfilling the role of glorifying God and bringing his purpose in creation into effect, but it is not the purpose itself.

In my previous works in this series, I have considered the concepts of covenant, as the basis by which God makes himself known to us, and kingdom, by which he expresses his rule in us and through us. Here, we are looking at the atonement as the means by which God effects man's reconciliation to him and his original purpose. Whilst all three lend themselves to independent analytical research, the link between them should not be overlooked. Under the current heading, we might even say that the kingdom of God is the hub around which his purpose in creation revolves, both having been unveiled to us in the context of covenant.

The purpose of creation and the promise of blessings that Adam was to receive "in his flesh" were inextricably linked by their common divine appointment. Though the latter was made known to Adam shortly after the process of creation had been completed, and in the context of covenant, the actual decision had been made within the covenant fellowship of the counsel of the Godhead before that process had begun, save in the mind of Almighty God. They are, thus, both of an eternal nature, despite the fact that their coming to fruition will invade the time/space continuum in some way.

The purpose of creation, then, whether in general terms or more specifically related to man, is ultimately the glory of God. It must clearly be understood, however, that to speak of the purpose of God in creation thus is not to imply incompleteness in the Divine Being prior to that creation having taken place. In other words, the creative act did not add to the essence of God in any of his attributes whatsoever. It was an action precipitated

---

27. Vine, *Expository Dictionary*, 1229.

exclusively by grace; it was a decree prompted by volition, not provoked by necessity.

Summary

No other creature enjoyed the status with which Adam was endowed by God. Necessarily and essentially different from all others, he was also entrusted with a mandate to exercise dominion over them on the Creator's behalf. How successful man became in this stewardship role was, in the final analysis, dependent upon how careful he was to maintain a right relationship with his Father, as the primary link between heaven and earth, and toward his wife, as co-worker in creation. That Adam so quickly rebelled against his Maker leaves us with little biblical evidence of how humanity might otherwise have progressed. What we are left with is the tragic story of mankind existing in alienation from the potential of fulfilling its created purpose—or so it seemed. The answer to whether it was feasible for it to have remained so depends largely upon whether it is possible for God's purpose to be ultimately foiled or frustrated.

THE FALL OF ADAM

Notwithstanding the view that regards the narrative concerning the fall of Adam as containing a significant proportion of symbolism, the general perception amongst most biblical scholars is that Scripture's presentation is historically valid. The New Testament writers certainly regarded Adam to have been a real person, the original man as created by God (see Luke 3:38; Rom 5:14; 1 Cor 15:22). This should not be taken to imply, of course, that there is no trace of imagery in the Genesis account, merely that the overriding feature as determined by the Bible itself must be acknowledged to be one of cardinal legitimacy.

This being the case, I propose to look at four key areas associated with the lapse of our first parent: in relation to the immediate consequences it brought about, the significance of Adam's federal headship and the responsibilities annexed to that governance, the wider effects of his sin, and how the whole of the created order was left tainted by his transgression.

Original Sin and Its Immediate Consequences

The most common Hebrew word translated "sin" in the Old Testament is *ht*, which conveys the idea of deviation from a required standard. Other connected usages include rebellion in terms of breach of relationship, deliberate perversion of truth, guilt arising from wrongdoing, erring through ignorance, and mischief done to others. Its New Testament counterpart is the Greek *hamartia*, which Vine takes to mean "literally a missing of the mark . . . the most comprehensive term for moral obliquity. It is used as a) a principle or source of action . . . b) a governing principle or power . . . c) a generic term . . . d) a sinful deed."[28]

The primary expression of sin in Scripture is that it is essentially a violation against God. In the words of Oliver Buswell: "sin originated in an act of free will in which the creature deliberately, responsibly, and with adequate understanding of the issues chose to corrupt the holy character of godliness with which God had endowed His creation."[29]

As far as the biblical evidence is concerned, its whole ethos seems to give credence to the thought that the Genesis narrative is more than simply a record of Adam's personal rebellion; it is also the account of sin's origin (that is, in the human realm). This being so, the principles of hermeneutics demand that this first documented episode should act as a pointer to our understanding something of the essence of sin. The most scriptural definition of sin, therefore, as encapsulated in the account of its origin, might be stated thus: sin is substantially a rapacious desire to seize spiritual, intellectual, and moral autonomy, which has as its foundation unbelief and dissidence. The escalating scale of the pervading influence of sin in our own day has frequently given rise to a rather philosophical approach, where sin is seen as little more than a proclivity to commit acts of misdemeanor, their severity being dependent upon personal circumstances, place in the social infrastructure, vocational or relational misfortune, environmental plight, and all manner of issues that may well exacerbate an existing problem. Such analyses, however, ultimately fail to do justice to the gravity with which the Bible speaks concerning the sinful nature of mankind.

Emil Brunner is in no doubt regarding the solemnity with which the sin principle should be viewed:

> The two expressions, the Fall and Original Sin—which only have meaning when they are placed together—suggest first of

---

28. Ibid., 1045.

29. J. O. Buswell, "The Origin and Nature of Sin," in Henry, *Basic Christian Doctrines*, 107.

all that sin is something far more powerful than moralism or Pietism . . . would have us believe. Sin is not a merely moral phenomenon, and it is not a merely subjective process. That which bears the name of sin, in the moralist's sense and in the subjective sense, belongs indeed to sin as a whole, but it is not the whole.[30]

He enlightens us further by concluding that:

Sin, from the Christian point of view, is primarily something which affects the nature of man as a whole. At this point the Christian view of sin approaches the Kantian doctrine of radical evil. Evil has not been understood if we think: "Now, at this moment, I have done something wrong, but previously, before the decision, I was either good or neutral." Whoever takes a view of this kind is not merely lacking in the scientific impulse to try to explain the existence of evil, but he is lacking in moral earnestness. We take sin seriously when to some extent we become aware of the depth of its roots. For I need to see that evil has its roots in the very depths of my nature in order to realize that "I" am really bad. Until I see this, I regard evil as something accidental, like a splash of mud, not like something which belongs to "the essence of my nature."[31]

With reference to its specialist theological use, Hodge points out that:

The phrase "original sin" is used sometimes to include the judicial imputation of the guilt of Adam's sin, as well as the hereditary moral corruption, common to all his descendants, which is one of the consequences of that imputation. More strictly, however, the phrase "original sin" designates only the hereditary moral corruption common to all men from birth.[32]

As we have seen, the most significant aspect regarding the biblical representation of *peccatum originis* is that it is fundamentally the rebellion of the creature against his Creator. The seed of truth inherent in this one act teaches us much about the subsequent condition of the sinful nature, for no sin, whether it is a deed of omission or commission, is negative; it is a positive denial of dependence. Indeed, this is the very heart of the sin issue: a lust for independence, which normally finds expression through insubordination, impudence, and generally ignoble behavior. It must be pointed

---

30. Brunner, *The Mediator*, 140.
31. Ibid., 141.
32. Hodge, *Outlines*, 325.

out that, though I am not at odds with the many theologians who hold that unbelief and not arrogance is the basis for all sin, I would beg to proffer that, in the context of the revelation of God's grace, unbelief is the most arrogant choice available to a nature seeking to exercise its assumed right of autonomy.

The strategy of the serpent in the downfall of Adam has continued to be Satan's policy throughout history. First of all, he promotes doubt: "Did God really say?" (Gen 3:1), moves swiftly to provoke disbelief: "You will not surely die" (v. 4), with the almost inevitable result of producing disobedience: "[Eve] took some and ate it. She also gave some to her husband who was with her, and he ate it" (v. 6).

Of course, the most immediate tangible consequence of the fall was the unfamiliar sense of shame that befell our first parents. But it would appear that Adam and Eve did not quickly identify their feeling of disgrace with its cause so much as the product of that cause. They admitted to being sensitive over the fact that they were naked, but it seems they had not yet associated that newly acquired sensitivity to their recent misadventure. Remorse was deficient because repentance was absent, their embarrassment presented only as the indignity of having their flesh so exposed.

God promptly gets to the crux of the matter, but not so instantly as to deny Adam the opportunity to see for himself wherein lay the cause of his own discomfort. How had he become aware of his nakedness? Therein was contained the answer to Adam's unease. He had not previously been afraid of his Maker's voice, though presumably he had been equally naked. What had changed? Even then, without directly answering the question set before him, Adam refused to acknowledge responsibility for his own action. Shifting speedily from subdued to contentious, he attempted also—albeit falteringly—to redirect the blame. But the guilt would not be so readily removed, as if to relocate some inanimate external object, for it began to gnaw away at him from the inside.

Arguably the most tragic consequence of Adam's rebellion was his forfeiture to unbroken fellowship with the Creator. It would appear from the biblical data that the first man had thitherto enjoyed unique access of communication with God and made a conscious choice that he must have known could jeopardize such privilege forever. Moreover, his race is thenceforth subject to the law of sin continually at work, whereby his nature has a tendency toward evil deeds. As a direct penalty for choosing the path of disobedience, Adam was disciplined with a constant struggle against the natural elements in his pursuit of eking out a livelihood, Eve had imposed upon her pain during childbirth, while humanity in general was given a life span to be terminated by death, where previously there had been at least the possibility of endless duration. It is also worth reminding ourselves that, though death itself was a product of the fall, the means by which this cessation of life was to be implemented came by removing man from the potential sphere of his continuing existence on earth, that is, the tree of life.

Adam's sin did not consist merely in the overt act of disobedience, but in the inner aspiration to "be like God" (Gen 3:5). Indeed, if the specific sin of Adam teaches us anything, then it is perhaps that the essence of sin appears to be a grasping by mankind for spiritual and moral autonomy. The consequences of the fall were both manifold and far-reaching. Obviously, man's attitude toward God changed dramatically, expressed so poignantly in Adam and Eve's desire to hide from the presence of their Lord. God's displeasure toward Adam's action, however, was but the natural response of his own intrinsic righteousness.

It is impossible to grasp the heinousness of sin except in contrast to the absolute purity of God's righteousness. Even then, our understanding of it is restricted by finite parameters. In the words of John Calvin, albeit in a slightly different context: "For while the measure of our capacity is too contracted to comprehend things of such magnitude, our tongue is equally incapable of giving a full and substantial account of them."[33]

It is not necessarily true that original sin assumes original righteousness, though I find it difficult to conceive of the former existing apart from as a direct contravention of the latter. Others, however, have not been quite so slow to imagine their independence. Pelagius, for example, did not hold to the opinion that Adam was created with positive holiness, but that his initial condition was one of moral neutrality, the direction of which was to be governed by the choices he made in the free exercise of his will. The choices themselves were neither good nor evil, but became one or the other dependent upon the consequence of them. That Adam chose to sin was only significant in that it elicited divine judgment upon the act itself, not upon the choice that governed the act. For Pelagius, there is no transmission of sin, because there is no original sin to transmit. To be born "in Adam" is to begin life as Adam did in his original condition of neutrality, free from guilt and pollution, with the freedom to make one's own choices, and yet into an environment that will invariably lead those choices to be made with a proclivity toward evil. Such an argument serves only to convince me that those who choose to ignore the linguistic evidence commonly do so in order merely to gratify their own sensitive disposition.

Augustine, on the other hand, regarded sin as the privation of good. He also considered Adam to have been created with the potential to become

---

33. Calvin, *Genesis*, 57.

immortal, conditional upon meeting the requirements set before him by his Creator, God. Louis Berkhof describes Augustine's position thus: "From the state of the *non peccare et mori* (the ability to not sin and die) he would have passed to the state of the *non posse peccare et mori* (the inability to sin and die). But he sinned, and consequently entered the state of the *non posse non peccare et mori* (the inability not to sin and die)."[34]

Such a view seems rational, if a little contrived. What appears to be more agreeable still, however, is Augustine's conclusion that man is thereafter incapable of exercising free will in the absolute sense, but has the parameters of his freedom dictated by an inclination toward sinful thoughts and deeds, in accordance with his acquired sinful nature. Where I truly find myself at odds with the Augustinian position is in his alignment to the realist theory of sin's transmission, though I am also aware that it may have been largely precipitated by way of an apology against the Pelagian view.

When speaking of the condition of man after the fall, Reformed theologians refer to him as thereafter "totally depraved." Objections to the doctrine of the total depravity of man frequently belie a misunderstanding of the term used. Hammond seeks to clarify the matter by advising us to first take account of its original use by earlier theologians. He suggests that:

> It was never intended to convey the meaning that man is as bad as he possibly can be, and that every trace of moral rectitude has been lost in fallen man. Total depravity is intended to indicate that the evil principle . . . has invaded each part of human nature, so that there is no part of it which can now invariably perform righteous acts or . . . think righteous thoughts. That is to say, the totality applies rather to the field of operation of the evil principle and not to the actual degree of evil in the individual. The depravity is also total in the sense that, apart from divine aid, it is irreversible. There is no means known to man by which he can alter the bias of his nature.[35]

A comment equally worthy of note regarding the total depravity of man is to be found amongst the writings of William Hendriksen:

> To be sure, man is "totally depraved," in the sense that depravity has invaded every part of his being: mind, heart and will. If he is to be saved, it is God who must save him. Man cannot save himself. This, however, does not and cannot mean that he is "*absolutely depraved*," as bad as he can be, as bad as the devil

---

34. Berkhof, *Christian Doctrines*, 134.
35. Hammond, *In Understanding*, 77.

himself. Did not Jesus also teach that there is a sense in which even the unconverted "do good"? (See Luke 6:33).[36]

The immediate consequences of Adam's rebellion, then, were twofold. The fact that, upon hearing the approach of their Maker in the Garden, he and his wife "hid from the Lord God" indicates an acknowledgment of a tarnished conscience. They had previously felt quite comfortable in the presence of their God as they fellowshipped with him in the cool of the day. There was now only a sense of unease, remorse, and misgiving at the prospect of coming face to face with the One whose image they had so foolishly and permanently sullied. This leads us to the other, perhaps more devastating, outcome of their folly: the curse and its effects. We shall, of course, be considering this more fully below under the heading of "Adam's Federal Responsibility." Suffice it to be said at this stage, however, that no longer would Adam or his race be free from toil or trouble, and the separation both he and Eve experienced at that time was but the seed of decay that, having once been sown, would finally end in physical death.

The oft-repeated objection that for the whole of humanity to be held responsible and creation to suffer for one man's lapse is unfair is seriously flawed for a number of reasons. First of all, it carries with it the implicit argument that God is unjust, perhaps even vengeful. Such a proposition contravenes everything we otherwise know about his character and nature. God is not only a just God and, therefore, able to dispense justice perfectly, but also the perfect essence of justice resides exclusively in him. This is not merely toying with words for literary effect: the difference is both real and potentially revolutionary to our understanding of divine justice.

When the mother of a teenage son, who has been mercilessly and randomly gunned down, pleads for justice, she probably has in mind punitive measures being brought to bear against the assailant so that some degree of moral equity may be seen to have been restored. If an elderly couple, who have been duped out of their life savings by a bogus enterprise company, cry out for justice, they do so in the hope that fairness will ultimately prevail. When we see television footage of countless children in African lands being the apparently innocent victims of a drought-induced famine, or familial homes being torn about by earthquake or tsunami, one of our first thoughts might be to challenge the injustice of their plight. But do we ever make the same automatic connection between justice and righteousness, each in their purest forms, that the contributory writers of Scripture do? It is unlikely.

Well, did the punishment fit the crime? More to the point, are we capable of making such a call? To conclude that we are sufficiently competent

---

36. Hendriksen, *Romans*, 100.

assumes that we are in possession of all the facts, that we are able to interpret them from an entirely objective position, and that our judgment of them is completely untainted by sin. Only he who is truly righteous can exercise true justice. If righteousness, even in a derivative or relative sense, is to be acknowledged as conformity to a required standard, then surely only God can be trusted to meet that standard, given that it emanates from his own intrinsic Being.

A friend and I were recently discussing the arguments in favor and against the theory of annihilationism, that is, the cessation of existence for the unbeliever after a period of post-death punishment. My friend supports the theory; I do not. One of the arguments he posited was that it seemed unjust for those who had lived an "ordinary life," yet without Christ, to suffer everlasting torment. My conviction regarding Scripture's account of original sin is such that I find myself—on this point, at least—to be fully in agreement with Karl Barth, that there is no "relic or core or goodness, which persists in man in spite of his sin."[37] After many hours of discussion and several weeks of e-mails being sent back and forth, my friend is still no more convinced by my position than I am by his; but we are still very good friends.

Adam's Federal Responsibility

Sin entered the world through the sin of Adam. Equally unequivocal is Scripture's teaching that, with the exception of Jesus, "all have sinned and fall short of the glory of God" (Rom 3:23). There are no other escapees from the principle of sin and certainly no biblical evidence to support such a belief. Indeed, the incarnation was such that Christ was born in a way that negated the propagation of the sin principle in him. It does not seem unreasonable, therefore, to assume that, in some mysterious way, the universality of sin in Adam's seed is entirely due to his personal act of disobedience. As members of the human race through natural generation, we do not enter life pure (as Adam did), with a clean bill of health until the moment we fail to resist temptation. Rather, we are somehow tarnished with sin at birth, but from the point of conception. How can it be, then, that this uniform product is so inextricably linked to that unitary cause?

To paraphrase George Bernard Shaw: "If all the theologians who had ever lived were laid head to toe, it is doubtful that even then they would reach a conclusion that satisfied them all." In fact, it seems to me that there are two types of apologist: those who seek to convince by the reasonableness

---

37. Barth, *Church Dogmatics*, 493.

of their argument and those whose position is so weak that their sole ambition is to confuse by a rambling tirade of unrelated statements. The reader is left to decide who falls into which category.

Thus, there are a number of theories concerned with the fall of Adam and how original sin—or, at least, the consequences of and guilt annexed to it—has been transmitted to the entire human race thereafter. Some of these are as intricate as they are inventive. I guess they would have to be given the paucity of detail we are given regarding the mechanics associated with how we are justly held responsible for another's transgression. The main three are the myth theory, the realist theory, and the federal representative theory.

The Myth Theory

The myth theory, as one might correctly envisage, suggests that the fall of Adam was not a historic episode at all, but is mythologically employed to convey spiritual truths that would be otherwise impossible to discern. Proponents argue that historicity—or the lack thereof—is relatively unimportant, as the lessons to be gleaned from the imagery remain intact without the need for them to be substantiated as events that actually took place.

Such a view admittedly seems to resolve some tricky areas that otherwise remain, such as absolving God of any perceived responsibility for holding successive generations accountable for what might be deemed the sin of another. By this theory, all are guilty of replicating the template of the couple in "the story" and, thereby, succumbing to their own private "fall." The moral truth of it is still conveyed in some measure and those who embrace it may feel some relief at not having to admit to a curse that has the potential for ridicule from unbelievers. If it did not really happen, we no longer come under any obligation to defend why we think it did. Talking snakes aside, this theory certainly paves the way for the current syncretistic trend to fuse the Bible's teaching on creation with the scientific evolutionary theory. However, one man's "Hallelujah!" can so easily be another's anathema.

The alleged exclusively parabolic nature of the fall raises a number of significantly overt objections, and not a few others by inference. The most obvious one is that it singularly fails to explain the universality of sin; it merely comforts us in the fact that we are not alone in our mire of transgression. Of all the people that have ever lived, why is it that none have avoided succumbing to the temptation to enter their own private fall? To counter that we are but products of our environment surely begs the further question: "How, then, did the environment become sufficiently sullied to effect such a polluted condition?"

The implications of holding to the mythological view of Adam's fall are arguably even more contentious than those it seeks to avoid. There is little suggestion that Scripture presents the episode as anything other than a factually accurate account of something that actually took place in history. Certainly, both Jesus and Paul do not appear to consider it to be anything less than that. If it was a mere myth, then are we left with any alternative but to apply the same criteria to other similar episodes in the Old Testament, and who is to be trusted with making the decision about where the axe between truth and myth may fall? Moreover, surely to accept such a view impinges greatly on many of the other doctrines annexed to the New Testament teaching of Paul that seem to depend so heavily on the historicity of Adam and his fall, not least of which is the subject before us: the atonement as God's means of effecting man's reconciliation.

The Realist Theory

Surely, the realist hypothesis must fare considerably better. Well, it does find greater approval and in some of the key areas where the myth theory so blatantly fails, but only marginally so. Those who hold to this view posit that we are all personally accountable for Adam's sin because we all (that is, every single human being that has ever lived and ever will draw breath) were individually present in Adam when he yielded to that first temptation. In an attempt to resolve the moral issue of being held personally responsible for an act committed outside of ourselves, its proponents argue that we were really there all the time in some pre-existent immaterial version of ourselves, mystically included in the person of Adam. Needless to say, the Bible provides no legitimate basis for such an idea.

First proposed by Augustine in the fifth century AD and otherwise known as the natural headship theory, the realist theory has found considerable support amongst some noted theologians. Augustus Strong is perhaps the most well known. His appeal is to that of the least unsatisfactory of the major theories being propounded, probably gauged as the one with which his understanding of Scripture finds the weightier support. The same could be said of the others by those who lay claim to their own particular theory of choice. I would be both foolish to brook that trend and dishonest to claim otherwise. I cannot help but agree with others, however, that if we are to be held personally accountable for Adam's sin because of some organic, mystically real association with him whereby we were actually present in him when he sinned, then why only this sin and why only his sin?

On the face of it, the realist theory does sound reasonably plausible, but in seeking to resolve one issue, it almost inexorably brings a number of others clambering to the surface. Those who lay claim to the so-called classic proof texts for this argument adopt a far more literal approach than is warranted and pay scant regard to what are obvious examples of Hebrew idiom. It is a similar fault of the Catholic doctrine of transubstantiation being founded upon Jesus taking the bread and saying: "This is my body given for you" (Luke 22:19). The texts in question on this occasion are to be found in Ezekiel (18:2–4) and Hebrews (7:9–10). The argument that looks to the former falls on its face, so to speak, within a very few verses (Ezek 18:19–20), while the latter is neither related nor relevant to the transmission of sin.

Although it would be clearly erroneous to speak of the collective will of humanity in Adam, it is by no means unjustifiable to acknowledge the plain biblical teaching that Adam sinned as the representative of all of humanity, and that the consequences of his action were not restricted to him only, but thereafter affected all his posterity also. In reply to the question, "Did all mankind fall in Adam's transgression?" the Westminster Shorter Catechism responds by speaking of a covenant having been made with Adam, not only for himself, but also on behalf of his offspring, whereby everyone who descended from him by ordinary generation "sinned with him, and fell with him, in his first transgression." The covenant of which it speaks contains the key to our understanding something of the federal responsibility of Adam. It is implied in the Genesis account, stated in the book of Hosea (6:7), and amplified by the Apostle Paul in the New Testament, especially so in his letter to the church at Rome (see Rom 5:18–19).

The Federal Representative Theory

As we have seen, Reformed theologians generally regard original sin as an instinctive tendency toward privation caused by the internal perversion of the human nature. Calvin's understanding of it was that of a divine precept being issued against humanity so that its effect is one of Adam's sin being attributed to his progeny in much the same way that Christ's righteousness is imputed to believers. Subsequently elaborated upon and modified by Calvin's successors, this doctrine has since become firmly established within the tenets of the Westminster Confession. Adam is thus acknowledged as being far more than simply the natural head of the human race; rather, he is seen as its federal representative. As a result, all mankind is born in pollution and corruption because they are symbolically embodied in the sin and guilt of Adam. This is the root cause of man's fundamental inclination toward sin: a federal identification, the fruit of which is manifestly evident in sinful acts.

As federal representative, the fall of our first parent ensured that the whole of Adam's posterity was thenceforth tainted with the principle of sin in them. It has been noted that: "The Fall had abiding effect ... upon all who descended from [Adam and Eve]; there is racial solidarity in sin and evil."[38] Richard Gaffin has the following to say:

> A perennially debated question is exactly how "through the disobedience of the one man the many were made sinners" (Rom 5:19a). In view of the sustained emphasis on the *one* sin of the *one* man (vv. 15–19), as well as the antithetical parallel way, here as elsewhere (see especially Rom 4:1–8), in which believers are justified, all men are sinners not only because they inherit a sinful nature from Adam, but primarily because his sin is imputed to them, or reckoned as theirs.[39]

Even though the account of Adam is restricted to comparatively few chapters of the Bible, the whole of the rest of the Scriptures can only be properly understood in the light of his influence upon them. Successive generations of willful transgression against God's law are seen to be the inevitable and unavoidable consequence of this one man's disobedience. The federal headship of Adam is no more clearly presented than when it is compared with that of Christ in Pauline theology (see Rom 5:12–21; 1 Cor 15:21–22, 45–49):

Adam	(Rom 5)	Christ
"the trespass"	v. 15	"the gift"
"judgment . . . and . . . condemnation"	v. 16	"justification"
"death reigned"	v. 17	"reign in life"
"one trespass"	v. 18	"one act of righteousness"
"disobedience"	v. 19a	"obedience"
"many were made sinners"	v. 19b	"many will be made righteous"
"sin increased"	v. 20	"grace increased all the more"

---

38. J. Murray and B. A. Milne, "Sin," in Douglas, *New Bible Dictionary*, 1117.
39. R. B. Gaffin, "Adam," in Ferguson and Wright, *New Dictionary of Theology*, 5.

| "sin reigned in death" | v. 21 | "grace [to] reign through righteousness [unto] eternal life." |

Adam	**(1 Cor 15)**	**Christ**
"death came through a man"	v. 21	"resurrection of the dead comes also through a man"
"in Adam all die"	v. 22	"in Christ all will be made alive"
"the first man Adam ... a living being"	v. 45	"last Adam, a life-giving spirit"
"of the dust of the earth"	v. 47	"from heaven."

I am particularly indebted—in this regard, at least—to the conclusions of Robert Lewis Dabney, who catalogues his findings under:

1. The parallel which is drawn between Christ and Adam (Rom 5:12–19; 1 Cor 15:22, 47). In almost everything they are contrasted, yet Christ is the second Adam. The only parallelism is in the fact that they were both representative persons.
2. The fact proves it, that the penalty denounced on Adam has actually taken effect on every one of his posterity (see Gen 6:3).
3. The Bible declares that sin, death, and all penal evil come into the world through Adam (Rom 5:12; 1 Cor 15:22).
4. Although the various other communications of the first three chapters of Genesis are apparently addressed to Adam singly, we know that they applied equally to his posterity, as the permission to eat of all the fruits of the earth; the command to replenish the earth; the threatened pains of child-bearing; the curse of the ground, and the doom of labor, etc.[40]

In his treatment on *Man in the Covenant of Works*, Louis Berkhof similarly asserts that:

> The parallel which Paul draws between Adam and Christ in Rom 5:12–21 ... can only be explained on the assumption that Adam, like Christ, was the head of a covenant. According to Paul the essential element in justification consists in this, that the righteousness of Christ is imputed to us, without any personal work on our part to merit it. And he regards this as a perfect parallel to the manner in which the guilt of Adam is imputed to us. This

---

40. Dabney, *Systematic Theology*, 304.

naturally leads to the conclusion that Adam also stood in covenant relationship to his descendants.⁴¹

The ultimate penalty for sin, of course, was the appearance of death. The principle of death is separation. Although physical death became a reality for us all because of Adam's corporate transgression, the fundamental aspect of death is in the spiritual sense of alienation from God. It is just because of this radical breakdown of relationship with the Creator that our moral nature is thus affected (Rom 3:23); our intellect is restricted within such boundaries (1 Cor 2:14); and our will is inclined toward self-centeredness, which in turn determines the desires (Rom 1:24), the emotions (2 Tim 3:4), speech (Jas 3:5–9), and actions (Gal 5:19–21). Berkhof thus concludes that: "The sinful state [of man] is the basis of sinful habits, and these manifest themselves in sinful deeds." Or, to put it another way, men are not sinners because they sin; they sin because they are sinners. I remember hearing the story many years ago of one man stating, with deliberate facetiousness, that he did not remember sinning with Adam. His Christian friend responded with equal aplomb: "No; I don't recall conquering its effects in Christ either, but I rejoice that the Bible assures me it is so."

When Adam sinned, then, we all sinned in him. Thus, the fall of the first man was the fall of humanity. There was no mystic realism attached to mankind's relationship to Adam, as some would have us believe. Rather, the covenant relationship in which Adam stood as the creature to his Creator was one in which he represented us all as potential beneficiaries or penalty bearers. Had he not sinned, we would have probably lived in the good of his obedience and been grateful to do so. The fact that he did sin means that we must somehow bear the price of his disobedience. I must, therefore, concur with Robert Sproul's observation that:

> . . . the federal view of the Fall is substantially correct . . . It satisfies me that God is not an arbitrary tyrant. I know that I am a fallen creature. That is, I know that I am a creature and I know that I am fallen. I also know that it is not God's "fault" that I am a sinner. What God has done for me is to redeem me from my sin. He has not redeemed me from his sin.⁴²

The man widely acknowledged as being responsible for the formulation of the doctrine of Adam's federal headship is the seventeenth-century German-born theologian, Johannes Cocceius (1603–1669). Building on the development of his predecessors, most notably Zacharias Ursinus and

---

41. Berkhof, *Systematic Theology*, 214.
42. Sproul, *Chosen by God*, 73.

Caspar Olevianus, Cocceius is rightly lauded for his contribution to covenant theology (Latin *foedus* means "covenant"). We must be careful that we do not go too far in our esteem of him, however, by imagining that he somehow "invented" the idea of our covenantal relationship to Adam, particularly in the context of the fall. Just as the early church fathers did not so much bring about the canon of New Testament Scripture as they formally ratified its constituent parts, so too Cocceius was merely the first to identify Adam's federal headship as a viable, valid, and vital hermeneutic by which to interpret God's dealings with the rest of humanity.

Although it would perhaps be too much of a stretch to posit that the embracing of Adam's federal headship will in and of itself resolve all hitherto hidden theological mysteries, I do share Arthur Pink's opinion that without an adequate understanding of it, much else is lost to us than need necessarily be the case. He makes his point thus:

> Adam was not only the common parent of mankind, but he was also their federal head and representative. The whole human race was placed on probation or trial in Eden. Adam acted not for himself alone, but he transacted for all who were to spring from him. Unless this basic fact be definitely apprehended, much that ought to be relatively clear to us will be shrouded in impenetrable mystery. Yea, we go further, and affirm that, until the federal headship of Adam be actually perceived, we are without the key to God's dealings with the human race, we are unable to discern man's relation to the divine law, and we appreciate not the fundamental principles upon which the atonement of Christ proceeded.[43]

The Wider Parameters of Sin's Effects

When referring to the Adamic fall, any Bible commentator worth his salt must surely mention the doctrine of total depravity or radical corruption. Not all will do so with any sense of conviction; some will be quite hostile to the very idea, but will feel just as compelled to vent their fury as those who are convinced of it will be forced to share their insights. Even among those who fall into the latter category, however, there is not always the unanimity of understanding we might expect. Consider the following examples:

> [The Bible] uniformly represents the unregenerate as totally depraved, and calls upon them to repent, to make themselves a

---

43. Pink, *Divine Covenants*, 13.

new heart; and never admits directly, or by way of implication, that they can do anything good or acceptable to God, while in the exercise of a wicked or selfish heart.[44]

The total lack of spiritual good and inability to do good before God has traditionally been called "total depravity."[45]

Total depravity . . . signifies a corruption of our moral and spiritual nature that is total, not in degree . . . but in extent. It declares that no part of us is untouched by sin and, therefore, no action of ours is as good as it should be, and consequently nothing in us or about us appears meritorious in God's eyes.[46]

Without the references, there is little there to cause much of an outcry to my theological understanding, though I might require further qualification on some of the quotations before relinquishing a hearty "Amen!" For example, Wayne Grudem includes his as a footnote, to which he adds: "but I will not use the phrase here because it is easily subject to misunderstanding. It can give the impression that no good in any sense can be done by unbelievers, a meaning that is certainly not intended by the term or by this doctrine."

Jim Packer adds a similar condition to his use of the phrase. Both he and Grudem find themselves labeled as Calvinists, though I suspect each would identify with me in supporting Jonathan Edwards' self-assessment that he did not slavishly endorse Calvin's views and, indeed, found him to be in error on some points. It just so happened that his understanding of Christian doctrine from the biblical evidence before him—and his interpretation of that evidence—coincided with many of the conclusions presented by John Calvin.

It was in his *Institutes of the Christian Religion* that Calvin initially discussed the effects of the fall on humanity as originally created in God's image. Although some of his followers may have subsequently taken his findings several steps further, it becomes clear that Calvin himself employed the phrase "total depravity" in the sense that "no aspect of man's original being or sensitivity has been left unaffected by sin." Calvin spoke of two spheres of life, the spiritual and the temporal, concluding that in relation to God: "mankind has been wholly deprived of all true knowledge and ability,"

---

44. Finney, *Lectures*, 249.
45. Grudem, *Systematic Theology*, 497.
46. Packer, *Concise Theology*, 83–84.

whilst "with regard to temporal . . . activities, the natural man still retains admirable qualities . . . by which to conduct his manifold human affairs."[47]

By way of contrast, Charles Grandison Finney was a staunch Arminianist. Are we to assume, therefore, that total depravity is not an exclusively Calvinistic doctrine at all? On some matters, what are often ungraciously derided as Arminianist doctrines are really no more so than those that are similarly disparaged for their Calvinistic heritage. The former often belong to a minority group with semi-Pelagian tendencies, while the latter may prove to be the treatises of hyper-Calvinists, which their forbear might have been ashamed to own. On this occasion, however, we need to understand that common use of terminology does not in itself guarantee universal application of understanding.

Finney's use of "total depravity" is aligned to a voluntary condition determined by individual will rather than constitutional sinfulness. Moreover, a certain intrinsic inconsistency needs to be pointed out in his argument. If, by such a personal choice, an individual places him or herself in a position of not being able to do "anything good or acceptable to God, while in the exercise of a wicked or selfish heart," then why would such a heart allow them to make the decision to "repent, and make themselves a new heart"? I do not criticize Finney personally and would never do so to the extent—as some have—of labeling him a heretic. I am grateful to God for the fruit of his ministry, despite what I consider to be his doctrinal idiosyncrasies.

It would be inappropriate to formulate or defend a doctrine on observation alone; Scripture must always be both our foundation and guide in such matters, even if our interpretation of it is subsequently proved to be wanting. Indeed, for those of us who purport to be Bible-believing Christians, if the determinant factor of our theology is anything other than Scripture, then perhaps the pattern of our understanding is in dire need of readjustment. However, what cannot be allowed to pass by unnoticed is that those who appear to most vociferously oppose the doctrine of total depravity are also the same who seem to have an inadequate view regarding the sinfulness of sin. Is this a mere coincidence? I think not.

Although many of the definitions that come from those of a Reformed persuasion ultimately amount to the same thing—though some spend so long outlining what total depravity is not that the reader is often left to deduce the definition from what remains—that used by Jim Packer (cited above) probably comes closest to my own understanding. What we do emanates from who we are. Thus, the noblest act of the unregenerate is that

---

47. R. S. Wallace, "Calvin, John," in Ferguson and Wright, *New Dictionary of Theology*, 122.

produced by a sinful nature and, therefore, of no eternal value. Our actions are unrighteous because our natures are sinful. It might even be said that there is a strange irony in the fact that so depraved is the human condition that, when faced with the notion of its depravity, it seeks to prove otherwise and, in so doing, attests only to its reality. Thus, the argument against total depravity is utterly deprived of merit.

Calvinism versus Arminianism aside, those who refute the idea of total depravity, even in its properly defined sense, do so on a number of grounds. We shall consider some of them. First of all, if man by his nature is so incapable of doing right in God's eyes, is he truly in possession of free will? In order to be able to answer that properly, we need to understand what is truly meant by free will. Before Adam fell, he had the freedom to exercise his will however he wanted and make absolutely unrestricted choices—or did he?

True freedom is governed by the capacity to act in accordance with the choices with which the will voluntarily engages. Only God has absolute power to bring unlimited choices of his will into being; even then, the options available to him are constrained by the parameters of his nature. He cannot, for example, choose to behave in a way that is inconsistent with who he is. Unfallen Adam was also bound by certain restrictions, which thereby impinged upon the choices available to his volition. He was a man; he could not wake up one day and decide to be a duck and expect it to be so. Fallen man is also bound within certain parameters, within which—and only within which—he may exercise "free" will. The fall of man brought with it the fallen nature of man, whereby there is now within us all a fundamental proclivity to choose that which the sinful human nature finds most agreeable. Moreover, man's natural judgment is so clouded that he would be wholly incapable of determining the righteous option, even if he had a propensity to do so.

Secondly, and this is related to the first objection raised, does not such inability to behave differently thereby negate our accountability for the actions that thereafter ensue? Again, this was annexed to the argument posited by Pelagius during the late fourth and early fifth centuries. It is not without its supporters today. Now, as then, the premise seems to be one of reason filtered through the lens of sentiment rather than an appropriate commitment to the pages of Scripture. God—through the Bible—declares us to be guilty. There is no higher court of appeal. Our only hope is not to cry "Injustice!" but to plead that we might somehow be rid of such guilt. We are deemed guilty because God says we are, but he has not left us without hope in becoming righteous once more, as we shall see in due course.

Thirdly, if nothing I do can ever find favor with God, then what incentive remains to even try? This seems to be the excuse of a naughty infant escalated upwards or the reasoning of a petty crook seeking to justify his decision to join the ranks of the serious criminal: "If daddy's going to be cross with me for trying to behave, then I may as well not bother"; "If I am to serve a maximum prison term, then I may as well make it worthwhile." If we were totally depraved in the sense by which that term is commonly misunderstood, there might be a legitimate point to such arguments. But, running alongside this truth of every area of our nature being adversely affected by the sin principle is the fact that we also retain some measure of the image of God, by which we inwardly yearn to be otherwise. This is surely the key to understanding the Apostle Paul's somewhat protracted and otherwise largely incomprehensible dilemma, as recorded in his letter to the believers at Rome:

> I do not understand what I do. For what I want to do I do not do, but what I hate I do. And if I do what I do not want to do, I agree that the law is good. As it is, it is no longer I myself who do it, but it is sin living in me. I know that nothing good lives in me, that is, in my sinful nature. For I have the desire to do what is good, but I cannot carry it out. For what I do is not the good I want to do; no, the evil I do not want to do—this I keep on doing. Now if I do what I do not want to do, it is no longer I who do it, but it is sin living in me that does it. So I find this law at work: When I want to do good, evil is right there with me. For in my inner being I delight in God's law; but I see another law at work in the members of my body, waging war against the law of my mind and making me a prisoner of the law of sin at work within my members. What a wretched man I am! Who will rescue me from this body of death?[48]

Paul provides the answer to his own question in the following verse, and this will form the subject of the following chapter.

But it is not just the depraved human nature that Paul finds so immensely tiresome. If the totality referred to its absoluteness, perhaps there would be no struggle. But it is the constant battle between the incapacity to do good and the intense desire to do so that is the problem. Or, to put it another way, radical corruption versus image retention lies at the root of Paul's dilemma. Just as the totality is in scope and not scale, so too the loss of the image of God in us has not left us utterly devoid of bearing some of that likeness. I realize, of course, that the apostle could simply be employing terminology with which his Jewish readership would be all too familiar. In this connection, Grant Osborne is correct to remind us that: "The Jews

---

48. Rom 7:15–24.

believed every person has an impulse or inclination to do good (*yetzer tob*) and an impulse to do evil (*yetzer hara*) and that every decision was made on the basis of interaction between these two forces."[49] Equally, it is not beyond the realm of reason that the Jews arrived at this construct on the basis of the inner conflict between the sinful nature and the partially retained image of God in man.

At first glance, the doctrines of man's total depravity and his retention of the image of God appear to be contradictory. A more detailed analysis of their finer points, however, reveals them to be but two sides of the same coin. Man's personality is clearly tarnished, but it is not destroyed; his innate sense of spirituality may well be polluted, but not completely muddied; though his moral integrity has been contaminated, there is yet some vestige of lawfulness and uprightness; the inherent authority of man has been abused, but this has not left him utterly desolate and devoid of compassion; whilst his creative aptitude is often egocentric, there are nevertheless remnants of beauty and ingenuity. Of course, these are of no salvific value. As has often been said, if a line is not perfectly straight, then it is crooked. And again, if it is incapable by its own means of becoming straight, then it is totally depraved, whether it is so by a millimeter or a mile. Without divine assistance, there is no means available to man by which he may change the proclivity of his nature. Or, as Isaiah the prophet put it in this context: "all our righteous acts are like filthy rags."[50]

Although the Bible refers specifically to man being created in the image of God, what this actually means is left to our powers of reason and deduction. The difficulty with this is that we are as capable of reasonably incorrect deductions as we are of being accurate in our assumptions. I have already noted a subtle, but nonetheless real, distinction between image and likeness. If man in God's image simply meant that he was like him, then the devil's temptation that eating of the forbidden fruit would make Adam and Eve like God would surely have been far less enticing. Of course, it is possible—even probable—that the likeness that existed and that which did not referred to different qualities. For as long as I can remember, those who have known us both have said that I am like my maternal grandfather. My sister says this is becoming increasingly true as I grow older, but readily concedes that there are some respects in which I could never possibly be like him.

Thus, likeness does not have to be perfect or absolute. Adam was created in God's image and shared some of his Creator's characteristics in measure. Theologians refer to these as the communicable attributes. He

---

49. Osborne, *Romans*, 186.
50. Isa 64:6.

was unlike his Maker in respect of his non-communicable attributes. These include omnipotence, omnipresence, omniscience, infinity, self-existence, and immutability. Amongst the communicable attributes, which Adam shared, we might mention spirituality, personality, knowledge, wisdom, veracity, goodness, holiness, righteousness, and resolve.

Although these aspects of the image of God in Adam were not perfect in the absolute sense of the word, they were innocent inasmuch that they were as yet unpolluted; the fall changed all of that. Where there had previously been harmony between man's spirit and that of his God, this was no longer the case; where Adam had hitherto been quite content to subject his personhood to the Fatherhood of the Almighty, he now wished to exercise a measure of autonomy; a knowledge that had been free from evil now embraced that also; into the field of heavenly wisdom was sown seeds that would eventually cause his descendants to choose instead to be worldly wise; veracity would relinquish its stronghold to guile and dishonesty, as would virtue to vice. Yes, the image was retained, but as in an old-fashioned mirror of polished metal: it was blurred and imprecise.

Before we conclude by identifying what I believe to be the key areas in which man retains some semblance of the image of God, in spite of his fallen nature, it is perhaps worth noting those features that have been culpably tarnished by sin. Man's ability to relate socially is somewhat affected because of his sullied personality; his sense of spirituality, desperate for expression, has become marred in its focus and is, therefore, frequently executed illegitimately; man's reason is perceptibly clouded by issues that he refuses to acknowledge; so-called "progressive morality" is usually based on social acceptability rather than finding its foundation in divine decree; God-inspired dominion far too easily gives way to fleshly domination; and man's inherent creativity is more often than not employed toward destructive ends.

All of this notwithstanding, man remains created in God's image. This being the case, it is possible to identify five specific areas where this retained image of God in man is yet discernible:

(i) the soul's qualities of personality, invisibility, and spirituality;

(ii) the psychical faculties of the rational intellect and will;

(iii) the moral integrity of man's nature;

(iv) the body as a suitable vehicle for exercising dominion; and

(v) man's invested authority as vice-regent over creation.

Sin Has Tainted the Created Order

Creation, too, is affected by the fruit of God's wrath against sin on the part of his vice-regent. Adam's sin was not an independent action, for its consequences were far-reaching, as we have seen. Not only was mankind alienated from God's perfect purpose, but also creation itself was similarly tainted. As God's representative in the earth, Adam's disobedience adversely influenced his living environment: "Cursed [was] the ground because of [him]" (Gen 3:17). Commenting on the divine sentence passed on man, Dietrich Bonhoeffer adds that:

> God's Word to Adam proclaims the destruction and division of the primal relation between man and nature. The ground, for the fruits of which Adam . . . previously only had to stretch out a hand, which had brought him what he needed, becomes cursed because of Adam's deed. It becomes Adam's concern, his pain, his toil, his enemy . . . This is . . . earth, cursed out of the glory of its creation, cast out of the unequivocal directness of its language and of its praise of the Creator into the ambiguity of the absolutely strange and mysterious. The trees, the animals, which had once represented the Word of God, the Creator, directly, now indicate in often grotesque ways the inconceivability, the arbitrariness of a despot hidden in darkness. Thus the work of man upon the cursed ground becomes the expression of the disunion of fallen man within nature; it is under the curse.[51]

Sin may well have taken place within the sphere of man's psyche, but the seeds of it were thence sown in the whole of creation. Both the evidence of Scripture and the reality of our experience testify to how deeply the natural world has been impacted by the disobedience of Adam. Where there had previously been harmony in the cosmos, there now resides discord; where pre-fallen creation knew of abundance, growth, and productivity, there was now death, decay, and repression. No longer would vegetation and the plant world willingly offer up their produce to the vice-regent over all the earth; instead, he would experience only strife, anxiety, difficulty, and hardship in providing for himself from his surroundings.

Thus, the fact that creation is currently subject to frustration is a matter of the biblical record (Rom 8:20a). That it is so through no fault of its own is equally clear (v. 20b). But its condition since the fall of Adam has not been one of static non-fulfillment of its potential. Rather, it has from that time on been bound to a process of lingering morpholysis (v. 21). This

---

51. Bonhoeffer, *Creation and Temptation*, 85.

progressive worsening is perhaps not quite so apparent in the KJV, which offers "corruption" as its translation, but the original Greek *phthora* "signifies a bringing or being brought into an inferior or worse condition."[52] It refers not so much to something being as to its becoming by degrees. It denotes more than merely arrested development; it speaks of a rigorous demise. It can be compared—in part, at least—to a potentially world-class pianist who, before having reached her prime, begins to notice the onset of premature degenerative arthritis in the knuckle joints of her fingers. At first, she ploughs on heroically, unable and unwilling to come to terms with the stark reality that faces her. In time, the painkillers cease to have their desired effect, the hands refuse to obey the will of the musician, the audience applause is no longer to be heard, and finally she refuses even to touch the keys, lest it remind her of what might have been. Her only hope is that some miracle cure may be found, but it has now been so long that, were that to be the case, would she even remember what to do?

This process of decay is also recognized by scientists as the principle of progressive entropy, which is the second law of thermodynamics. Although in this context it refers to the transfer of heat energy within a given system, the definition is surely more widely applicable: entropy is the quantitative measure of disorder in a system. Qualify this further by introducing the consistent degeneration process, where the system in question is the universe, and one is left in no doubt that the effects of sin on the created order may clearly be described as entropic. Strictly speaking, such chaos is irreversible; the process can be redirected, but only by the presentation of an energy source from outside of the system to be thus affected. This is surely the whole premise of Paul's argument relating to the restoration of man and, by extension, the renewal of the created order by the demands of the penalty placed upon them having been met by an external Mediator.

But we must not abandon our lesson in New Testament Greek just yet. In the previous verse, Paul speaks of the creation being subject to frustration, as we have seen. This is how the NIV translates the Greek *mataiotes*. The KJV has "vanity," though as Hendriksen points out,[53] it is difficult to render this in the sense of "inflated pride" in the passage under consideration. But can we be any more certain that "frustration" does more justice to the original intent? The corresponding verb and adverb forms are linked to "making empty as a consequence of another act" or "to no desired purpose."[54] In this milieu, it is not so much "vanity" in the sense of being puffed up, but "in

---

52. Vine, *Expository Dictionary*, 235.
53. Hendriksen, *Romans*, 268.
54. Vine, *Expository Dictionary*, 1193.

vain," that is, without having achieved the purpose for which the effort was engaged. To say that we tried in vain does not mean that we endeavored with great pomp, but that we did not attain that for which we set out. The frustration on the part of the created order, therefore, is one brought about by the temporal incapacity to realize its potential.

The sin of Adam has adversely affected the rest of the created order on two distinct levels. Perhaps the most obvious of these lies in the fact that God annexed his judgment upon Adam with the ground whence he was taken (Gen 3:17–19). Those who take the view that such a judgment is somehow unjust must pause to consider the alternative. Prior to the fall, there is sufficient grounds to presume that the created order was blessed because of Adam's righteousness; why, then is it any less fair that it be cursed on account of his sin? We must also be aware, however, that part of Adam's prelapsarian responsibility was to engage in an ambassadorial stewardship role over creation on God's behalf. Can we really imagine that his sin did not have a negative outcome on his capacity to fulfill such a task as effectively as would have been the case had he remained without sin? We may never know for sure, of course, but I doubt whether our initial instincts would be so very far removed from the truth of it.

It must also be noted that the stewardship mandate was not rescinded; it remains in force. Although Scripture is generally silent regarding how this directive is now to be obeyed, we may be reasonably sure that some of the ways that the earth and its other inhabitants have been treated by humanity over the centuries fall some way short of the divine expectation. Despite all the expertise and research analysis available to us today, it hardly needs stating that the vitiating of man's stewardship over the rest of the created order is more obvious now than it has ever been. Certainly, the effects of his abuse and exploitation are more palpable. Moreover, and without exception, every aspect that mankind may be seen to be failing in this regard can be traced without too much difficulty to a disposition that leans toward greed, extortion, pride, abuse, and expedience; in a word, sin.

Before I go any further, let me first of all qualify my position regarding the potential man has for the destruction of the planet, lest I be misunderstood. Since Eden, the whole of creation has been on a one-way journey to decay. Psalmist and prophet alike testify to the heavens and the earth wearing out "like a garment" (Ps 102:26; Isa 50:9; 51:6), in stark contrast to our unchanging and immutable God. The New Testament writers were no less persuaded of the fact (see Heb 1:11). That the old worn out garb will be replaced is equally sure. But our times are ultimately in his hands (Ps 31:15); the end of the age will only come at his appointed time (Eccl 3:1; Rom 9:9), and in accordance with certain criteria having been met (Matt 24:14; 1 Cor

15:24). We do not know when that time is to be, nor are we encouraged to speculate on such matters. Christians can hasten the day in some respects by working toward the necessary conditions being met in us and through us, but God will be the one who makes the decision to "roll up the garment."

That notwithstanding, humanity retains its creational mandate to be wise stewards of the earth and its resources. Those who include the Genesis account of creation among their holy Scriptures should need no reminding of their obligations in this regard. Amazingly, however, the ones who seem to take such a responsibility most seriously are those with little or no religious infrastructure upon which to hang their convictions. Biological studies, environmental analyses, research into climatic changes, and a continually developing understanding of the effects of the so-called carbon footprint on our planet all contribute to a knowledge that is hitherto unsurpassed. No longer does one need to be a Christian, a Jew, or a Muslim to realize that mankind has generally been less than dutiful in caring for his surroundings.

Does the acquiring of such information place us all under an even greater obligation? Well, to imagine that it does implies also that ignorance lessens our responsibility. The evidence of Scripture is far removed from such a proposition. Sin is an abrogation of God's righteous requirements, irrespective of whether or not we are aware of that fact.

Of course, we can only truly gauge the effects of the curse on man's environment by making a direct comparison between the relative situations before and after Adam's sin. This knowledge is largely unavailable to us. We can only imagine the difference between the two, though there are certain clues to aid us in our quest. For example, we know that thereafter the earth resisted man in his endeavors and that this is presented in terms that make it appear to be a product of his rebellion. It does not seem unreasonable to assume, therefore, that in its unaffected state the earth was compliant, even perhaps offering up its harvest with little effort required on the part of Adam and Eve. In short, the correlation of maximum yield for minimum exertion has been dramatically and irrevocably reversed.

Thus, the curse on creature and nature alike, to be inferred from both the Genesis account and Paul's reminder to the Roman believers, is one of devastating endurance. If we only had the former record to go by, then we might easily believe the sentence to be exclusively punitive. The context of Paul's reference to it, however, suggests not only hope for the created order, but anticipation of that hope, as if creation was fully aware that it would eventually fulfill the destiny for which it was designed. Disorder will once again give up its claim to divine order, imbalance will surrender to organic unity, and the original purpose of God in creation—that is, the whole of creation—will finally be realized.

In the meantime, however, the link between human sin and divine judgment is firmly established. Neither should we be tempted to think that it is only referred to in this context, as if there might be some as yet unrevealed scribal error belonging to such an age of antiquity. The sin of those of Noah's generation evoked a similar response from God to the one we see in Eden (see Gen 6:5–7:5). Similar sentiments are also expressed many years later through the prophets of old. Isaiah is particularly forthright, speaking as he does of devastation, ruin, being completely laid waste, total plunder, languishment, withering, defilement, being consumed by a curse, broken up, split asunder, and thoroughly shaken (Isa 24:1–20). Even the most noted planetary light-bearers will be dimmed in the face of God's justice being dispensed (v. 23). And the cause of such vivid language? It was the catalogue of human sin as outlined by the prophet in the previous eleven chapters or so.

But not only is creation a victim of God's punishment against sin, it is also very often a channel by which that judgment is meted out. We need only to be reminded of the plagues of Egypt immediately prior to the exodus of God's covenant people to be convinced of the veracity of that statement (see Exod 7:14—11:10). But this is not just a matter-of-fact incidental, especially in the context of what we are considering here. No; this, too, is testament to the fact that Adam's sin has tainted the created order, for it is now expected to fulfill a function that was never included in the blueprint. How many among our respective workforces—whichever side of the Atlantic you may happen to be domiciled—are frustrated to find themselves in jobs that fail to allow them the creativity that was promised at the interview? And, as if this is not in itself cause for more than mild annoyance, how much more perturbed must they be to discover that many more menial tasks are to be expected of them than was initially made clear? Now escalate the sense of that exasperation to encompass the whole of creation.

There is perhaps an element of fanciful speculation to Martyn Lloyd-Jones's musing on the subject, but I also think it captures the sense of frustration experienced by creation perfectly well when he asks:

> I wonder whether the phenomenon of the Spring supplies us with a part answer. Nature every year, as it were, makes an effort to renew itself, to produce something permanent; it has come out of the death and the darkness of all that is so true of the Winter. In the Spring it seems to be trying to produce a perfect creation, to be going through some kind of birth-pangs year by year. But unfortunately, it does not succeed, for Spring leads only to Summer, whereas Summer leads to Autumn, and

Autumn to Winter. Poor old nature tries every year to defeat the "vanity" of the principle of death and disintegration that is in it. But it cannot do so. It fails every time. It still goes on trying, as if it feels things should be different and better, but it never succeeds. It has been doing so for a very long time . . . but nature still repeats the effort annually.[55]

Part of creation's frustration, then, is undoubtedly because of human negligence, but I cannot concede more ground than that to those who claim that this is the sole cause of such dissatisfaction. Inadequate policies of cosmic management coupled with practices that pay scant regard to the need to preserve and protect, even from a selfishly anthropocentric perspective, cannot be underestimated, but neither should they be inappropriately overstated, as some have been in the habit of doing.

This is perhaps where the evidence for the pervading influence of sin is most clear. Of course, the main premise of the argument in this section is how Adam's original sin adversely impinged upon man's surroundings and his earthly nonhuman cohabitants thenceforth. But we hardly need a degree in environmental studies to convince us that it continues to be so affected in no small part due to mankind's propensity for sinful acts. We are still called to be stewards of the earth and its resources. How long they continue to be negatively influenced by the effects of divine curse is largely out of our hands. What remains in some measure within our capacity is to ensure, as far as is practicable, that sinful deeds on our part do not add to the creation's misery.

Those who seek to trivialize sin or recategorize it as a simple mistake or merely an error of judgment would be better advised to consider the consequences of sin before they too hastily remove it from their vocabulary. Where the pinnacle of God's creation had previously known only peace, harmony, and joy in his relationships with God, his family, and that over which he was vice-regent, there was thereafter embarrassment, dysfunction, and toil. If that fails to impress upon us the seriousness of sin, then consider what it took to bring a satisfactory resolution to the heart of God on its account.

Sadly, some of those who would otherwise describe themselves as evangelical, even church leaders, have not been exempt from the tendency to devalue, and sometimes encourage, the practice of so-called "cheeky little sins." Cohabitation sounds far more sanitized than "living in sin," but it is no less alien to the principles of godly relationships for all that. This might appear to be a more obvious example, but what about the flagrant disregard

---

55. Lloyd-Jones, *Romans 8:17–39*, 59–60.

for our God-provided habitat? Is it any more tolerable to sin in this way? Surely, the matter is *res ipsa loquitur*.

Summary

The world in which we live is not merely the stage upon which humanity plays out the developmental acts of life, but it is in very real terms the soil from which that life is produced. There is a natural affinity between mankind and the rest of the created order that transcends even the profundity of the fact that we share God as our Creator. The whole of the creation process was begun with the idea of relationship, stewardship, and interdependence. When Adam sinned, his actions were tragically more extensive than to strike solely at humanity, disastrous though that undoubtedly was. As a system designed to bear good fruit in accordance with the divinely instituted principle of sowing and reaping, sin did not simply negate that decree, but introduced to its core an alien seed of evil origin, against the fruit of which creation itself has thereafter been subjected and frustrated.

SUMMARY

Many Christians today rejoice in their salvation without really knowing what it entails or what is encompassed by it. The reality and benefits of the atonement await our discovery in subsequent chapters, but it is my conviction that our appreciation of them would be much enhanced by a more informed understanding of precisely what necessitated them. I remember my former lecturer in evangelistic studies reinforcing the idea that it was necessary to precipitate a crisis in the minds of the listeners before you could reasonably expect them to take advantage of a satisfactory resolution. A similar principle applies in the matter we have considered here.

There are, of course, many features regarding the status of Adam as originally created and the mechanics concerning his subsequent fall that are beyond our understanding, largely because they have not been made known to us. In such cases, the most advisable policy is to affirm those things of which we may be sure, posit reasonable conclusions from the revealed truth within recognizable parameters, and avoid uncorroborated—and generally also both unhelpful and unwelcome—speculation.

What we can assert on the basis of Scripture's revelation is that man was created in the image of God. He was not created perfect, but he was perfectly created. What do I mean by that? Well, the fact that he did sin means that he obviously was capable of doing so. It is inconceivable to consider that this would be a possibility for God. I have commented elsewhere that the idea that God can do absolutely anything is not strictly true: he cannot behave in any way that is inconsistent with his intrinsic nature. Moreover, I believe that the 1689 Baptist Confession—even with John Piper's helpful assistance—is somewhat in need of further qualification. To posit that man was created perfect in knowledge, righteousness, and holiness could lead us to assume that Adam was in possession of these qualities in absolute measure. What we actually mean by such an assertion, however, is that within finite boundaries there was no imperfection to Adam's knowledge, righteousness, and holiness.

We cannot possibly know the exact limitation imposed by these boundaries, but we do know that they were as yet unaffected by sin. The entrance of the sin principle into God's creation had such a devastating effect, and yet we can only imagine the true extent of it, because we cannot fully appreciate how different things were before that event. Again, what we do know is that thereafter man's relationships with his Creator, his partner, his cohabitants, and his environment were drastically and radically altered. It had all looked so good for Adam at the beginning. In fact, the divine pronouncement was "very good" (Gen 1:31). How quickly things change! On the sixth day of creation, we find man in desperate need of a mate (2:18–24); within a few short verses, we are faced with a race in dire need of redemption (3:15).

2

The Reality of the Atonement

The effects of Adam's sin were universal in the truest possible sense of that word. Not only has every human being from that point in history been adversely affected by their forefather's actions, but both the physical world and the spiritual realm also became contaminated thereafter. In many ways, the origin of sin remains a mystery. What we can be sure of, however, is that it entered the world through Adam's disobedience and thence began its virulent influence upon all with which it came into contact. Mankind now seemed irreversibly separated from God. If there was the remotest possibility of their relationship being restored, then it was clearly outside of man's capacity to produce such a rapprochement.

Thank God he did not just leave us as a race in need of redemption without taking the required steps to meet that need. Or to put it another way, those of us who have availed ourselves of the opportunity must ever be grateful that the necessity was met by the reality on the part of the only one capable of so doing: his Son, Christ Jesus. We must also be clear, however, that he was under no forensic obligation to take upon himself the penalty that should have been ours. It was a uniquely voluntary act by Almighty God.

Whatever scientific filters may condition our understanding of the age of man, there can be no doubt for the Christian that—even allowing for the shortest time possible—the period from Adam to Christ was one of constant bondage to both the effects of sin and the sin principle itself. Thus, we may say that the whole of the Christ event is the hinge upon which the door of history turns. Until very recently, this fact has traditionally been attested to by our designation of dates as either BC or AD. Even the modern trend to speak rather of Before Common Era and Common Era cannot eradicate the pivotal act in history that such terms represent.

In this crucial chapter, then, we will focus our attention on Jesus Christ as both the ultimate restorer and the final conqueror. We will look, first of all, at some of the terms normally associated with the atoning work of Christ. We will see that words such as "redemption," "justification," "propitiation," and "reconciliation" are not merely technical nouns, but they are biblio-ecclesiastical words used to express the reality of something that actually has taken and will take place. Neither are they synonymous terms, but each relates to a specific feature of the atonement, the identification of which can only enhance our understanding of what Christ's sacrifice truly achieved. Although the long-term benefits of the atonement belong to the following chapter, we will also consider the immediate effects as direct consequences of the reality of the atonement. Among these are included the defeat of Satan and his hordes, the death sentence being passed upon the principle of death, and the beginning of the restoration process for creation.

JESUS CHRIST—THE ULTIMATE RESTORER

We have seen that, because of the nature of man's predicament, God alone could take the initiative to rectify the situation. He did so by sending his Son to effectively remove the curse from fallen humanity. Theologically, this is known as the atonement. In many ways, the atonement is the central doctrine of Christianity, for without it all else becomes somewhat meaningless. The word "atonement" is almost unique in that it is one of the few theological terms to be Anglo-Saxon in origin. Its meaning is essentially "to make one" and it translates the Greek *katallage*. Biblically, the concept of this word grouping is employed to define the conciliatory work of Christ in dealing with the sin issue. In general speech, the idea of atonement indicated a course of action whereby parties who were formerly estranged were brought into a place of unity. Similarly, within the realm of theology it has come to signify the ministry of Jesus in bringing sinners into a right relationship with God.

The Doctrine in Scripture and History

A Biblical Perspective

Leon Morris accurately asserts that: "The need for atonement is brought about by three things: the universality of sin, the seriousness of sin, and man's inability to deal with sin."[1] Thus, the incontrovertible gravity of the fact of the atonement can only be correctly understood in view of man's acknowledgment of the otherwise untraversable chasm that existed between himself and his Maker. Emil Brunner describes it this way:

> The more seriously guilt is regarded, the more it is realized that "something must happen," just because forgiveness is not something which can in any way be taken absolutely for granted. The more real guilt is to us, the more real also is the gulf between us and God, and the inviolable character of the law of penalty; the more real also the obstacle between God and man becomes, the more necessary becomes the particular transaction, by means of which the obstacle, in all its reality, is removed. The more serious our view of guilt, the more clearly we perceive the necessity for an objective—and not merely subjective—Atonement.[2]

Moreover, he adds:

> The converse ... is also true: only in Christ, and not till then, has humanity been able to perceive this burden of guilt, this necessity for an objective act of Atonement. The gulf of separation, all that blocks the way between man and God, did not become fully evident in its immensity until the actual Atonement had taken place, through the Cross. In the revelation of Christ, in this one event, question and answer, need and the knowledge of need are present simultaneously. Only at the Cross of Christ does man see fully what it is that separates him from God; yet it is here alone that he perceives that he is no longer separated from God.[3]

And yet, the very notion of the atonement stems from the heart of a holy, loving Father God. His love, however, is not superseded by justice, nor is there any sense in which his inherent righteous demands have somehow become overwhelmed by an emotional plea from the Son. The two go hand in hand; God's love and justice are complementary rather than contradictory. As the gospel writer puts it: "God so loved the world that he gave his one and only Son" (John 3:16). Thus, Christ's dying for us was the full expression of God's love toward us (see also Rom 5:8).

We have seen that the total inability of man in sin rendered the atonement absolutely necessary. The unmitigated perfections of God also meant that the atonement was the only way possible for him to both pardon sin

---

1. L. L. Morris, "Atonement," in Douglas, *New Bible Dictionary*, 104.
2. Brunner, *The Mediator*, 451.
3. Ibid., 452.

and satisfy his own intrinsic holiness. God's divine nature, consistently represented throughout Scripture as being abhorrently opposed to sin (see Exod 34:7; Nah 1:2–3; Rom 1:18), would allow him but one route that would at the same time justify the sinner and maintain his own sense of justice: the atonement. The seriousness of sin's condition in man completely and utterly disarmed him in any aspirations he might have had toward finding acceptance with God. Not only did this mean that someone else would have to take man's place, but there was only one who could: Jesus. As Dr. Hodge points out: "This sacrifice would be most painfully irrelevant if it were anything short of absolutely necessary in relation to the end designed to be attained—that is, unless it be indeed the only possible means to the salvation of sinful man. God surely would not have made His Son a wanton sacrifice to a bare point of will."[4]

The gift of satisfaction conferred upon mankind as of sufficient value to atone could only be God himself. But in order to amply demonstrate his identification with the race he was to redeem, he had to share its nature without relinquishing his own; he had to be human as well as divine. He also had to be one without whom the taint of Adam's sin had personally tarnished. Only the *Theanthropos* (that is, the God-man) could truly render ineffective the curse upon man. There is much merit to Dabney's view, when he says:

> It may be very true that it is good . . . for one of us to forgive injury without satisfaction, and to extirpate our indignation for the sake of rescuing our fellow-creature from suffering the punishment; but the reasoning does not hold when applied to the Supreme . . . It is a more proper and noble thing that God should please Himself in the acting out of His own infinitely holy and excellent attributes, than He should please His whole creation by bestowing impunity on guilty creatures.[5]

Jesus was to submit himself in complete obedience to God throughout his earthly life. Although this compliance in some way contributed toward him retaining his status as the ideal representative, we must be careful that we do not imagine his obedience as helping to pay the ransom in and of itself, for such compliance was man's duty before the fall. Rather, he did so in order that he might thereby die a substitutionary death on behalf of others, since he was under no obligation to do so for himself. Such an act warranted merit but, as the Son of God, the divine *Logos* was not so needy. Hence, the imparted, the imputed, and—indeed—the immediate benefits of

---

4. Hodge, *The Atonement*, 237.
5. Dabney, *Systematic Theology*, 489.

the atonement were forgiveness of sin and assumed righteousness for those who, by faith, meet the criterion of the gospel of Christ: repentance.

Despite the rather crude way in which many proponents of the substitutionary theory have presented their case, it cannot adequately be refuted that there exists in the biblical account of the atonement an element of substitution. That "he was pierced for our transgressions . . . [and] crushed for our iniquities" (Isa 53:5), and "gave his life as a ransom for many" (see Mark 10:45; 1 Tim 2:6) to my mind points unequivocally to a representative dimension. Paul also hints at this aspect of Christ's death when he speaks of "God [making] him who had no sin to be sin for us, so that we might become the righteousness of God" (2 Cor 5:21), and "Christ [having] redeemed us from the curse of the law by becoming a curse for us" (Gal 3:13). Similarly, the writer to the Hebrews consistently applies Old Testament phraseology to the work of Jesus in terms that can only properly be understood as vicarious (see Lev 16:8; Heb 9:7, 12, 28). On the basis of such evidence, I can only conclude that those who believe otherwise have allowed their minds too much space into which their erroneous thoughts might spread. As Vincent Taylor has observed: "The thought of substitution is one we have perhaps been more anxious to reject than to assess, yet the immeasurable sense of gratitude with which it is associated . . . is too great a thing to be wanting in a worthy theory of the Atonement."[6]

The atonement, then, can be viewed from Scripture both objectively and subjectively, as I trust the following table will clarify:

Objective fact of Christ's atonement	Subjective factor of Christ's atonement
Atonement for sin— "that he might make atonement for the sins of the people" (Heb 2:17).	*Association* with Christ's sufferings— "I fill up in my flesh what is still lacking in regard to Christ's afflictions, for the sake of his body, which is the church" (Col 1:24).
Bruised for sin— "he was pierced for our transgressions, he was crushed for our iniquities" (Isa 53:5).	*Branded* for Christ— "I bear on my body the marks of Jesus" (Gal 6:17).
Cursed for sin— "Christ redeemed us from the curse of the law by becoming a curse for us" (Gal 3:13).	*Conformed* to Christ's death— "I want to know Christ and the power of his resurrection and the fellowship of sharing in his sufferings, becoming like him in his death" (Phil 3:10).

---

6. Taylor, *The Atonement*, 30.

Delivered for sin—
"He was delivered over to death for our sins" (Rom 4:25).

Dead to sin—
"so that we might die to sins and live for righteousness" (1 Pet 2:24).

Endured the cross—
"Let us fix our eyes on Jesus, the author and perfector of our faith, who for the joy set before him endured the cross" (Heb 12:2).

Enduring for Christ—
"it is commendable if a man bears up under the pain of unjust suffering . . . if you suffer for doing good and you endure it . . . [then to] this you were called" (1 Pet 2:19–21).

Finished the work—
"Jesus said 'It is finished'" (John 19:30).

Finishing the race—
"I have fought the good fight, I have finished the race, I have kept the faith" (2 Tim 4:7).

Giving of himself—
"I live by faith in the Son of God, who loved me and gave himself for me" (Gal 2:20).

Giving of ourselves—
"And they did not do as we expected, but they gave themselves first to the Lord and then to us, in keeping with God's will" (2 Cor 8:5).

Healing—
"This was to fulfill what was spoken through the prophet Isaiah: 'He took up our infirmities and carried our diseases'" (Matt 8:17).

Healing—
"by his wounds you have been healed" (1 Pet 2:24b).

Historical Recognition

As far as theology is concerned, it was Athanasius who penned the first known attempt at a systematic treatment on the atonement. Although the Apologists had already spoken of Christ as the Redeemer, this was almost exclusively in the context of humanity being liberated from the power of the devil. Gnostics referred to mankind as having been delivered from the contaminating influence of the world of matter, while Marcion represented the death of Christ as a price to be paid by the God of love to purchase humanity from the Demiurge or Creator of the world. Irenaeus, Clement, and Origen were no less vague in their efforts, and so it was left to Athanasius to produce his *De Incarnatione*.

Athanasius began by stating that the purpose of the incarnation—as distinct from the necessity of the atonement—was so that the *Logos* could refurbish man with the perfect knowledge of God, thitherto prohibited by the veil with which sin had masked it. The Christ of God was destined to become man's substitute, who thereby paid the debt owed to God on behalf of fallen humanity by willingly embracing the penalty for sin: death. Athanasius adopted the earlier teaching of Irenaeus, though in a somewhat modified form, that placed particular emphasis on the *Logos* assuming human flesh in order to bring deity to humanity, immortality to mortal man. His work was further elaborated upon by the Cappadocian Fathers: Basil, his brother Gregory of Nyssa, and their friend Gregory of Nazianzus.

Gregory of Nyssa seems to have been the one responsible for promoting the idea that not only is death to be ultimately destroyed, but so too sin. The conclusion he drew from this was that Satan would also enjoy the benefits of the atonement, as it will finally result in his salvation also. Thankfully, this theory finds little favor today. John Chrysostom and Cyril of Alexandria went on to insist upon the incalculable value of Christ's death as that of a divine Person, though John of Damascus appears to have formulated his own treatment by identifying with the more palatable contributions from his Greek patristic counterparts.

Whilst acknowledging the efforts of Athanasius and his fellows, it was to be almost five hundred years before anyone dared once more to tackle the theological implications of the necessity of the atonement. In his work *Cur Deus Homo*, Anselm of Canterbury sought to challenge the assumptions that had attached themselves to the doctrine. Could not God have just as readily issued a verbal command to redeem humanity? Could he not, perhaps, have simply delivered a pardon without the need for his sense of justice to be appeased? And if the atonement was so necessary, then why was it imperative that the *Logos* become the means of mediation?

Well, Anselm found his answers in the attributes of God. By dishonoring God through rebellion, man undertook a debt that could be repaid only in a manner befitting his Maker's mercy *and* justice. Retribution and satisfaction were the only two options available to the integrity of the Divine Being. The former would have defeated the object of his purpose, for only death could be regarded as an adequate punishment. That it remained outside of man's capability to satisfy the conditions of God's demands was amply demonstrated by his failure to keep even the legal requirements of the written code.

Though not without certain shortcomings—such as neglecting the atoning value of Jesus' sufferings in life and doing immense disservice to the mystical union of Christ and believers—there can be no denying the significance of Anselm's treatment on the doctrine of the atonement. Some 450 years later, Martin Luther expressed its vicarious aspect thus:

> Our most merciful Father . . . sent his only Son into the world and laid upon him . . . the sins of all men, saying: Be thou Peter

that denier; Paul that persecutor, blasphemer and cruel oppressor; David that adulterer; that sinner which did eat the apple in Paradise, that thief which hanged upon the cross; and briefly, be thou the person which hath committed the sins of all men; see that thou pay and satisfy for them. Here now cometh the law and saith: I find him a sinner . . . therefore let him die upon the cross. And so he setteth upon him and killeth him. By this means the whole world is purged and cleansed from all sins.[7]

The Perfect Sacrifice

Almost without exception, the New Testament writers perceived Jesus' death as being the perfect fulfillment of all that had been foreshadowed under the Old Testament code of offerings. Whereas it was beyond the realm of conceivability for the blood of animals to deal effectively with the issue of human sin, the voluntary act of self-sacrifice by Jesus did accomplish this (see Heb 10:4–10). The word "sacrifice" is actually our English translation of the Greek *thuo*, which is used essentially of the sacrificial slaying of a victim. Indeed, he is "the Lamb of God, who takes away the sin of the whole world" (John 1:29, 36), mankind having been "redeemed . . . with the precious blood of Christ, a lamb without blemish or defect" (1 Pet 1:18–19). And again, "the Lamb who was slain, to receive power and wealth and wisdom and strength and honor and glory and praise" (Rev 5:12).

Jesus' death is often referred to in terms of a specific sacrifice like the Passover Lamb (1 Cor 5:7). A more general reference is most frequently employed, however, such as "Christ [loving] us and [giving] himself up for us as a fragrant offering and sacrifice to God" (Eph 5:2). In the words of Fritz Laubach:

> The blood of Jesus Christ (1 Pet 1:2), the blood of Jesus (Heb 10:19; 1 Jn 1:7), the blood of Christ (1 Cor 10:16; Eph 2:13; Heb 9:14), the blood of the Lord (1 Cor 11:27), the blood of the Lamb (Rev 7:14; 12:11) occupies a central position in N[ew] T[estament] thought. It derives its meaning particularly from the sacrifices of the Day of Atonement (Lev 16). It is sacrificial blood that Christ, in perfect obedience to God (Rom 5:19; Phil 2:8; Heb 5:8), presented in giving himself on the cross (Heb 9:12ff). In his suffering and death, Jesus offered the true sacrifice

---

7. Luther, *Commentary*, 272.

for the removal of sins. In place of all the sacrifices that had been brought by men, he brought the perfect sacrifice of his life.[8]

The sacrificial system of God's people can actually be traced back as far as man's very first act of disobedience (Gen 4:4). When introduced to Israel as a religious observance (see Lev 17:11), it is clear that the sacrificial offering was intended to be a two-way communication between God and man. Although it is true that in the act of presentation the offerer gave to God that which he had prescribed for the continuation or restoration of fellowship, it must not be forgotten that God himself took the initiative to provide that which he found to be both appropriate and acceptable for the purpose. It was never meant to be a screen behind which to hide, but a provision in which boldly to enter. Death had taken place by the innocent on behalf of the guilty. Where animal sacrifice expressed this in principle, the perfect reality is seen only in the death of Christ Jesus.

Although the gospel accounts record how Jesus initially went to great lengths to demonstrate who he was, this should be viewed as but preparatory to him defining his mission in life. In other words, the vital significance of who he was can only properly be grasped by finite understanding in the context of what he came to do. It is perhaps interesting, therefore, that having established his Personhood to the disciples (Mark 8:27–30), Jesus then goes on to emphasize the importance of the fact that "the Son of Man must suffer many things" (v. 31; see also 9:31; 10:32–34).

The vicarious nature of the atonement consisted in Jesus' active and passive obedience. For him to be an acceptable substitute, fully meeting the judicial obligations on man's behalf, it was necessary that he was not himself subject to those demands, whether that be through Adam's pollution or personal offence. The immaculate conception by the Holy Spirit coming upon Mary rendered Christ untarnished by the transmission of the sinful nature, and the dual aspect of his obedience in life unto death meant that he truly was the perfect sacrifice. Although these twin elements cannot be separated in reality, they may nonetheless be summarized as comprising, on the one hand, Jesus voluntarily offering himself as the Suffering Servant (active obedience) and, on the other, that he lived in unmitigated submission to the law's requirements (passive obedience). Berkhof wisely calls attention to the fact that:

> Christ's active and passive obedience should be regarded as complementary parts of an organic whole. In discussing it, account should be taken of a threefold relation in which Christ

---

8. F. Laubach, "Blood," in Brown, *Dictionary of New Testament Theology*, 1:223.

stood to the law, namely, the natural, the federal, and the penal relation. Man proved a failure in each of these. He did not keep the law in its natural and federal aspects, and is not now in a position to pay the penalty, in order to be restored in the favour of God. While Christ naturally entered the first relation by His incarnation, He vicariously entered . . . the second and third relations.[9]

The sacrificial theme of Jesus as accomplishing both the obligations and office, penalty and priesthood, of the atonement account for a large proportion of the New Testament writings. Paul's works especially provide sufficient evidence of the significance of Christ's ministry as fulfilling the conditions of the Old Testament requirements. As an erstwhile student under Gamaliel, Paul was well versed in the Hebrew Scriptures. Little wonder then that he constantly refers to the Christian's standing in Christ as being on account of his shed blood (see Rom 3:25; 5:9; Eph 1:7; Col 1:20). As prophet, priest, and king, he alone was divinely equipped to appropriately mediate "between God and men, [this] man Christ Jesus, who gave himself as a ransom for all men" (1 Tim 2:5–6). Paul is not alone in making the association, of course; Peter (1 Pet 1:19) and John (1 John 1:7; Rev 5:9) are similarly inclined.

To the Greek mind, the idea of sacrifice was an all too familiar one. Its mythical origins were designed to appease the gods in the hope of somehow currying their favor. This concept is most notably evident in the Roman cultic maxim *do ut des* (that is, "I give so that you also may give"). A similar meaning is conveyed by *quid pro quo*, though not with any necessarily sacrificial content. What was entirely absent from Hebrew, Greek, and Roman thought was the notion that such a sacrifice could be so rich in value as to render all subsequent offerings, not so much invalid as, unnecessary. This is a constant theme of the New Testament writers cited above, though it is perhaps more thoroughly investigated by the writer to the Hebrews, who couches the death of Jesus in terms reminiscent of the Jewish religious system. Consider the following:

> For Christ did not enter a man-made sanctuary that was only a copy of the true one; he entered heaven itself, now to appear for us in God's presence. Nor did he enter heaven to offer himself again and again, the way the high priest enters the Most Holy Place every year with blood that is not his own. Then Christ would have to suffer many times since the creation of the world.

---

9. Berkhof, *Systematic Theology*, 380.

> But now he has appeared once for all at the end of the ages to do away with sin by the sacrifice of himself.[10]

And again:

> Day after day every priest stands and performs his religious duties; again and again he offers the same sacrifices, which can never take away sins. But when this priest had offered for all time one sacrifice for all sins, he sat down on the right hand of God.[11]

Why? Because "we have been made holy through the sacrifice of the body of Jesus Christ once for all" (v. 10b). All that remained was for the perfect sacrifice to await the outcome of that for which he had offered himself. Ray Stedman has this to say: "This would, of course, involve his mediation of the new covenant and his intercession for believers. No further sacrifice of any kind was required or needed. Enough had already been done to deal with every form of sin or rebellion. He could remain figuratively seated until his enemies had been totally rendered impotent."[12]

To speak of Jesus' death as an atoning sacrifice can often lead to a misunderstanding that seems to preclude its objective direction, for it is essentially an offering made to God on behalf of man. Thus, it is in the divine realm where the change primarily—though by no means exclusively—takes place. Such a viewpoint is admittedly not without difficulties; neither is it exempt from the possibility of misunderstanding. However, the conclusive fact of the death of Christ is that sin as a principle of life, which incurs penal and punitive recognition, is thereafter repealed so that God and man might be reconciled. The most flagrant protest offered in recent times has centered on a refusal to accept the twofold mediatorial role of Christ. Scholarly debate continues as to whether it is rationally conceivable that Christ can be both God's gift to man *and* a sacrifice offered for man to God. The early Christians, among them some highly distinguished theologians, willingly embraced both ideas without question and display no evidence of being in any doubt as to their equal validity. Certainly, the writer to the Hebrews spoke with similar conviction on both aspects of Christ's offering.

It must surely be acknowledged that the basis of man's restored relationship toward God has little to do with a morally upright Jew of two thousand years ago. This is not to underestimate or devalue the human nature of the Messiah, but it should be seen in the context of who he really is.

---

10. Heb 9:24–26.
11. Heb 10:11–12.
12. Stedman, *Hebrews*, 105.

Once again, I must applaud the efforts of Emil Brunner in this regard, who informs us that:

> The life of Jesus, the story of Jesus of Nazareth . . . is a significant event within the human sphere, but it is no more. But the "coming" of the Son of God in the flesh, the fact that the Son was sent forth into the world, this event which moves between time and eternity is, as the origin of Christ, as the mystery of His Person, the proper concern of faith. For this coming constitutes the Person of the Mediator: for here and nowhere else can Jesus be known as the Christ. All other knowledge is on the historical plane and is represented as an extension of humanity, as a human phenomenon—however sublime this may be. The fact of His coming, the shining thread which extends from eternity into time, and is perceived by the eye of faith—it is this which distinguishes faith in Christ from an admiration for an historical character.[13]

We have seen that the New Testament clearly teaches of the vicarious sufferings present in the death of Jesus. These were not merely the sympathetic actions of a very close friend, nor could they have been. Not only is Christ's sacrifice perfect, but it is uniquely so. Only one who was perfectly sinless could possibly have taken the place of those born into sin. Any attempt on our part to offer God an alternative to embracing the atoning work of his Son is much like the Old Testament sacrificial system: futile, fruitless, and utterly devoid of faith. Regular church attendance will not suffice as a means to earn God's pardon. Offering our service to the congregation is worthless, whether that be in handing out hymn books, working the laptop that generates the preacher's PowerPoint presentation, or baking scones for the monthly church lunch. Going round our local housing estate, pushing gospel invitations through letterboxes cannot bridge the gap between us and God. If any of these could have had such soteriological merit, then God would surely have chosen them instead. No, the price of God's forgiveness was the perfect sacrifice of his Son.

Propitiation

A number of the more technical terms associated with the atonement are often used as if they were synonymous. Though closely linked, this is not, in fact, the case. We will now discuss the peculiar distinctions that exist between some of them.

13. Brunner, *The Mediator*, 309.

The first to come under scrutiny is "propitiation," and we must begin by once more consulting the Greek text that we may thus be aided in our understanding. As we do so, we find that the word employed is *hilasmos*, which according to Vine is "akin to *hileos* (merciful, propitious) . . . [it] signifies an expiation, a means whereby sin is covered and remitted."[14]

Propitiation has traditionally been understood as the quenching of God's wrath against sinners. Scholars who prefer to use "expiation" frequently do so on the grounds of their objection to the concept of God's wrath. This dilemma appears not to have been quite so problematic for the Old Testament saints, who proclaimed with fervor a holy reaction to sin in the strongest possible terms. Although it is true that Scripture declares God to be "slow to anger" (Neh 9:17; Num 14:18; Ps 86:15), his opposition to evil should never be underestimated. This is the proper context in which to view the biblical concept of propitiation: God is diametrically opposed to evil, such opposition may appropriately be described as wrath, and this wrath can only be averted by the propitiatory work of Christ. For a learned discussion on the theological difference between propitiation and expiation, we need look no further than the works of Colin Brown:

> In propitiation the action is directed towards God or some other offended person. The underlying purpose is to change God's attitude from one of wrath to one of goodwill and favour. In the case of expiation, on the other hand, the action is directed towards that which has caused the breakdown in the relationship. It is sometimes held that, while God is not personally angry with the sinner, the act of sin has initiated a train of events which can only be broken by some compensatory rite or act of reparation for the offence. In short, propitiation is directed towards the offended person, whereas expiation is concerned with nullifying the offensive act.[15]

Dr. Martyn Lloyd-Jones puts the argument into its doctrinal perspective when he says that:

> Propitiation carries . . . [the] notion that there is someone who has been offended, someone who has done the offending, that there is an offence, and that something is necessary on both sides. Something has got to be done from the side of the One who has been offended as well as from the side of the offender; and this great and glorious doctrine teaches us that the very God

14. Vine, *Expository Dictionary*, 896.

15. C. Brown, "Reconciliation," in Brown, *Dictionary of New Testament Theology*, 3:151.

whom we have offended has Himself provided the way whereby the offence has been dealt with. His anger, His wrath against sin and the sinner, has been satisfied . . . and He therefore can thus reconcile man unto Himself.[16]

The biblical presentation of the doctrine of propitiation indicates that it is, indeed, necessitated by the wrath of God. A denial of the existence of wrath within the Divine Being, as if it were somehow incongruous with his pure character is surely tantamount to a failure to recognize the gravity with which God's holiness responds to sin. The largely outdated argument that fails to conceive of the harmony between God's love and his wrath has prompted Randolph Tasker to comment thus: "It is an axiom of the Bible that there is no incompatibility between those two attributes of the divine nature; and for the most part the great Christian theologians and preachers of the past have endeavoured to be loyal to both sides of the divine self-disclosure."[17]

Any aversion to the idea of personal wrath in God is inclined to be provoked by anthropomorphic association. In other words, we do not like to think in terms of God being angry because when we see that emotion being expressed in the natural realm it is often accompanied by ill temper, hostility, violence, and/or hatred. It is expedient to observe, however, that God's anger is always in perfect accord with his intrinsic holiness and, as such, is wholly devoid of those aspects that both effect and are affected by human indignation. In the words of John Stott: "Human anger is usually arbitrary and uninhibited; divine anger is always principled and controlled. Our anger tends to be a spasmodic outburst, aroused by pique and seeking revenge; God's is a continuous, settled antagonism, aroused only by evil, and expressed in its condemnation. God is entirely free from personal animosity or vindictiveness; indeed, he is sustained simultaneously with undiminished love for the offender."[18]

James Denney speaks in similar terms when commenting on the Apostle Paul's treatment of the doctrine. Having established that the Father initiated forgiveness through the blood of his Son, Denney goes on to graphically present the sacrifice of Christ Jesus as "One who has felt all the waves and billows break over Him in which God's reaction against sin comes home to us sinners." He finds no discord between the goodness of God in salvation and what he refers to as his "inexorable repulsion of evil." Indeed, so fundamental is this commensurate loving of righteousness and

16. Lloyd-Jones, *Romans 3:20—4:25*, 78.
17. Tasker, *The Wrath of God*, 7.
18. Stott, *The Cross of Christ*, 106.

hating of wickedness to Denney's understanding of the biblical revelation of God's nature, that he feels compelled to conclude: "This is as important to Paul as that God should be a forgiving or justifying God. He must also be a true God, to whom sin is what it is, nothing else and nothing less; and in the propitiation, which deals with sin as it is with a view to its removal, He is revealed in both characters at once."[19]

In a comparable vein, I am again beholden to the learned findings of Leon Morris, formerly principal of Ridley College, Melbourne. He cites both Paul (Rom 3:25) and John (1 John 2:2) as using the Greek noun *hilasterion* in the sense of propitiation, taking great pains to assert his choice of interpretation thus:

> In modern times, scholars who reject the idea of the wrath of God suggest that we should understand such passages to mean expiation rather than propitiation (cf. RSV). But the linguistics are against this (the *hilaskomai* word group is used for the turning away of wrath, not expiation). Furthermore, Scripture requires the concept. Expiation is an impersonal term; we expiate a sin or crime. But propitiation is a personal word; we propitiate a person. And the problem in bringing about our salvation is that by our sin we have put ourselves in the wrong with the living God. We have aroused his wrath, that is exercised against evil, and this must be reckoned with. Hence, one biblical way of looking at Christ's saving work is to see it as averting the divine wrath, that is to say, as a propitiation.[20]

And so, in much the same way that a financier refuses to publically acknowledge the possibility of a stock market crash, an athlete will admit that the best of his competitive edge is fast becoming but a memory, or my wife will concede that I am not as able to multitask as she would like, so too some Christians decline to entertain the idea of God's wrath. They are all aware of the possible existence of that which they shun but, just like Victorian English gentlefolk in relation to sexual impropriety, they somehow believe that by not mentioning "it," "it" will not be aroused from slumber. It is not unlike the oft-employed argument of the atheist, which usually begins: "I cannot believe in a God who would allow such and such to happen." Whatever culturally sensitive proposition replaces the words "such and such," the whole premise that lies behind it is nonsensical, unreasonable, and—ultimately—falsifiable. It is akin to me saying that I refuse to believe in the existence of

---

19. Denney, *Reconciliation*, 159.

20. L. L. Morris, "Sacrifice," in Ferguson and Wright, *New Dictionary of Theology*, 609.

a musical genre that is repetitive, utterly lacking in melody, and completely uninspiring; hip-hop exists whether I believe in it or not.

Upon a candid and objective examination of the Bible text, however, it becomes apparent that to spurn the existence of the wrath of God pretty much amounts to refuting the divine revelation concerning sin. What is perhaps understandable, however, is the basis of such rejection when considered in the context of a frequently overzealous defense of the doctrine of propitiation, which has at times seemed to represent God's displeasure as almost synonymous with a fickle temper tantrum or restless aggression. Whilst the wrath of God is most certainly fuelled by a passionate hostility toward sin, proportionately disposed by his own intrinsic righteousness, this is in no way intended to portray God as One who is prone to impulsive or gratuitous bouts of behavioral disorder.

There are many even in our own day who, denying the biblical validity of the concept of the wrath of God, favor the use of the word "expiation" instead of "propitiation." It must also be pointed out that amongst those who have been entrusted with the responsibility for accurately translating the Scriptures without partiality, some have often been guilty of allowing their particular theological bias to dictate their work rather than be willing to formulate their doctrinal position on the basis of the linguistic evidence before them. That such eminent commentators as C. H. Dodd[21] and A. T. Hanson[22] see fit to expound the New Testament use of the phrase "wrath/anger of God" in exclusively impersonal terms is much to their discredit. By stark contrast, Leon Morris[23] refers to God's wrath as both his "personal divine revulsion to evil" and his "personal vigorous opposition" to it.

Lest I be completely misunderstood, it must be pointed out that the argument is not merely for propitiation versus expiation, as if acknowledging the former automatically disallows the latter. Those who favor expiation only make their choice solely on the grounds that they find the idea of propitiation so distasteful. Proponents of propitiation, however, usually embrace the idea of expiation within the concept they support. In other words, though it is possible to conceive of the expiation of sin as standing alone, the propitiation of God's wrath against the sinner includes also the expiation of the sin that evoked it.

Allowing for accurate translation, the word "propitiation" appears four times in the New Testament (see Rom 3:25; Heb 2:17; 1 John 2:2; 4:10). On three of those occasions, the context suggests its application is restricted to

---

21. Dodd, *Romans*.
22. Hanson, *The Wrath of the Lamb*.
23. Morris, *The Cross*, 190–91.

the elect of God. The exception is to be found in the second chapter of John's epistle, though some have countered that even here a twofold propitiation may be inferred. The less obscure interpretation is surely that "the whole world" means precisely that—or does it? Or, more specifically, what else could possibly be meant by "the whole world"?

The more obvious meaning to us would be the entire human race, without exception. This would certainly make the concept of unlimited atonement more credible. It would also lead us to one of two possible conclusions: either a universalistic ideal or that propitiation does not in itself save, but makes salvation possible. The latter alternative changes our understanding of propitiation from one of efficacy to that of sufficiency. Thus, what now condemns the unregenerate is not sin *per se*, but the deliberate rejection of God's propitiatory provision (see 2 Thess 2:7–10).

Other plausible renderings include the "world" that was most familiar to John (that is, Asia Minor), though that seems to negate rather than support the use of "not for ours only." Also, we have no such difficulty in reading John's sense of this phrase "the whole world" in generic terms elsewhere (e.g., John 3:16), so why here? Similarly, the view of the eschatological universalist seems more than a little contrived. That "the world" should refer to all that are left after the judgment has taken place and the unsaved have been removed from its sphere of influence is not unlike me having an aim for the entire global population to appreciate my preferred choice of music and achieving that aim by making it the only one that is accessible, by whatever means such an objective might be realized. Yes, it is farfetched.

The ethnological argument has more in its favor, though even that does not escape some difficulty by way of implication. Advocates posit that the context of "the whole world," both in 1 John 2:2 and John 3:16, is to emphasize Christ's universal impact and place the work of God's Messiah outside of an exclusively Jewish milieu. God, as Creator of all that is, has sent his Son to be the Savior of all that is, whether Jew or Gentile. This certainly seems to be the meaning of *kosmos* as applied by the Apostle Paul, and without any apparent need for further qualification or explanation (see Rom 11:11–15), so why not by John here too? Thus, the argument is that "the world" is to be perceived in contrast to natural Israel only, or from amongst all nations (see Matt 28:19; Rev 15:4; 22:2).

Redemption

According to Vine, the biblical concept of redemption is based upon the Greek verb *lutroo*, which means "to release on receipt of [a] ransom . . .

lutroo signifies the actual deliverance, the setting at liberty."[24] In the Old Testament, the idea of redemption embraced the paying of tribute by a family member (that is, the kinsman-redeemer) to secure the release of someone or something that might otherwise become lost. All such references are but shadows of the work of the Son of Man, who came to give his life in return for those who were under the sentence of death (that is, sinners). Amongst the recorded prayers of the Reverend George MacLeod, we find the following poignant lines:

> Almighty God, Redeemer:
> The sap of life in our bones and being is Yours,
> Lifting us to ecstasy.
> Not always in the beauty: the tang of sin, in our consciences.
> The dry lichen of sins long dead, but seared upwards in our minds.
> In the garden that is each of us, always the thorn.
>
> Yet all are Yours as we yield them again to You.
> Not only our lives that You have given are Yours:
> But also our sins that You have taken.
> Even our livid rebellions and putrid sins:
> You have taken them all away and nailed them to the cross!
> Our redemption is enough: and we are free.[25]

There is an unfortunate tendency when speaking of redemption to somehow imagine God as having been blackmailed by Satan. This is especially so in view of its association with a ransom having been paid. This notion is entirely missing from Scripture, such an idea owing more to the current trend in society than to the biblical revelation. In the words of Howard Marshall, then Professor of New Testament Exegesis at the University of Aberdeen:

> Redemption is a concept found in the [Old Testament] to express the action of a relative in setting free a member of his family or buying back his property . . . or in general that of purchasing something for a price. A ransom-price is paid to secure the release of what would otherwise be forfeit . . . There is dispute whether, when the action of redeeming is ascribed to God, he is regarded as paying a price to set his people free; certainly cost and effort are applied, but the thought of a price being received by somebody from him is absent.

He goes on to conclude that:

---

24. Vine, *Expository Dictionary*, 935.
25. MacLeod, *The Whole Earth*, 8.

> In the [New Testament] the starting-point for the concept is found in the sayings of Jesus, which state that no-one can give anything in exchange for his life . . . but that the Son of Man came to give his life as a ransom for many . . . whose lives are forfeit and thus sets them free . . . Thus the term "redemption" can be used in quite a broad sense to express the general concept of salvation and deliverance.[26]

The death of Christ is certainly represented in Scripture as the price by which man is redeemed from slavery to sin. Rudolf Tuente refers to this as a "metaphor of sacral manumission [which] is here united with the idea of a change of masters." He further explains that:

> Believers "having been set free from sin, have become slaves of righteousness" (Rom 6:18; cf v 22). This manumission from the bondage of a supposed independence into *eleutheria* (freedom) does not lead to a new independence. Rather, the one manumitted is set free for the "obedience of faith," which he presents to his Lord, Jesus Christ, as his servant (Rom 12:11; 16:18; Col 3:24; cf 1 Thess 1:9; Rom 7:6). Yet this new relationship of master and servant is dominated, not by "the spirit of slavery (*pneuma douleais*) to fall back into fear"; believers "have received the spirit of sonship (*pneuma hyiothesias*)" (Rom 8:15).[27]

Therefore, any inherent idea of a ransom being paid should be regarded as language consistent with the analogy and must be seen as no more than that. Certainly, the genre allows it to be understood as a metaphor for Jesus offering himself in obedience to the Father as a substitutionary sacrifice in satisfaction of God's righteousness, without it becoming necessary to interpret such an action as in any sense making a payment to the devil. Paul's use of the noun *apolytrosis* (that is, redemption) also carries with it the notion of deliverance (see Rom 3:24; 1 Cor 1:30; Eph 1:14), with the added emphasis of substitutionary sacrifice (Eph 1:7), Jesus' blood being the means of that redemption. As the hymn writer puts it:

> Blest inhabitants of Sion, washed in the Redeemer's blood:
> Jesus, whom their souls rely on, makes them kings and priests to God.
> 'Tis his love his people raises over self to reign as kings,
> And as priests, his solemn praises each for a thank-offering brings.[28]

---

26. I. H. Marshall, "Redemption," in Ferguson and Wright, *New Dictionary of Theology*, 560.

27. R. Tuente, "Slave," in Brown, *Dictionary of New Testament Theology*, 3:597.

28. John Newton, 1725–1807.

The underlying theme of redemption in the New Testament is that God has inaugurated a plan on behalf of humanity, designed to provide a route of transfer from the realm of darkness to the kingdom of light. The biblical evidence is such that this is necessary because man is incapable of bringing about such a transformation in and of himself. Although the use of redemption terminology can be somewhat restricted, the concept of it is nevertheless crucial to the idea of the atonement. The words *agorazo* and *lyo* (and their respective derivatives) reflect the context of a marketplace scenario, specifically conveying images of the purchase and release of slaves. The associated thought pattern in terms of soteriology, therefore, is that of deliverance from bondage or captivity.

In response to those who reject the necessity of the death of Christ as the only possible means of redemption, Denney scornfully contests that:

> . . . the question, "If Christ had not suffered, would He nevertheless have redeemed us?" is puerile and unreal. The work of redemption has actually been done by Christ who died, and the consent of all Catholic theologians, that He would have redeemed us all the same even if He had not died, adds nothing to our knowledge or understanding. Intelligence is given to us, not to ask and answer fancy questions about a world which has never been and never will be, but to interpret the actual world and things as they are. The fact being that Christ has redeemed us to God by His blood, to argue that He would have redeemed us nevertheless, though there had been no cross or Passion, is neither profound nor sublime, but irrelevant.[29]

Although I am inclined to be in agreement with the fundamental basis of Denney's objection, he does seem to miss the opportunity to answer the real argument: that the death of Christ was actually the only tenable means of redeeming humanity from its bondage to sin. As wonderful as this undoubtedly is, however, it remains only half of the gospel message. Were it the whole story, mankind would simply thereby find itself back in the status of pre-fallen Adam, with the potential to repeat our first parent's folly. But there is so much more provision for us. Not only were our sins placed on Jesus at the cross; his righteousness is also put to our account. For those who are "in Christ Jesus [he] has become . . . our righteousness, holiness and redemption" (1 Cor 1:30). This is what is known theologically as "the great exchange," that "God made him who had no sin to be sin for us, so that in him we might become the righteousness of God" (2 Cor 5:21).

---

29. Denney, *Reconciliation*, 269.

When speaking of redemption in covenantal terms, Jim Packer points out that this brings clarity to three foundational truths:

1. The love of the Father and the Son, with the Holy Spirit, to lost sinners is shared, unanimous love. The tritheistic fantasy of a loving Son placating an unloving Father and commandeering an apathetic Holy Spirit in order to save us is a distressing nonsense.

2. As our salvation derives from God's free and gracious initiative and is carried through, first to last, according to God's eternal plan by God's own sovereign power, so its ultimate purpose is to exalt and glorify the Father and the Son together. The man-centred distortion that pictures God as saving us more for our sake than for his is also a distressing nonsense.

3. Jesus Christ is the focal figure, the proper centre of our faith-full attention, throughout the redemptive economy. He, as Mediator of the Covenant of grace and of the grace of that covenant, is as truly an object of divine predestination as are we whom he saves... The legalistic sub-spiritual... theology of Mass and merit, whereby Christians are required by the Father, and enabled by the Son, to take part in the achieving of their own salvation, is a further distressing nonsense.[30]

We have already considered precisely what it is that we have been redeemed *from* in the previous chapter. In terms of privilege, we shall be looking at what we have been redeemed *to* in the following chapter. Perhaps here would be a good place to briefly remind ourselves that such rewards are not divorced from responsibility. Thus, there is an oft-overlooked aspect of what we have been redeemed *for*. The purpose of redemption, therefore, is essentially trifold: we are saved from sin and its due penalty; we are saved that we might thereby receive the inheritance that has been set aside for us as adopted sons of God in Christ; but we have also been saved that we might thus become thoroughly equipped to do every good work required of us as ambassadors of him who works in us and through us. Redemption, then, is not only about eradicating the past and/or equipping us for the future, but also enabling us in the present.

If I was to be pressed to draw a particular distinction between redemption and the other terms in this section, it would have to be that whereas justification, propitiation, and even—to a degree—reconciliation may all be said to be liberating, only redemption can appropriately be employed as a synonym for liberation *per se*. Again, we must be careful not to isolate the sense of our redemption to only that which we have been liberated *from*,

---

30. Packer, *The Saving Work of God*, 15–16.

that is, bondage. We have also been liberated *to* freedom and *for* service. To speak of liberty and servanthood as co-existent states for the Christian believer might seem a strange paradox, and yet it is one that Scripture does not seek to avoid (1 Pet 2:16).

To be free to serve in this way is to be free to be governed aright and in accordance with godly principles. This is why the grace of God in Christ succeeded where the law of God outside of Christ failed, because it dealt with the sin issue that was preventing such allegiance. By virtue of the atonement that is to be found in God's Son on the cross, Christ has reasserted the fundamental underpinning of God's kingdom rule in the social order, to be directed through the church in every age. The law incarcerated because it fashioned a dilemma in the strictest etymological sense of that word: it told us what we must do, but also convicted us of our utter helplessness; it insisted upon the unattainable. The atonement of Christ sets us free in part by empowering us to meet the law's requirements.

Redemption rightly comes under the overarching umbrella of the atonement. The former is an aspect of the latter. It might even be said with certain qualifications that redemption is a particular way of looking at the atonement, a specific metaphor, if you will. However, where the atonement originated in the love of God, redemption took place by virtue of that concept in the mind of God becoming real in and through the Son of God. Of course, we might just as easily say the same of each divine idea preceding its reality, if for the sake of finite understanding we might so limit infinite matters. Here we must distinguish between consequence and cause. Redemption is the consequence of the atonement having taken place; thus, the latter is the cause of the former. In turn, we might also say that redemption causes our liberty, sonship, and servanthood. They each, in their turn, may also be the basis by which other things are caused. However, none of these things are primary causes, but are consequential upon their own cause. The primary cause of them all, of course, is the love of God.

Justification

The word in the New Testament that is translated "justification" is the Greek *dikaiosis*, which "denotes the act of pronouncing righteous."[31] Because it is essentially a forensic term, attested to by both the Hebrew verb-form (*hiphil*) and its Greek counterpart (*dikaioo*), there is an inherent sense of acquittal without necessarily bringing about any change in the moral condition. Scholars who argue in favor of a state of sinless perfection often

---

31. Vine, *Expository Dictionary*, 614.

present their case on the basis of a misunderstanding of the biblical text. This usually involves a historico-graphical claim on the Latin *justifio*, rather than adopting a sound exegetical application of the original language. The Vulgate translation of the Bible appears to be the chief proponent of this unfortunate delusion.

Our English word "justification" is, in fact, a translation of the Latin *justificare*, which is itself a composite of *justus* and *facere*, thereby meaning "to make righteous." In its biblical context, the verb-form "to justify" has the sense of effecting a state of righteousness by means of a judicious decree. This may be executed in one of two ways:

i) by acknowledging the right of the claimant to warrant such a decision (that is, the just deserve to be justified); or

ii) by crediting those who lack merit with the righteousness of another.

The consistent emphasis of justification in the New Testament embraces the latter alternative. Indeed, according to Tom Wright, who at the time of writing was lecturer in New Testament Studies at Oxford University:

> Justification denotes, primarily, that action in the lawcourt whereby a judge upholds the case of one party in dispute before him (in the Hebrew lawcourt, where the image originates, all cases consist of an accuser and a defendant, there being no public prosecutor). Having heard the case, the judge finds in favour of one party, and thereby "justifies" him: if he finds for the defendant, this action has the force of "acquittal."[32]

In his observation of Paul's treatment on the subject, William Hendriksen points out that:

> ... justification ... is in no sense whatever the work of man. On the contrary, it is:
>
> (a) God's gift, (Rom 5:15–18);
>
> (b) the product of his grace, (3:24; 4:16; 5:15);
>
> (c) free, (5:16);
>
> (d) not of works, (3:20);
>
> (e) the opposite of condemnation, (8:1, 33, 34);
>
> (f) that which deprives man of every reason for boasting, (3:27);

---

32. N. T. Wright, "Justification," in Ferguson and Wright, *New Dictionary of Theology*, 359.

(g) appropriated by faith, even that faith being God-given, (Eph 2:8).[33]

The Apostle Paul's understanding of the doctrine of justification is not such a radical departure from the forensic view prevalent within Judaism at that time. It may be seen in a twofold aspect. First of all, the pronouncement as just of those who are justified releases them from any penal liability that would otherwise have been theirs had the declaration been that they were unjust. Secondly—and perhaps more positively—there is the implied feature that the recipients of justification are also entitled to all the privileges incurred by obedience to the law. This may loosely be designated as the vindication. So, those who are justified in the theological sense of the word are not only thus reconciled to God, as wonderful as that undoubtedly is, but they are also made the recipients of all that the imputed righteousness of Christ avails for them.

It is not difficult to see why theologians of the Reformation period viewed the doctrine of justification as the article of faith by which the church would either stand or fall. In the words of Jim Packer: "Justification by faith has traditionally . . . been regarded as one of the two basic and controlling principles of Reformation theology. The authority of Scripture was the *formal* principle of their theology, determining its method and providing its touchstone of truth; justification by faith was its *material* principle, determining its substance."[34]

So pivotal is the doctrine of justification to Emil Brunner's Christology, he is compelled to declare that:

> Justification is the most incomprehensible thing that exists. All other marvels are miracles on the circumference of being, but this is the miracle in the centre of being, in the personal centre. Justification means this miracle: that Christ takes our place and we take His. Here the objective vicarious offering has become a process of exchange. Apart from this transaction, forgiveness is not credible; for it contradicts the holiness of God. Justification cannot be separated from the "objective atonement," from the expiatory sacrifice of the Mediator. Indeed, justification simply means that this objective transaction becomes a "Word" to us, the Word of God.[35]

Justification, then, is not determined by the works of man, but is entirely dependent upon a judicial act of sovereign grace in Christ Jesus, faith

---

33. Hendriksen, *Romans*, 133.
34. Packer, *The Saving Work of God*, 137.
35. Brunner, *The Mediator*, 524.

being the hand that receives it as a gift. H. D. McDonald offers the following comprehensive definition:

> Justification is that . . . act of God's free mercy whereby He pronounces guiltless those sinners condemned under the law, constitutes them as actually righteous, once and for all, in the imputed righteousness of Christ—on the grounds of His atoning work, by grace, through faith alone apart from works—and assures them of a full pardon, acceptance in His sight, adoption as sons, and heirs of eternal life, and the present gift of the Holy Spirit; and such as are brought into this new relation and standing are by the power of this same Spirit, enabled to perform good works which God hath before ordained that we should walk therein. Yet, such works performed, as well as the faith out of which they spring, make no contribution to the soul's justification, but they are to be regarded as declarative evidences of a man's acceptance in the sight of God.[36]

Strictly speaking, to say that we have been justified is not exactly the same as being forgiven, any more than it would be outside of a particularly Christian milieu. To be justified, in any given arena, means to be pronounced not guilty. It is true that we can only be declared justified in God's sight in relation to the sin issue because we have first been forgiven, but we must be careful to distinguish between the two.

Indeed, to speak of justification solely in terms of divine pardon hardly touches the surface of its full implications in the biblical perspective. We might even say that justification is barely justified by such an approach. To be pardoned implies that the one to whom the debt is owed has, by a decree of arbitrary benevolence, simply chosen to overlook an act of indiscretion or misdemeanor against his person. The necessity of the atonement renders such an idea obsolete in this case. Paul's appreciation of the matter is such that sinners are justified by God on a just ground, this being that the demands of his righteous law upon them have been fully met, the essence of the Divine Being remaining unreservedly intact. The law was neither adapted nor postponed for this transaction to take place, but it was perfectly accomplished by Christ on man's behalf. Believers are reckoned to be righteous by God because he divinely credits them with the merits of Jesus' obedience. This is no mere fanciful playing with words, for God actually charges to our account that we have fulfilled the law's obligations, not personally, but representatively in and through Christ Jesus.

---

36. H. D. McDonald, "Justification," in Henry, *Basic Christian Doctrines*, 214.

If I have arranged to meet my wife at the railway station at a given time, perhaps to bring her home after a visit to her sister and family, and I arrive later than planned, my first attempt at any conversation—rightly or wrongly—is not to greet her, or ask how our nephew's exams went, or how our niece is coming along in her driving lessons, or even if she enjoyed her stay, but to excuse my tardiness. "There were unexpected roadworks," "I failed to allow sufficient time for the volume of traffic," "the phone rang just as I was about to leave," "the cat got stuck in the tumble dryer," or "I urgently needed the bathroom before I set off" are just some of the reasons Barbara might find acceptable. To say that I was listening to the radio sports commentary and wanted to wait until half-time in the featured match would not be a popular excuse. She might even suspect that to be the real reason, even if I offered one that I knew would get me off the hook. However, if on our arrival home she discovered that there was no game being played tonight and that the cat really did show signs of recent distress, I would then be justified in her eyes. I would be forgiven for arriving late because my reason was perfectly justifiable; I had been proved right all along. This is how God sees us in his Son—justified, innocent of any wrongdoing; not because we are guiltless in ourselves, but because we are so in Christ.

Thus, justification in theological terms is one of the immediate benefits of the reality of the atonement having taken place; it is not the atonement itself. Or, to put it another way: it is the pronouncement that we are Christian, without any reference to how we came to be that way. Of course, because it could only be on account of Christ's finished work, we might argue that it is implied anyway, but that is only because we know something of the mechanics and how they interrelate. The fact that the terms and the reality of what it signifies stands alone in this way is important for a number of reasons, not least of which are the forward implications. If justification is the declaration that we are righteous without saying how we became so, then it also makes that same assertion without necessarily being annexed to any demands to maintain such a status.

This does not mean, of course, that there are no behavioral expectations of one who has been declared justified. Nor should it be inferred that, having had such a pronouncement made, we thereafter have it within our gift to make a mockery of such an affirmation by conducting ourselves contrary to the findings of the Almighty. Shall sin continue so that grace may abound all the more? God forbid! But righteous acts do not add to our justification as if in some way the atoning work of Christ was incomplete; by the same token, neither can their absence diminish its value.

It would not be inappropriate, therefore, to consider the scriptural concept of justification to be both etymologically and theologically set in complete antithesis to blameworthiness. This is why the Apostle Paul can so confidently assure his Roman readership that "[t]here is now no condemnation for those who are in Christ Jesus" (Rom 8:1). The fact that they are "in Christ Jesus" through faith signifies that they are justified, declared righteous, the penalty for their sin having been paid "JUST as IF they had dIED." Although it is not a theme that is exclusive to Paul in the New Testament, his writings do account for around seventy-five percent of the use of the verb "justify" and its derivatives to be found there. So much so, in fact, that from amongst his works the following definition of the biblical concept of justification in the context of the atonement may be affirmed: "Justification is God's deed and decree to graciously forgive the sin of the convicted penitents and credit them to be righteous, of his own volition and by his grace, according to a response of faith in Christ, not on the basis of works, but of the mediatorial keeping of the law and substitutionary death of the Lord Jesus Christ in their stead."

And so, the basis of our justification is the atonement. One of the many benefits of our justification is assurance. This, too, is of manifold expressions. We are comforted in the fact of our status of having been justified, but there is also an intrinsic pledge that such a decision cannot be rescinded on appeal, simply because of the supremacy of the One who has made the declaration; it cannot be taken to a higher court. The guarantee of such a promise is, of course, the Holy Spirit. However, to posit that the assurance of justification we have as believers by way of the Holy Spirit in respect of him convincing us thus is true, but only partially so. Or, to put it another way, it is the truth, but not the whole truth. To present it as such is demeaning of his function, disrespectful of God's purpose, and is to disregard the biblical revelation. The fact of the matter is that the giving of the Holy Spirit (or, from the believer's perspective, the receipt of him) is in and of itself a token of our assurance, a "deposit guaranteeing what is to come" (see 2 Cor 1:22; 5:5; Eph 1:4).

By way of summary, then, the following points may be observed in relation to justification:

1. participation or otherwise is determined by covenant membership, irrespective of national identity, cultural background, racial distinction, social standing, or gender (Gal 3:26–29);

2. the basis for the judicial decision is none other than the substitutionary death and subsequent resurrection of Christ Jesus (Rom 3:24–26; 5:8–9);

3. the blessings of justification in the present meticulously anticipate the divine decree at the end of the age (Rom 2:1–16);

4. the corporate recipient of justification is the church, its individual members having undertaken a personal commitment to its head, Jesus Christ (see Gal 2:21; 5:4–6); and

5. justification is essentially by grace through faith (Rom 3:22–26; Titus 3:7).

Reconciliation

Re-conciliation implies that there is a wrath to be averted in order to restore good relations. Indeed, Scripture points out that, as sinners, we were enemies of God (Rom 5:10; Col 1:21). This is not merely the use of vivid language to express the distinction between a passing acquaintance in contrast to a close friend; there was positive animosity between us. In order to become "at one" with God, therefore, the root cause of the quarrel needed to be dealt with. The sole purpose of Christ's voluntary sacrifice was to bear the curse of the law so that man and God could thereby be reconciled. It is also important to maintain that God's righteousness is not the problem in the equation, for that is wholly immutable. Man's sin is the complication, man is the one at odds with his Maker, and it is essentially he who must be reconciled to the Father, not *vice versa*.

The Greek word *katalasso* ("to reconcile") and its corresponding noun *katallage* ("reconciliation") occur infrequently in the New Testament, Paul being the sole exponent of the terms. It would be a mistake, however, to suggest that the doctrine of reconciliation is thus only hinted at in Scripture, for when these words are used it is with such precision that no one can be in any doubt as to their rudimentary value to the basic concept of Pauline Christology. Although not an exclusively religious term (see 1 Cor 7:11), the foremost use of the idea of reconciliation has God as its object (2 Cor 5:8–21). This being the case, it must be noted that man does not effect a change in his relationship by any merit on his part to persuade God to respond with such favor. On the contrary, it was while we were opposed to God in every meaningful aspect that he initiated the foundation upon which reconciliation becomes attainable.

With this association in mind, Vine offers the following comprehensive definition of *katalasso*:

> With regard to the relationship between God and man, the use of this and connected words shows that primary reconciliation is what God accomplishes, exercising His grace towards sinful man on the ground of the death of Christ in propitiatory

sacrifice under the judgment due to sin . . . By reason of this, men in their sinful condition and alienation from God are invited to be reconciled to Him: that is to say, to change their attitude, and accept the provision God has made, whereby their sins can be remitted and they themselves be justified in His sight in Christ.[37]

Emil Brunner links the act of remission with that of rapprochement in the following learned fashion:

> . . . reconciliation through the cross of Jesus Christ . . . is the event in which God makes known His holiness and His love simultaneously, in one event, in an absolute manner. We can, however, only perceive its full significance as a real act of forgiveness if we see that it is far more than a symbol, however impressive . . . that it is *the* revelation, which . . . constitutes the basis of our faith in forgiveness. This is what is meant by reconciliation, if the word is taken in the Biblical objective sense.[38]

It was Athanasius (ca. AD 297–373) who first developed the idea of the inextricable relationship between the incarnation and the atonement. For him, soteriology was the pervading influence of the biblical revelation, and so his theology had the constant thread of the salvation theme running through it. In his *On the Incarnation*, Athanasius elaborated on the doctrine of creation and the significance of man's role within the divine decree. He maintained that man had lost the life of God, thereby bringing upon himself the process of decay, pollution, and a progressive diminishing of the image and knowledge of God. The only possible solution for such a disaster, he argued, was for the Creator to take it upon himself to effect man's reconciliation. The essence of God's Being dictated that this could only be viable by him taking human flesh, revealing himself as the Savior of mankind and executing the penalty for sin in righteous judgment by bearing the shame of the cross, and yet proclaiming its victory in the power of the resurrection.

In later years, Athanasius revised his concept of the *Theanthropos* considerably. While sustaining the prominence of the absolute necessity and inseparability of the incarnation and the atonement, he further reinforced the notion that reconciliation took place initially within the Person of the Christ, or more specifically, in the hypostatical union of the two natures of Christ. It would perhaps be worthwhile at this point to refer the reader to the introduction of Dr. Moule's argument that: "The one really distinctive

---

37. Vine, *Expository Dictionary*, 932.
38. Brunner, *The Mediator*, 450.

thing for which Christians stood [in the early church] was their declaration that Jesus had been raised from the dead according to God's design, and the consequent estimate of him as in a unique sense Son of God and representative man, and the resulting conception of the way to reconciliation."[39]

Time was when the concept of reconciliation in terms of the atonement required little explanation in Christian circles. Although there were minor differences of understanding, they generally followed either the classical or the Latin pattern. In the former, the victory of Christ over demonic forces at the cross is the primary focus. The perceived mythical content became a stumbling block to those in pursuit of truth and for whom the imagery conveyed was presented as real. The Eastern Orthodox Church remains a chief proponent of the classical position, as one might expect. Those who favored the Latin approach made their choice on the basis of its emphasis being more annexed to the divine satisfaction against the sin(s) of humanity. Anselm of Canterbury (1033–1109) was an early advocate, his *Cur Deus Homo* (that is, *Why God Became Man*) forming the starting point for expressing the role of the *Theanthropos* in redemption history. The sharp contrast between Christ's obedience and humanity's waywardness was central to this argument, though the polarization soon paved the way for human guilt to become the subject of personal penance.

Perhaps unusually in such matters, a third way also failed to do justice to the biblical position. Rather than taking the more valid elements of those theses that preceded it, it followed instead an even more humanitarian approach. According to its chief protagonists, reconciliation becomes first of all attainable by the life of Christ as much as by his death and then, by extension, possible also by a life lived in accordance with the example Jesus set, without any necessity to initially embrace the atoning work of his death and resurrection. Just for the record, can I state my conviction that reconciliation without repentance is anathema to the biblical revelation of both concepts. Moreover, sanctification that fails to acknowledge salvation as its gateway is wholly unattainable by us. Any attempt to walk that path is both doomed to failure and may rightly be identified with endeavoring to enter the sheep fold by an unprescribed way (see John 10:1).

More recently still, John Stott identifies four images of salvation, each presenting a different illustration of the same truth. Concerning the symbolism that is reflected in the idea of reconciliation, he informs us that this:

> . . . is probably the most popular of the four because it is the most personal. We have left behind the temple precincts (propitiation), the slave-market (redemption) and the law courts

---

39. Moule, *The Phenomenon*, 18.

(justification); we are now in our home with our family and friends. True, there is a quarrel, even "enmity," but to reconcile means to restore a relationship, to renew a friendship. So an original relationship is pre-supposed which, having been broken, has been recovered by Christ.[40]

In the four major conciliatory passages (Rom 5:10–11; 2 Cor 5:18–21; Eph 2:11–22; Col 1:19–23), Paul's common approach is also one that suggests an act of putting right a relationship that had previously been one of acrimony and antagonism. Although God's forgiveness is free and final, it should not be perceived as merely the turning of a blind eye to petty mischief. The cause of our impaired relationship is sin and the basis for its restoration is the effective management of that problem. Hence, "Christ died for our sins" (1 Cor 15:3). Speaking on the meaning of the word "reconcile" as employed by Paul, Martyn Lloyd-Jones draws the following conclusions:

1. It means . . . a change from a hostile to a friendly relationship.

2. It does not merely mean a friendship after an estrangement . . . it means really bringing together again, a reuniting, a re-connecting.

3. It is a word also that emphasizes the completeness of the action. It is not the patching up of a disagreement. It is not a compromise . . . it is a complete action [which] produces complete unity and accord where there was formerly hostility.

4. This word that the apostle uses implies that it is *one* of the parties that takes the action, and it is the *upper* one that does it . . . [and] it suggests an action that comes down from above.

5. The word carries the meaning that it is a restoration of something that was there before . . . They were conciled before; they are now re-conciled, brought back to where they were.[41]

The benefits of having been reconciled belong to the following chapter. However, there are certain obligations and it would be remiss of me not to allude to them here, or at least to challenge one or two erroneous assumptions. In Paul's second extant epistle to the believers at Corinth, he speaks of our status "in Christ" as being akin to "a new creation," before identifying both the source and the responsibility it places upon us thus: "All this is from God, who reconciled us to himself through Christ and gave us the ministry of reconciliation: that God was reconciling us to himself in Christ,

---

40. Stott, *The Cross of Christ*, 192.
41. Lloyd-Jones, *Ephesians*, 285.

not counting men's sins against them. And he has committed to us the message of reconciliation" (2 Cor 5:18-19).

Three obvious questions might be asked of this text:

- Who are the "us" that the apostle refers to as having this ministry?
- What does the ministry of reconciliation entail?
- What is the message that is associated with that ministry?

First of all, then, to whom does the "us" refer? Is the apostle referring to apostles in general, to the team under his specific apostolic guidance, or is it more all-embracing than either of those options? Well, both the immediate and the overall context suggest the latter. It would be linguistically unusual if the "us" who have been given this ministry were not the same "us" whom God has reconciled to himself.

Secondly, the "ministry of reconciliation" that we convey to others can surely be no different to the one we ourselves have received. We do not become reconciled by one means and then develop a ministry that does not build on that same foundation. As if to offset the possibility of such a misinterpretation, Paul gives further clarity: "that God was reconciling us to himself in Christ." Thus, the ministry of reconciliation is to proclaim that we have been reconciled on the basis that propitiation has taken place.

That, too, is the message. The ministry is to make the message known and the message is that made known by those entrusted with such a ministry: all of us who have thus far been reconciled.

For the reconciliation of two parties to take place, a change must occur. There are a number of possibilities. The passage of time can remove the sense of grievance, those things that may have caused us offence as a younger person may not be quite so injurious in later years, a genuine apology on the part of the one causing the damage might placate the one offended, the closer one is to death the less important some matters might seem by comparison, and our perceptions often alter with age and maturity. No such change occurred in the person or nature of God, nor could it do so. His hatred of sin did not gradually diminish in intensity, he had not got over his hostility as the centuries elapsed as if his wrath had originally been no more than a fit of pique, no expression of sorrow on our part could possibly satisfy the righteous indignation of a holy God against sin. What changed was our standing in relation to sin and righteousness, and what effected that transformation was the atoning sacrifice of God's Son, Jesus Christ.

The basis of such reconciliation, therefore, is the atoning work of Jesus. In other words, it was essentially and necessarily the atonement that effected the transformation in God's relationship toward mankind. This is not to imply, of course, that any part of God's nature underwent change, but that he himself activated the process whereby his own intrinsic sense of justice could be satisfied by a single act of conciliatory love toward the world. Again, it must be understood that God's position was not such that his love was bound up against his will until these righteous demands could be fully met, but the very sacrifice of his only Son to meet the penal obligations of the law was itself ample evidence of so deep a love.

Summary

Sadly, there seems to be a bias within man's understanding of the atonement to view it from an entirely anthropocentric perspective, thereby completely underestimating the divine approach to such a reconciliatory act. The fact remains, however, that the substitutionary sacrifice of Jesus Christ points to One who, though born of a woman, could choose to be the first—and only—man to render perfect obedience to the will of God. The cross of Christ as the climax to the redemptive act, therefore, brought together those facets of God's nature that may well appear to be contradictory to finite minds. In him reside justice and love, righteousness and mercy, without even a trace of conflict. Remission of sin is not the winking of a holy eye to frivolous misdemeanor; God's intrinsic sanctity must remain intact. The purpose of the atonement was so that the penal demands of the law could be fully satisfied on our behalf, thereby effecting the reconciliation of relationship between God and man, Creator and the pinnacle of his creation.

CHRIST JESUS—THE FINAL CONQUEROR

Modern society seems to bear witness to the theory that those who oppress others often share a history of having been victimized themselves. Evidence for this may be observed in terms of playground bullying, child abuse, inappropriate punishment for minor misdemeanors, racial aggression, and hostile marital relationships. Although perpetrators of sinful deeds have an obligation to be held accountable for their actions, this does not gainsay the fact that for many there is a painful inner disposition in desperate need of healing and restoration to wholeness. In the beginning, Adam and Eve chose to defy God and were thereby held personally responsible for the consequences of their rebellion. It cannot be denied, however, that they were also in some measure victims of the serpent's guile. In order for man to be truly free to exercise the liberty that is now available to him by virtue of the atonement of Christ, then those things that would seek to keep him bound also needed to be dealt a death blow.

The Defeat of Satan

An Enemy with a Battle Plan

The biblical presentation of Satan is as one who is the enemy of God, his very name meaning "adversary." It would appear that his battle strategy is fuelled by envy at God's decision to set man as vice-regent over creation, and so he seeks to oppose humanity, thus frustrating God's purpose. His objectives are clear, as are his tactics: to make members of the human race either his envoys or his victims, thereby causing them to fail to fulfill their potential in God.

Scripture informs us that the devil's sole purpose is "to steal and kill and destroy" (John 10:10). His mode of attack is usually threefold. First of all, he is committed to bringing about destruction wherever and to whomever he can. This is perhaps nowhere more clearly seen than in the principle of death that he effectively managed to inaugurate, which is presumably why Jesus labeled him as "a murderer from the beginning" (8:44).

However, God has mercifully restricted the devil's ability to inflict suffering and discomfort. The consequence of this divinely appointed prohibition is that the devil thus becomes little more than a tormentor, as can graphically be seen in his dealings with Job in the Old Testament (see Job 2:5–6). The New Testament also gives numerous accounts of God's people being subject to demonic oppression (see Luke 13:16; Acts 5:16; 2 Cor 12:7–9).

Satan also engages in battle for the mind by seeking to bring about confusion and mental instability. It is perhaps significant that when the Apostle Paul was commissioned by God to work amongst the Gentiles, his ministry was described in terms of him being sent "to open their eyes and turn them from darkness to light, and from the power of Satan to God" (Acts 26:17–18). In other words, it seems that God regarded the Gentiles as a people who had been so blinded by confusion that they had until that point been incapable of perceiving truth. Surely there can be little doubt that intellectual perplexity remains a primary device of the enemy as he seeks to lead "the whole world astray" (Rev 12:9). For the Christian, however, the battleground is not unchartered territory. Nor is the conflict one of evil thoughts tussling with godly ones with both hopeful of gaining the upper hand. Though the encounter remains nonetheless real, the combat zone already belongs to God (see 1 Cor 2:16).

In complete antithesis to the devil, who is the oppressor of mankind, Jesus came to deliver humanity from that oppression. Indeed, "[t]he reason the Son of God appeared was to destroy the devil's work" (1 John 3:8). Thus, Jesus tackled the enemy in the three key areas of his own battle plan head on. Where Satan seeks to bring confusion, Jesus confused Satan by gaining victory at his weakest and most vulnerable point at the cross (1 Cor 2:8); where the devil hopes to torment, the Christ will have him tormented in hell forever (Rev 20:10); and where the adversary plans to wreak destruction, he will be personally destroyed by humanity's Messiah (Heb 2:14).

The First Temptations of Christ

From the biblical text, we are able to identify Jesus' overthrow of Satan at three strategic points of reference in his life. According to the Synoptic Gospel accounts, the temptation of Christ in the wilderness follows on immediately from his baptism in the Jordan River. There is nothing particularly unique in that, as I'm sure many Christians could testify to a similar occurrence of their own. What is exclusive to Christ, however, is the nature of the temptation, especially in the context of the Father's especial declaration as Jesus emerged from the water. Compare the enemy's words with those of the Father:

> "You are my Son, whom I love; with you I am well pleased."[42]

> "If you are the Son of God . . ."[43]

The significance of these three attempts by Satan to tempt Jesus should be neither underestimated nor downplayed. The devil tried to cause "the last Adam" to fall even as the first Adam had, though in vastly different circumstances. Perhaps in the economy of God's purpose and in order to radically reverse the effects of the sin issue, Jesus was obliged to triumph in this relatively minor skirmish before embarking on the major battle ahead. There seems little doubt that—in the mind of the Tempter, at least—this was an ideal opportunity to cause Jesus to distrust his Father's provision and thereby to look to his own means.

With the obvious exception of the cross, this was arguably Jesus' most vulnerable moment in life. First of all, the basic element of life sustenance

---

42. Luke 3:22b.
43. Luke 4:3, 9.

was involved. Having fasted for forty days, some might be excused for thinking that it almost insults our intelligence to have to be told that "he was hungry" (Luke 4:2b). There is a mocking tone to the devil's words that is not fully conveyed in translation. The implication is one of ridicule: "You're the Son of God and you're hungry? How can this be?" Again, the comparison between this incident and that of Adam's failure is an all too obvious one. That both involved the desire for food is not without significance, if albeit a minor one. The real issue, however, is that on each occasion the one being tempted is challenged in relation to his confidence in the Father's capacity to sustain him. Seeds of distrust are sown in the hope that they become full grown into a harvest of unbelief. In Adam's case, they were watered by an aspiration toward autonomy; for Jesus, the seeds could establish no root in the fertile soil of his interdependent relationship with the Father.

Secondly, the devil offered Jesus the authority and splendor of all the kingdoms of the world (Luke 4:5–6), if only he would submit to his rule (v. 7). Much debate has ensued as to the validity of such a temptation given that, as the Son of God, Jesus would probably have seen straight through the lie. Whether this was hidden from him can only ever be confined to the realm of speculation. Where Scripture avoids precision of detail it is wise to shun conjecture. This is especially so where the message is unhindered by its absence and would not be enhanced in any way by it being more readily attainable. If it were otherwise, then it would have been made plain to us. To my mind, the vision theory is both the most likely and the most consistent with other similar instances that are known to us in the Bible (see Ezek 40:2; Rev 1:10).

What can be asserted with more certainty, however, is that for Jesus' triumph in the desert to be anything but shallow, then the temptation can have been nothing but real. Similarly, the actual nature of the temptation is unambiguous: enjoy the splendor without the suffering. The implied suggestion that the Christ could have access to the crown of glory with no need to endure the cross of ignominy must surely have been an appealing proposition. Thankfully, it was one to which the Son of God refused to yield.

Finally, Jesus is enticed to prove the legitimacy of his confidence in the protection of the Father (Luke 4:9–11). In stark contrast to Israel's trial of Yahweh at Massah and Meribah (see Exod 17:1–7), Jesus declined to abuse his trust in the love of the Father by deliberately placing himself in a position of natural danger. His reply is consistent with Moses' reflection of this same episode (Deut 6:16).

The likelihood that the third temptation faced by Jesus also took the form of a vision cannot summarily be disregarded, but neither does that possibility make it any the less real. The Scripture posited by Satan was a legitimate one, if incomplete (cf. Luke 4:10; Ps 91:11). The omission of "in all your ways" is an important one, but perhaps not vitally so. The essence of the temptation—or, at least, the guile behind it—is immediately picked up by Jesus: "It is also written . . ." Texts taken out of context so easily become pretexts to support an alleged proof text that was never intended in the original. Thus, our interpretation of Scripture must always be subject to internal harmony. Where this is not immediately apparent, we must reserve judgment until it becomes so. In other words, we should never cite Scripture to support a premise when to do so would impinge unfavorably upon other known revelation. Neither can the latter be temporarily suspended to accommodate the former, as the devil seemed to be doing here.

There is much similarity—and not a little contrast—between this episode in Jesus' life and the fall of Adam, with whom Satan had employed precisely the same strategy, questioning the legitimacy of the word received by God's created "son." The major difference between the two, of course, is that whereas our first parent succumbed to the enemy's temptation, Jesus resisted the promise of all earthly authority and splendor on the basis of "It is written . . ." In his observations on the relationship between the first and last Adam, Dietrich Bonhoeffer offers the following: "To be precise, the Bible tells only two temptation stories . . . of the first man and . . . of Christ, that is the temptation which led to man's fall, and the temptation which led to Satan's fall. All other temptations in human history have to do with these two stories of temptation."[44]

It is also in this one event, perhaps more so even than the cross, that Christ's trifold ministry is perfectly evident. As priest, he suffered truly, each of the three incidents being progressively more intense than the last, even though it is beyond our comprehension to fathom the reality of the sinless being truly tempted; as prophet, he boldly declared God's word as the appeal by which he fought the assaults being made upon him; and as king, he triumphed over the would-be usurper to his crown.

Throughout Jesus' Life

Because the next time we see such an obvious example of Jesus and the devil in direct conflict is at the cross, it would be easy to imagine their paths never having crossed between those two events. Far from it: the pattern of obedience to God established in the desert continued throughout the public ministry of Christ. The wilderness experience had been one of Satan attacking Jesus at his most vulnerable in an attempt to disarm and render ineffective.

---

44. Bonhoeffer, *Creation and Temptation*, 101.

As such, Jesus had been pretty much on the defensive. Thereafter, however, it is Jesus who takes the fight to the enemy.

The remaining three and a half years of Jesus' life are replete with episodes of his reversing the works of Satan: healing the sick, conquering strongholds, exorcising demons, releasing those held captive, loosing the bandages of infirmity, raising the dead, bringing hope in the midst of despair, effecting peace where there had previously been only hostility, and generally exercising his authority to overthrow the devil's strategies, schemes, and systematic uncleanness. The evil one had steadily and steadfastly oppressed, afflicted, and brought immense suffering to humanity from Adam onwards, but Jesus "went around doing good . . . [to] all who were under the power of the devil" (Acts 10:38).

On this basis, it is perhaps more appropriate to speak of Jesus' public ministry as a declaration of his victory over Satan than further evidence of the battle having been joined. That notwithstanding, however, it is to the cross that we must look for the place of the final triumph, Christ's cry of "It is finished!" testifying to the fact.

Calvary

Thus, it was at the cross of Calvary that the decisive blow was struck. In the context of the previous section, it would be understandable to consider what actually took place at Jesus' crucifixion in terms of the agony he suffered, the Father's wrath being averted and, thus, our reconciliation being made possible on the grounds of faith. It is right and proper that these should be the main foci of our attention. But, in so doing, let us not forget the effect the cross of Christ had on Satan. Of course, this is not to imply that from that point in history the devil has either ceased to exist or been totally ineffective in seeking to frustrate the saints in their pursuit of holiness. He is no less evil than before, any more prone to goodness, or driven by anything other than a desire to steal, kill, and destroy.

So, what change—if any—did take place? Well, the writer to the Hebrews puts it like this: "Since the children have flesh and blood, [Jesus] too shared in their humanity so that by his death he might destroy him who holds the power over death—that is, the devil—and free those who all their lives were held in slavery by their fear of death."[45]

That word "destroy" appears in other translations as "render powerless" (NASB, Weymouth), "break the power of" (NLT), "bring to nought" (ERV, ASV), and "annul" (Darby). The original Greek so translated is

45. Heb 2:14–15.

katargeo, which carries the meaning "to make of none effect" or "to render useless for practical purposes." It is a compound of two words which, when brought together in this way, would literally be "to reduce to inactivity."[46] The same word is translated elsewhere in the New Testament as "abolish" (see Eph 2:15).

The cross of Christ, therefore, really was the crucial turning point in history, the hinge upon which the door of salvation revolves, after which the enemy can no longer exercise legitimate dominion over the lives of those who are "in Christ" (see Rev 12:11). One hymn writer expressed it this way:

> Mighty victim from the sky,
> Powers of hell beneath thee lie;
> Death is conquered in the flight;
> Thou hast brought us life and light,
> Now thy banner thou dost wave;
> Vanquished Satan and the grave;
> Angels join the praise to tell—
> See o'erthrown the prince of hell.[47]

Whilst it is true that Peter advises us through his writings to be alert because of the enemy's predatory instincts directed against the church (1 Pet 5:8), it would be inaccurate for us to regard ourselves as mere pawns in some sort of dualistic battle between God and Satan, the outcome of which remains debatable. Although the devil possesses superhuman capabilities, he is not free to exercise his own choice of destiny. Indeed, what freedom he has is tightly bound within the parameters of God's sovereign will. He was totally defeated at the cross. The difficulty we as believers are now faced with is how to reconcile in our minds the certainty of Christ's victory over the adversary with the undeniable level of control that he still seems to exert on the earth. The answer must surely lie in the fact that it is only for the individual in relationship with Jesus that such victory is assured. The very word "Christian" means "in Christ"; it is not simply a name behind which to hide in seasons of difficulty, but a lifestyle to adopt in obedience to him and his principles, constantly drawing upon the resources at our disposal through the Spirit of Christ.

Shortly after the turn of the last century, these poignant words were written by way of an attempt to offer some insight into the hope we profess:

> The fallen race of Adam which God said must be "blotted out"
> because "every imagination of the thoughts of the heart was

---

46. Vine, *Expository Dictionary*, 5.
47. Seventh century, traditionally ascribed to Robert Campbell.

only evil continually," was nailed to the Cross in the person of the Second Adam, and by the Cross the Lord from heaven triumphed over the Prince of darkness. "*Through death*"—the very result of sin; "*through death*"—the very weapon by which the evil one held his subjects in bondage; "*through death*"—drinking the cup of death to its dregs for the whole world; "*through death*"—the Prince of life destroyed "him that had the power of death, that is, the devil." Satan has fallen from heaven. He is "cast out," his power destroyed, his kingdom shaken, at the place called Calvary.[48]

There is much current Christian literature that focuses on the reality of demonic activity, which conveys the underlying message: "Beware, the devil . . ." The perceived element of fear, however, has surely been replaced by one of confidence since Christ defeated Satan at the cross. This is not to say, of course, that believers are immune from the attacks of the devil. Far from it! The warnings of Paul to the church at Ephesus that the saints there might be adequately attired in spiritual armor serves as both a vital lesson and a sober reminder to us that we, too, might avail ourselves of the opportunity to "extinguish all the flaming arrows of the evil one" (Eph 6:16). And what of James' advice that if only we: "[r]esist the devil . . . [then] he will flee from [us]" (Jas 4:7), providing that we have first of all submitted ourselves to God? Again, John repeatedly assures the young men amongst his readership that, because of their standing "in Christ," they "have [that is, past tense] overcome the evil one" (1 John 2:13–14).

Similarly, the Christian believer is not encouraged so much to engage in personal combat with the devil as to declare his or her standing in the one who has already conquered. This is what it means to be "in Christ" (1 Cor 15:22; 2 Cor 5:17). Such an understanding is also presumably the background to Paul's teaching to the believers at Ephesus in the context of taking up spiritual armor that we may stand our ground, being "strong in the Lord" (Eph 6:10–19). The King James Version translates this as "withstand," which seems to better convey the original sense of resistance inherent in the Greek *stemi*. It is to stand fast no matter what assaults designed to cause us to fall may come against us.

It is inappropriate to dismiss the devil as a mere inconvenience; it is also a mistake to treat him only as an object of derision and ridicule. He is far too wily, subtle, scheming, and—well—devilish for that. But neither should we afford him more credit than he is due. He is dangerous, but he is also defeated. He has strength, and yet he is subject to the sovereign will

---

48. Penn-Lewis, *Warfare with Satan*, 44.

of God in Christ Jesus. He may gain some sense of perverse pleasure from winning minor skirmishes, though the overall battle outcome was decided long ago.

What we have here, then, is the idea that the power of Satan, which ultimately resides in the principle of death as the consequence of original sin, has been completely and utterly disarmed by the dying of one who was not personally bound by its conditions. We shall be returning to this in more detail a little later in the chapter. For now, we can but echo the opening line of John Donne's *Divine Sonnet X*: "Death, be not proud!"

Powers Are Overcome

In many ways, Jesus' defeat of Satan was preparatory to his overcoming what the New Testament describes as "the rulers of the age" (1 Cor 2:6–8), "the rulers of the kingdom of the air" (Eph 2:1–2), the "authorities in the heavenly realms" (3:10), the "powers of this dark age and . . . the spiritual forces of evil" (6:10–13), and "the basic principles of this world" (Col 2:20). Other terms used include "powers," "dominions," and "thrones." There is no explicit definition for any of these individually, and so it is pure speculation to think of them in terms of some demonic territorial structure of hostility. Some commentators regard them as being exclusively personal demons, others consider them simply to be human tyrants, while still others argue for a combination of the two. What we do know, however, is that their collective strength under Satan's guiding hand is no match for Jesus even at his most susceptible.

As the reader will have deduced from the Scripture references cited above, it is chiefly in the writings of the Apostle Paul that we find such terms being used. The significant aspect in Paul's understanding seems to be that where believers were formerly victims, the effects of Christ's victory over Satan are such that we are now not merely passive spectators, but are those who "have divine power to demolish strongholds" (2 Cor 10:4). Jesus expressed a similar sentiment upon Peter's confession of him as the Anointed One, when he declared that the gates of Hades would not be able to withstand the onslaught of the conquering church (Matt 16:18). Some have interpreted this assurance in terms of the future stability and security of the church in the face of all that hell can throw against it, as if its strength lies in unflinching resistance. The sense of the Greek verb *katischuo*, however, is more offensive than defensive; it is generally used to convey the idea of a forceful advance on enemy territory. One nineteenth-century hymn writer expressed it thus:

> Christian, dost thou see them on the holy ground,
> How the powers of darkness rage thy steps around?
> Christian, up and smite them, counting gain but loss,
> In the strength that cometh by the holy Cross.
> Christian, dost thou feel them, how they work within,
> Striving, tempting, luring, goading into sin?
> Christian, never tremble; never be downcast;
> Gird thee for the battle; watch and pray and fast.
> Christian, dost thou hear them, how they speak thee fair?
> "Always fast and vigil? Always watch and prayer?"
> Christian, answer boldly, "While I breathe I pray!"
> Peace shall follow battle, night shall end in day.[49]

When we think of rulers, authorities, and powers, we usually have in mind human structures of government and leadership. Paul is clear to point out, however, that "our struggle is not against flesh and blood, but [is one being fought out] in the heavenly realms" (Eph 6:12). There is an implied struggle for supremacy between the people of God and these unseen powers, which certainly seems to suggest satanic influence. Indeed, it is most likely the devil who is the one described as "the ruler of the kingdom of the air" (2:2). But who precisely are the plurality of "rulers of this age" who joined forces to kill "the Lord of glory" (1 Cor 2:8)? It could simply be a reference to the combined efforts of Pontius Pilate, Caiaphas, and Herod Antipas, though the context seems to allude to something altogether more sinister. Although the Bible never gives any specific identification of demonic powers with human structures of political rulership, there seems to be some evidence to reflect an ongoing scheme whereby the evil realm is particularly tangible where human authority is subject to abuse.

Personally, I believe the evidence is insufficiently conclusive to rule with any sense of absolute conviction. If pressed, I would have to admit a leaning toward both being possible on the basis of the passage in 1 Corinthians. My objection to those who insist it must be human rulers only is not so much that I find the idea itself unconvincing, but rather the reasons that are usually cited for having arrived at such a conclusion. To say that it must be human rulers because the idea of evil spirits is far-fetched, or even preposterous, cannot be maintained on the basis of Scripture's testimony elsewhere. Jesus' own public ministry and the authority he invested in his closest disciples are surely ample evidence for that. Moreover, the references cited in Paul's other works, especially in his letter to the church at Ephesus, cannot so readily be understood in solely human terms.

---

49. John Mason Neale, 1818–1866.

At the cross, Jesus broke the reign of all such powers. He has asserted his Lordship, thereby establishing his supreme authority over all other systems of rule. Having been raised from the dead, Scripture testifies that he is now "seated . . . in the heavenly realms, far above all rule and authority, power and dominion, and every title that can be given . . . God having placed all things under his feet" (Eph 1:20–22). Although the destruction of demonic powers is yet future (see Rev 11:18), its guarantee is presently assured. Even they themselves acknowledge an appointed time of torture still to come (Matt 8:29), graphically referred to in the gospel account as "eternal fire prepared for the devil and his angels" (25:41).

In his commentary on the theme of forgiveness in the book of Colossians, Ralph Martin offers the following exegesis into the implications of chapter 2, verse 15:

> . . . the first line declares how the crucified Christ dealt effectively with the enemies which conspired to cause his death. These demonic agencies . . . tried to cling to [his flesh] but he stripped them from his person and discarded their pretended authority over him, as a person divests himself of clothing. In so doing he disgraced them by showing them up in their real character, as usurpers and rebels against God. They presumed to attack him as weak and helpless . . . [but] he repelled their assault by turning them into captives and conquered rebels . . . He led them in a public procession, just as the victorious Roman general paraded his captives of war in chains through the streets of the city at the conclusion of a foreign campaign. So these demonic powers are Christ's "prize of war," held up to public spectacle as he mounted the cross.[50]

Where I do find myself drawing the line between reasonable possibility and ostentatious conjecture is over those who promote the so-called strategic level spiritual warfare (SLSW) theory. Whether proponents of SLSW have tapped in to an existing popular fascination, have helped to create an unhealthy obsession, or the truth lies somewhere between the two, there can be little doubt that the past twenty years or so has seen what can only be described as a diversionary increase in the Christian vocabulary of terms like "spiritual mapping," "territorial spirit domination," and "identificational repentance." That none of these terms has any biblical basis—nor, indeed, have the activities associated with them—seems largely immaterial to those so enchanted by them. In purely fictional terms, the sales of Frank Peretti's novels have no doubt been escalated by this apparently coincidental interest,

---

50. R. P. Martin, "Forgiveness," in Banks, *Reconciliation and Hope*, 118–19.

though I'm not sure that everyone who has enjoyed his work would be able to so easily divorce the fiction from the perception of an unseen reality.

Arguably the most notable name to be associated with the promulgation of the SLSW manifesto is that of Peter Wagner. By his own admission, the tactics he endorses "were virtually unknown to many Christians before the 1990s."[51] That is quite a neat way to sidestep the issue of having to provide a sound biblical basis for an argument, especially for a work that carries the subtitle: *How the New Testament Church Experienced Strategic-Level Spiritual Warfare*. To my mind, such works exploit an almost medieval fear of the unclean supernatural instead of cultivating genuine faith in the one who has overcome.

It is no accident that most of the biblical references cited earlier are to be found in the book of Ephesians. First-century Ephesus was the occult center of its day, worship of the pagan goddess Diana (Greek Artemis) was particularly rife (as was the trade in associated cult objects; see Acts 19:23–28), while witchcraft had enjoyed a long and relatively unhindered existence. It was into such a coven of pollution that the new covenant people of God were to demonstrate their allegiance to the one pure God. How they were instructed to do so was not by coming to understand more fully the deep secrets of Satan, but by developing their relationship with the risen Christ. Paul's prayer for the believers at Ephesus was primarily that they might know Jesus better, not that they should seek further revelation concerning the "ruling spirits" of the area into which God had placed them (Eph 1:17). Even when he does get to mention authority, power, and dominion (and I must here allow for at least the possibility that this is some structure of demonic activity), he does so in the context of Christ's supremacy over them (vv. 18–22).

The preoccupation with naming spirits and identifying geographical locations over which they are alleged to hold sway is, in my opinion, one of Satan's most subtle ploys to both disarm God's people and rob them of enjoying the inheritance that is truly theirs by virtue of what Christ achieved in the atonement. "Let us fix our eyes on Jesus," writes the author of the letter to the Hebrew Christians. Why? Because he is the "perfecter of our faith, who for the joy set before him endured the cross, scorning its shame, and sat down at the right hand of the throne of God" (Heb 12:2). This verse is rich in meaning, especially in the present milieu. Too many believers have averted their gaze away from their Redeemer and focused instead on the would-be tormentor of their souls. Why do we need to know the names of demons when it is that of Jesus that is the name above all names, to which every knee

---

51. Wagner, *Confronting the Powers*, 21.

must bow (Phil 2:5–11)? Again, why? Well, Paul makes it very clear, as does the writer to the Hebrews in the aforementioned passage. Consider the following: "And being found in appearance as a man, [Christ Jesus] humbled himself and became obedient to death—even death on a cross! Therefore [that is, 'because of this' or 'for that reason'] God exalted him to the highest place and gave him the name that is above every name . . . " (vv. 8–9).

The parallels are surely obvious: humility leading to exaltation might be a general application, but for Christ it was the extent of the one that was commensurate with the degree of the other. His death paved the way for being afforded the highest honor possible. Only here in the whole of Scripture do we find the verb *huperupsoo*. The NASB and KJV seem to be better translations of the original at this point than the NIV, for it is not so much that Christ was lifted up to a higher location, which might be inferred, but that he was highly or super-exalted. To be exalted to the Father's right hand established Jesus' identity as the only legitimate ruler of the universe. Thus, not only was he given "the name that is above every other name," but in so doing he was acknowledged to be the power above all other claimants to power.

So, where does this leave the SLSW theory? Well, as a valid hypothesis it probably deserves our consideration. Finally, however, it—like all other such deliberations—must be subject to the rigors of sound biblical exegesis. I would even be forced to concede that I can see how the idea might have developed from the texts that are often cited in support of its legitimacy. But an awful lot of context must be sacrificed to allow the concept of SLSW to sit comfortably in my conscience. It is, I believe, the responsibility of every Christian to simply rest in the assurance of Christ's victory over Satan and his disarming of the powers associated with him at the cross. We are not encouraged to fear the devil, nor should we believe his propaganda of deceit. The armor of God is at our disposal and every item of it is important, but it is made available to us as children of God, the sonship of whom has been wrought by the atonement of God's Son at Calvary. It is to this that our attention must be directed.

I do not for one moment doubt the evangelistic fervor of those who so strongly advocate "binding the strong man" or so enthusiastically rally prayer amongst God's people for the nations, some of which do seem to have more of a proclivity toward evil than others. Of course, the church is not unused to finding itself confronted with practices with which it finds itself uncomfortable. I am as grateful to God as anyone that some legitimate, yet long-neglected, truths have been restored to their place of vitality and vibrancy even during my relatively short Christian experience. But we must be careful that our attempts at exegesis do not spill over into eisegesis, nor the purity of our theology be dictated by mythological fragments.

What appears to make Strategic Level Spiritual Warfare so attractive (or, for that matter, Ground Level and Occult Level Spiritual Warfare) is that its target is perceptibly the enemies of God in the spiritual realm. Why would we not wish to engage in such a battle? Well, largely because—and despite pleas to the contrary—it is based on premises that find no biblical warrant. Indeed, if one were to take more than a merely superficial glance, closer analysis would reveal that Wagner's theology is governed by—I'm almost tempted to say "squeezed into"—his experiential worldview. His understanding of Scripture is, thus, almost entirely subjective. Now, I am fully aware that there is an equal danger in so promoting the cerebral that we distance ourselves from the practical application that intellect is able to grasp, but that should not be an excuse for falling into the trap of allowing observation and/or experience alone to formulate our doctrine.

Much of the evidence for SLSW is derived from extrabiblical documentation and anecdotal evidence. That writings by known occultists should inform our strategy in prayer is itself some cause for concern. Similarly, to cite the alleged confronting of a Bavarian oak tree, in which was supposed to be housed the Norse god Thor, by some eighth-century self-styled "apostle" is hardly a model that inspires confidence for the truly evangelical. But there can surely be no more convincing damnation than to then read Scripture through the polarizing filter of a predetermined agenda that has SLSW firmly in view. Not only are Peter's experiences with Simon Magus (Acts 8) and Herod (chapter 12), along with Paul's encounters with Bar-Jesus (chapter 13), the Philippian slave girl (chapter 18), and at Ephesus (chapter 19) assumed to be classic examples of SLSW activities, but Wagner also regards himself to be sufficiently informed to assert that the reason for Paul and John Mark going their separate ways was because of the younger man's disapproval of the apostle's involvement in SLSW. These episodes only become susceptible to such interpretation by those who are predisposed to validate their otherwise spurious claims.

At the risk of sounding like just another grumpy old theologian—though I much prefer to be labeled a "student of theology," even it is to be insisted that I am a grumpy old one—I have been a Christian for almost forty years and have seen and often actively embraced many new techniques. In so doing, I have observed that novel methods that fail to take account of established values are often consigned to history as just another example of certain factions of the church being blown about by the latest wind of doctrine. The prophet Joel is often cited by those of a more charismatic persuasion, most notably perhaps his prediction that "Your sons and daughters will prophesy, your old men will dream dreams, your young men will see visions" (Joel 2:28). I am at an age where I find myself to be increasingly sensitive to such declarations.

It may or may not be significant that Peter reversed the order between young and old when he addressed the enquiring crowd on the day of Pentecost (Acts 2:17). If there is any import to be attached, then I believe it is this: each is interdependent upon the other. If a young man's vision is not tempered by an old man's dream, he will rush headlong into unnecessary danger and, possibly even, unfulfilled obscurity. Similarly, if an old man's dream is not harnessed to a young man's vision, he will gather to himself only those of a like disposition whose collective motto might be "All Our Yesterdays." In much the same way, newly devised procedures are most effective when they are undergirded by acknowledged and recognizable biblical principles.

"For we are not unaware of [the devil's] schemes," writes Paul to Corinth (2 Cor 2:11). He would, indeed, seek to outwit us. His device is as it has always been with man: to seek to make us think that we are less dependent upon God by whatever means are at his disposal. If such a mechanism can be cloaked in the garb of religious pursuit, then so much the better. Let the following words of Martin Luther serve as a timeless warning to us:

> Woe betide all our teachers and authors, who go their merry way and spew forth whatever is uppermost in their minds, and do not first turn the thought over ten times to be sure it is right in the sight of God! These think the devil is away for a while in Babylon, or asleep at their side like a dog on a cushion. They do not consider that he is around them and all his venomous flaming darts which he puts into them, such superlatively beautiful thoughts adorned with scripture, that they are unaware of what is happening... Thus, the devil has the advantage that no teaching of fancy so clumsy can arise but he can find disciples for it, and the clumsier the more quickly he can find them![52]

Chapter 6 of Paul's epistle to the Ephesians cannot be divorced from the context afforded by chapters one and three of the same book. Taking the fight to the enemy must always be on God's terms as revealed to us in his word, which includes diligent prayer, proclamation of the gospel message, and a practical application of all that the atonement of Christ on the cross has achieved for us. He has disarmed the powers; all that believers are now required to do is simply to stand firm and declare his victory over them. How the devil and his hordes would like to sidetrack the church from doing just that!

52. Luther, *Works* 37, 17, 19.

Jesus has effectively re-established the basic foundation of God's kingdom rule in society through the church. Where believers live their lives in obedience to the principles of God's authority, they can—and should—be an influence for good. Godly structures in the family, community, government, and artistic expression, so long abused and subject to disorder, tyranny, and exploitation, can again become areas where righteousness reigns, as Christians begin to display a lifestyle that is regulated by Christ's rule.

Although believers are not immune from the effects of social decadence, rebellion, and disarray, we are free from the slavery that such evil promotes. As "the salt of the earth" (Matt 5:13), the function of the church has always been twofold: preserve the good and purify the bad. Although it must be acknowledged that we can expect only comparatively limited success, it is equally evident from Scripture that the world has yet to benefit from the full impact of a committed company of believers in the earth, the significance of whose influence in projects that foster godly standards, whether that be in the home, education, legal system, business enterprise, or political arena, can be quite substantial.

The Death of Death in the Death of Christ

For something so universal, the subject of death is as unwelcome a topic of conversation as its reality is to even the most prepared of hearts. Throughout the ages and in every culture, death has arguably been the most feared of phenomena. The uncertainty, apparent finality, emptiness, and sense of abject loss usually associated with passing from this life always seem to arouse the strongest of unpleasant feelings, fostering nightmares, panic attacks, and sometimes emotional breakdown. For many Christians, their salvation has largely failed to remove the fear factor, though this is no doubt primarily due to a misunderstanding of how we presently stand in relation to death. It is to this that we must now turn.

The biblical revelation on the origin of death is, as we have seen, that it is the penalty imposed by God upon mankind for the unfaithfulness of Adam in the garden of Eden. Indeed, it is with three distinct emphases that Scripture speaks of death. Physical death is obviously the one most commonly considered and refers to the termination of natural bodily activity. In this regard, Louis Berkhof remarks that: "death is not the cessation of existence, but a severance of the natural relations of life . . . [therefore] life and death are not opposed to each other as existence and non-existence, but are opposites only as different modes of existence."[53]

---

53. Berkhof, *Systematic Theology*, 668.

Whereas spiritual death denotes man's relational alienation from God, as brought about by original sin, eternal death (or "the second death") describes the future destiny of all who refuse to be reconciled by the only prescribed way (that is, the atoning sacrifice of Christ Jesus). The penalty for Adam's sin was death for humanity in all its aspects, insomuch that the way to eternal life was thereafter barred. The Apostle Paul speaks of this in terms of Adam's federal headship when he affirms to the Roman believers that it was "by the trespass of one man [that] death reigned" (Rom 5:17). Whatever mysteries there may yet be surrounding death, there can be no doubt that the reality of death came as a direct result of Adam's transgression.

The outstanding feature of the New Testament treatment on the subject of death is that the bias is almost always toward life. Indeed, when speaking of death in regard to believers, the emphasis consistently seems to be on the resurrection: "The wages of sin is death, but the gift of God is eternal life in Christ Jesus, our Lord" (Rom 6:23). And again: "For as in Adam all die, so in Christ all will be made alive" (1 Cor 15:22). That Jesus took upon himself man's sinfulness "so that by his death he might destroy him who holds the power of death—that is the devil" (Heb 2:14) is surely cause enough for great rejoicing. The realm of death had previously been Satan's territory, and yet here is Jesus taking on and defeating the enemy in his own backyard, so to speak. And the victory was complete, for "[t]he death he died, he died to sin once for all" (Rom 6:10).

The fact remains, however, that we still die, Christian and unbeliever alike. It is perhaps significant that whenever Scripture speaks of death for the Christian, it employs the word "sleep" (Greek—*koimaomai*), for the second death has no rule over us (Rev 2:11; 20:6). Although we are by no means encouraged to hasten that day, neither are we taught to fear death, for the horror of the grave no longer reigns. The sting of death has been removed. Once again, I am indebted to the erudite findings of Emil Brunner:

> If human death . . . is the effect of sin and the divine wrath . . . of man's perverted relation to God, then conversely, the consequence of the newly established communion with God in Christ is the re-establishment of "existence-unto-eternal life." Jesus Christ is the great Transformer: He reverses the perverted meaning of human existence and once more gives it its original meaning . . . which it had in the intention of the Creation. This is precisely the significance of His death upon the Cross. As the coming of God into the curse of our sinful existence not only reveals to the sinner the unconditional love of God, but also provides a new ground of existence, so also His acceptance of death and His passage through it in the Resurrection is not only

revelation, but it also constitutes the new possibility for every believer, the beginning of the realization of eternal life.[54]

He summarizes his argument thus:

> The point here is not merely that through Jesus Christ the Christian receives the certainty of eternal life, nor that through Jesus Christ his immortality is assured afresh; it is rather that Jesus Christ is the Saviour from death, and that faith in Him is already the beginning, the "dawn" of Eternal Life.[55]

The death of Jesus is sometimes portrayed as the termination to a life of perfect obedience. Without wishing to completely tarnish that image, may I respectfully and reverently suggest that his death was but the final act of that obedience, the cardinal test of his submission to the will of the Father? Abandoning himself to death produced something positive in the realm of obedience, without which it may well have remained inadequate. To suffer in service to God, and in the midst of hostility and oppression, without wavering or allowing any vestige of sin is beyond anyone but the Son of God. We rightly marvel at it. But Christ also knew that for any of that to have redemptive value required that he relinquish his life in perfect trust as an apparent failure, in divine ignominy and degradation, "despised and rejected by men" (Isa 53:3), more so in death than even in life, and so spiritually outcast that he felt both the physical and psychical pain of separation from the Father as if forsaken by him (Matt 27:46). "In our Lord's death," wrote John Lidgett, "both the trial and the triumph were unique."[56]

The good news of the gospel is that believers do not have to wait until after physical death to attain all the benefits of eternal life. For example, we can enjoy the wonderful blessings of having been set "free from the law [that is, the principle] of sin and death" in the present (Rom 8:2). Jesus' promise to those who are faithful that they "will never see death" (John 8:51) is not to deny the reality of bodily death, but rather it indicates the glorious truth that the Christian has passed from a state of death into an altogether different realm, which is initiated by new birth. The sting of death is no longer effective. The death of Jesus truly spelled the death of death.

In much the same way that sin no longer has a rightful claim to dominion over those who are in Christ Jesus, so too the reign of death has come to an end. For the Christian, death should hold no fear, for it carries with it no penalty for sin. It has lost its power. Even for those of us who

---

54. Brunner, *Man in Revolt*, 475.
55. Ibid.
56. Lidgett, *Atonement*, 280.

must pass through a painful and traumatic experience of dying into the fulness of our eternal inheritance, it can have no legitimate claim. We can be both as convinced and as confident as was Paul that: "[n]either death nor life, neither angels nor demons, neither the present nor the future, nor any powers, neither height nor depth, nor anything else in all creation will be able to separate us from the love of God that is in Christ Jesus, our Lord" (Rom 8:38–39).

Whilst there is no fear of dying for the Christian, death itself will not be shown to have been finally destroyed until Christ's return (1 Cor 15:26). Prior to that time, it remains an enemy and we are thus excused for the expression of mournful emotions whenever we may lose a loved one. We are also mindful, however, of the fact that Christ has delivered a death blow from which it will never recover. We, too, may echo Paul's words that "to die is gain" (Phil 1:21), not because there is nothing left to live for and so we view death as a state of non-existent annihilation, but because death is for us merely the passage to a better dwelling. As Paul also puts it elsewhere: "we . . . would prefer to be away from the body and at home in the Lord" (2 Cor 5:8).

In his closing remarks on 1 Corinthians 15:26, Davis McCaughey observes that:

> Just as the Christian proclamation must begin with a backward look to the death and resurrection of Jesus Christ, so it must finish with a forward look, not indeed to a parallel death and resurrection for man, but to acts of God's sovereignty exercised through the reign of Christ. There is no reason to think that that reign is or will be exercised other than in the manner of the risen crucified one; but nor is there any reason for the Christian to forget the strange victory which was won in precisely this manner. The Christian looks to the future with hope, not because of anything inherent in the world but because of his faith in Jesus the *Kyrios*, who points to and makes effective the sovereignty of God.[57]

He concludes:

> In a day when the secular expectation looks to "the death of man," the Christian does not respond with a theology of "the death of God"; nor does he try, by induced mystical experience or the exercise of psychic powers, to demonstrate the presence of God in the midst of life and death. He speaks rather of a

---

57. J. D. McCaughey, "Hope," in Banks, *Reconciliation and Hope*, 260.

future and a hope. The death of death depends not upon experience but a promise.[58]

The unnaturalness of death is depicted in Scripture by the type of language it employs. It is described as the devil's domain (Heb 2:14; Rev 20:13), an unwavering despot (1 Cor 15:26; Rev 6:8), and a condition of captivity from which Christ sets its incarcerated free (Rom 8:2, 38–39). The unleashing of emotions normally associated with death tells its own harrowing story. It is the enemy of humanity. Even the most hardened of souls cannot help but be touched with sorrow at the passing of a loved one. Grief, despair, anguish of heart, tears, and painful memories all conspire to overwhelm us without invitation when we suffer such loss. And Christians are not immune from this kind of dejection, even when the sadness is eased by the knowledge that the deceased is now with Christ. Far from being dissuaded from feeling such desolation, there is some comfort in the fact that, after the death of his close friend Lazarus, Jesus too wept (John 11:35).

As believers, the only perception we are prompted to have of death is as a release from our natural, deteriorating, earthly, bodily frames. Death is also presented as the gateway to the fulness of our eternal inheritance (1 Pet 1:4), whereupon we are to be clothed with spiritual garments that will not perish (1 Cor 15:51–54). There is no dismay because there is no longer any uncertainty. There is no fear because faith has overcome. There is no anxiety because Christ's perfect love has driven it out (1 John 4:18). Just as the first Adam introduced the death principle by his actions at the beginning of history, so the resurrection of Jesus as the last Adam has established the foundation of eternal life, he being the "firstfruits" of an eschatological harvest to take place at the end of time.

I make no apology for borrowing the title of this section from John Owen's lauded tome of the same name. I am comforted by the words of my close friend, Byron Evans, who assures me that "there is no room for sentiment in the pursuit of truth, nor seasoning in the presentation of it." The personification of death in this way, of course, is not unique to seventeenth-century Puritan theologians. The New Testament writers had beaten Owen to it, and they, too, were found following in the wake of their Hebrew forbears. Given the authority of Scripture, we might even be tempted to say that the idea is of eternal origin. "Death," announced the prophet Hosea in predictive tones, "where is your sting?" (Hos 13:14). It is surely no accident that the apostle recalls these words when reminding the Corinthian believers of the significance of Christ's resurrection in the context of them anticipating their own (see 1 Cor 15:50–58).

58. Ibid.

To regard Owen's words as merely a clever literary device created to attract attention to his treatise is somewhat to miss the point. It also risks our becoming blinded, not so much to the truth of the doctrine he posits, but certainly to the irony therein encapsulated. Jim Packer seems to be fully aware of the satire when he comments:

> Every scriptural analogy and the whole attitude throughout the Old Testament to these animal sacrifices shows that the shedding of blood means the pouring out of life in a death of which the shed blood is witness. It is to exhibit death that the blood is presented at the altar. This alone is the basis on which God promises forgiveness of sin to his Old Testament people when they transgressed. So this alone is the meaning of blood-shedding in sacrifice. It is the laying down of life in death which atones.[59]

How apposite, then, that in filling out to their fullest potential all to which the Old Testament sacrifices pointed, Christ's initiating of the new covenant in his blood, the laying down of his life in death, not only wrought atonement, but in so doing put an end to the life-robbing principle of death itself!

In an earlier section of this chapter, I referred to John Donne's much lauded *Divine Sonnet X*. Although some poetic license must be granted, the biblical grounds for the message Donne seeks to convey cannot be denied:

> Death, be not proud, for some have called thee
> Mighty and dreadfull, for thou art not soe,
> For those whom thou think'st thou dost overthrow
> Die not, poore death, nor canst thou kill mee.
>
> From rest and sleepe, which but thy pictures bee,
> Much pleasure then from thee, much more must flow,
> And soonest our best men with thee doe goe,
> Rest of their bones, and soules deliverie.
>
> Thou art slave to Fate, Chance, kings, and desperate men,
> And dost with poyson, warre, and sicknesse dwell,
> And poppie, or charmes can make us sleepe as well,
> And better then thy stroake; why swell'st thou then;
> One short sleepe past, wee wake eternally,
> And death shall be no more; death, thou shalt die![60]

---

59. Packer, *The Saving Work of God*, 129.
60. John Donne, 1573–1631.

The suggestion that death is dependent upon other allies, to whom it is also bound as a slave, begs the further question: how can it survive when those things upon which it relies are no more? Although the poem cannot be described as a reasoned argument *per se*, the striking manner in which the numerous points are stacked one upon another does help build toward an effective climax. Although the first three quatrains serve as an inquisitive apostrophe, albeit in positively mocking tones, the final couplet resolves the question in the greater context of death itself succumbing to its own end.

John Stott raises the cogent point that it would perhaps be more accurate to speak of Christ as having conquered death by his resurrection, rather than by his death.[61] Thus, in order to reflect Stott's proposition, might a more valid title for John Owen's work—and, therefore, also this section—be "The Death of Death in the Resurrection of Christ?" I believe we need to look more closely at the biblical evidence for clues, which thankfully Stott goes on to pursue, in order to find a satisfactory resolution to his own question. So rarely is the death of Christ separated from his resurrection in Scripture that it is reasonable to assume both as comprising the one event, which may well have been Owen's intention in identifying them together under the one heading "Death" as a form of shorthand. The evidence of his work certainly seems to suggest that this is the case, though the main purpose of his treatise, of course, was by way of an apology against the idea of universal redemption.

The writer to the Hebrews does, indeed, affirm that it was by Christ's death that he destroyed him who holds the power of death, and thereby—one must assume—death itself (see Heb 2:14). Is this to be understood as the same kind of shorthand or does the writer actually intend to isolate Christ's death for the purpose of such analysis? Well, it is probably the latter in this case, but are we really to imagine that the victory would have been just the same had the resurrection not also taken place? It would be difficult to maintain such a position. The fact remains, however, that Christ died and he rose again, so the issue is not one that can be consigned to anything other than conjecture. "He was delivered over to death for our sins," writes the apostle, "and was raised to life for our justification" (Rom 4:25).

There is much merit to be found in the passion of those who speak of Christ's death in exclusively soteriological terms providing we understand it in the way I have described, that is, as shorthand for the twofold aspects contained in the single event. If they do not intend for us to regard it in this way, then all such value with which it might otherwise be credited surely

---

61. Stott, *The Cross of Christ*, 275.

flounders on the testimony of Paul's counsel that: "if Christ [had] not been raised . . . [then we] are still in [our] sins" (see 1 Cor 15:14–17).

In the Bible generally, though especially so in the New Testament, the subject of death is not viewed as a biological necessity, but its certainty is presented as essentially theological in nature. Similarly, there is no trace of supposition or surmise regarding the cause of death: it is the wages of sin. Of all the New Testament writers, none pays more attention to the connection between the corrupt nature of man and his mortal destiny than does Paul. It may well be argued that the gospel, of which he confidently affirmed to be unashamed (Rom 1:16), is principally one of victory over death. The terminology employed by his contemporaries clearly indicates that the early Christians did not perceive the death of Jesus as merely an historic event whereby the life of a profound religious leader came to a rather abrupt and ignominious end. Neither was Christ's death seen as simply the unfortunate product of a gross miscarriage of justice. The irresistible evidence supports the soteriological implication that this was a foundational issue in the divine plan of redemption. In other words, Jesus died for the benefit of fallen humanity (see Rom 5:8; 1 Cor 15:3).

Creation's Restoration Process Begins

We have previously noted that Adam was not alone in suffering the consequences of his disobedience; nor, indeed, were the members of the race he represented the sole victims of their forefather's sin. All of creation was thereafter polluted. In the same way, however, Scripture clearly teaches that the obedience of Christ Jesus offers restoration to both humanity and the created order. For this reason, and "[i]n keeping with his promise, we are looking forward to a new heaven and a new earth, the home of righteousness" (2 Pet 3:13), the context suggesting that believers are in a position to hasten that day as they set about accomplishing the purposes of God in the present realm (v. 12). John paints an even more graphic picture of what we are to expect of creation in the age to come (see Rev 21:1–5).

In the meantime, we live in a transitional period where the coming age has broken into the present, though not in its fulness. In this overlap, as it were, the devil has been disarmed, though not yet rendered completely powerless; powers of evil have been exposed for what they really are, but await total destruction; death has been overcome, but not utterly eliminated; and, though the sin issue has been fully dealt with on man's behalf, humanity is not yet sinless. And neither has creation become the recipient of all the potential there is in store for it on account of the atonement.

In the eleventh century, the scholastic theologian Anselm presented the doctrine of reconciliation from a platform that was both systematic and scientific. *Cur Deus Homo?* ("Why did God Become Man?") deals with the Christ event rationally and reasonably, qualities that do not always rest easily with those who believe that such issues are exclusively a matter of faith and not philosophy. The impetus for Anselm's work, however, coupled with the fundamental argument that his research unearthed, has made a lasting contribution to the doctrine of the atonement.

In a nutshell, *Cur Deus Homo?* seeks to—and succeeds in—establish(ing) that God became man because the principle of sin meant that he could only thus effect man's salvation and, at the same time, restore his own initial purpose in creation as a whole. God had created man as the pinnacle of the created order to walk in fellowship with him and Adam's disobedience had jeopardized the realization of this. That God's intent might be finally frustrated was an impossible position for Anselm to accept, for it implied a denial of divine omnipotence.

Although from a vastly different branch of Christian tradition and otherwise dissimilar theological persuasion, I find myself in somewhat uncomfortable agreement with Bishop Butler when he says:

> It seems reasonable to hold that this consummation relates not only to man but to the whole of creation. Indeed, it is difficult to conceive of a redemption of humanity that would not also involve the environment in which he lives and which, in some real sense, both enters his very constitution . . . and fashions him into what he becomes as he lives out his life in response to the ever-changing situations in which he finds himself.[62]

Thus, the extent of Christ's atonement is at least as broad as the parameters of Adam's sin. For Adam, his rebellion brought death to himself, his race, and his surroundings. As for Christ, his obedience has wrought life. For himself, this was demonstrated in his own resurrection: the grave had no claim over him. As far as humanity is concerned, eternal life is accessible by faith to all who would acknowledge him as Savior. But what of the rest of creation? Is there any evidence that the process of decay is to be reversed? And if so, can we legitimately claim that such a restorative course of action has already begun?

Of course, the whole concept of new creation rightly belongs to the realm of eschatology, that is, the study of the end times and thereafter. However, the clear evidence of the New Testament writers is such that eschatology and soteriology are inextricably linked. So much so, in fact, that we

---

62. Butler, *An Approach to Christianity*, 243.

might rightly say that eternity has broken in upon temporality. We, thus, live in the age of "the now and not yet." Glimpses of the future state may be seen, experienced, even enjoyed right now. One has only to consider the prologue of John's gospel account for clues as to how this might affect creation itself. The domain of death and darkness is progressively being invaded by light and life, terms reminiscent of the Genesis account of that first creation before Adam's rebellion wrought decay and decadence. We have seen that sin and death and hell's forces are powerless to resist against the force of Christ's righteousness, resurrection, and heavenly might. Could we possibly imagine that the death-induced created order could fail to respond positively to the life-giving power of the Creator once death has been defeated?

But we must be careful with the terminology we employ. Or, at least, be cautious to avoid phrases that might convey the wrong idea without further qualification. I must freely admit that the word "restoration" could convey images of a mere patch-up job being done to the existing creation, a sort of divine papering over the cracks. The word "re-creation" might also conjure up the idea that the new creation shares little or no similarities with that which it is intended to replace. Even the word "renewal" is not entirely devoid of unhelpful associations.

As with all such matters, it is often beneficial to look to the original language and how it was used in the Bible. When we do so, we find that the verb *anakainoo* ("renew") and its noun forms are invariably used in the context of making an adjustment, which has a transforming effect (see Col 3:10; Titus 3:5), while *apokatastasis* ("restoration"—NIV; "restitution"—KJV) is "to set in order again" (e.g., Acts 3:21). Such restoration is not necessarily to be annexed to a former condition, though neither is that by any means absent (Matt 12:13; Luke 6:10). In the sense in which the New Testament writers use it and similarly translated verb forms (*apokathistemi* and *apokathistano*) there is usually an associated meaning of being or having been restored to the original intention in God's mind.

In more recent times, the word "restoration" has been shunned by many in theological circles. This has been largely—though not exclusively— due to the emphasis placed upon the concept by the so-called "shepherding movement." The perceived excesses associated with that movement have almost blinkered other Christians to the biblical truth that lies at the heart of a valid understanding of restoration. In the context before us, it would not only be inappropriate, but also grossly remiss of me to allow such prejudice to dictate the steps taken along the path of increasing my understanding of the atonement in this regard. The Bible speaks of a coming restoration of all things (see Matt 17:11), so I must seek to determine, as far as is practicable, what may be meant by that.

There are those who posit that Christ could come again at any time. The revelation of Scripture, however, is such that he will return at God's appointed time. In fact, it was those of the "any time" mentality that Jesus found himself being obliged to correct on more than one occasion (see John 2:4; 7:1–8). Indeed, the literal meaning of the Greek *kairos* is a fixed or designated time; when used in the New Testament it is usually in accordance with God's predetermined purpose. It is equally clear that this "time" is known only to the Father (Matt 24:36), but will come about when certain stipulations have been met. Broadly speaking, these conditions constitute the fulfilling of all that has been promised by the prophets of old (Acts 3:21).

It has generally been acknowledged that there are two possible translations of the above text from the original. Either Christ's coming awaits the fulfillment of the prophets' utterances or that his *parousia* will be in order to fulfill them. It might even be argued that his actual coming will be a fulfilling of them in part. Different versions seem to opt for one line or the other, usually governed by the personal doctrinal stance of those responsible for the translation. I am not entirely convinced that it is necessary to choose one to the exclusion of the other. Both are possible, both are plausible, and both are permissible. Again, this is linked to the "now and not yet" dimension of the coming of God's kingdom rule. In the context of the subject presently before us—that is, creation's restoration process—it is not unreasonable to suggest, on this basis, that its fulfillment awaits a future date, but that the effecting of that fulfillment has already begun. One such prophecy that fits into this category is that of Isaiah:

> The wolf will live with the lamb, the leopard will lie down with the goat, the calf and the yearling together; and a little child will lead them. The cow will feed with the bear, their young will lie down together, and the lion will eat straw like the ox. The infant will play near the hole of the cobra, and the young child put his hand into the viper's nest. They will neither harm nor destroy on all my holy mountain, for the earth will be full of the knowledge of the Lord as the waters cover the sea.[63]

The way this passage is presented in its original form suggests a certain amount of imagery may be involved. We do well to exercise caution, therefore, before we so readily defend an absolutely literal application. However, the use of such language is always intended to convey an otherwise imperceptible truth. The context implies that these are component features of the Messianic age, the repeated references to other events taking place "[i]n that day" should again be taken as a period of time, rather than necessarily on

63. Isa 11:6–9.

a specific twenty-four hour day. The question before us, then, is: should we understand the truth of this and other similar passages as occurring after Christ's return or as a prelude to that one event? And what truth therein is being conveyed?

The answer to the first question will, for each of us, be in some measure conditioned by our perception of eschatology. Pre-millennialists will argue with post-millennialists, a-millennialists will be content to stand aside in the vain hope that the other two groups can manage to knock some sense into each other, while the pan-millennialists won't even bother to turn up for the debate, believing it will all simply pan out in the end. There are, of course, significant numbers of intelligent, well-informed, highly respectable, godly scholars who would faithfully number themselves among the proponents of each position. Under normal circumstances, I would most readily identify myself with the latter group, but on this occasion I am sufficiently curious to dig just a little deeper.

Isaiah uses the same terminology toward the end of the prophetic book that bears his name (see Isa 65:17–25). Here, the context is perhaps a little more clear: the creation of new heavens and a new earth. In such an environment, Isaiah envisages variety being lauded at the expense of uniformity and the weak no longer being perceived as defenseless victims, but rather complementarily necessary to those who are naturally stronger in interdependent relationship. The key to all this, of course, is "the knowledge of the Lord" (11:9). Again, the original does not allow us to regard this as mere mental awareness, but rather as knowledge that is annexed to personal intimacy. It is a knowledge that both directs us toward and is discovered on God's "holy mountain" (see also 65:25).

But if the context of the later passage is the creation of new heavens and a new earth, does this presumably re-creation not negate the idea of restoration? I have already posited that the term "restoration" is to be understood more in relation to that under consideration being restored to the original idea in God's mind; rather how we would set about restoring a piece of antique furniture, for example. There is no reason to suppose, on the basis of the evidence we have from Scripture, that this "new" creation will differ greatly from what the old creation would have become had it not been for the sin of Adam. Much of this obviously belongs to the following chapter. Suffice to say, however, that the key to resolving many of the questions that beset us here are to be found in Paul's letter to the Roman believers, to which figurative status can surely not be ascribed.

Having contrasted man's unrighteousness with the righteousness of God, and then described how the latter can be received by faith on account of Christ's finished work, the apostle begins to unfold what this might mean in the future. Man is not to be alone in benefitting from what Christ achieved, but the whole of the created order will be set free from that which has bound it within parameters of aggravated unfulfilment (Rom 8:19-22). At a specific time, yet to come, the entire creation is to be finally and fully released to achieve the purpose for which it was originally made—the glory of God.

Frustration usually exists when motivation lacks either means or mobility (or both), where a sense of destiny is unaccompanied by a specific destination, and where potential is held captive by fear or discouragement. Although it is true that God has, indeed, "set eternity in the hearts of men" (Eccl 3:11), it is equally valid that "in Adam" (1 Cor 15:22) that dimension of God-awareness in us is incarcerated by the limitations of our inherited loss according to the sinful nature. The biblical revelation of Jesus coming into the world, however, is that he did so as a second Adam and, thereby, the federal head of something completely new (v. 45). It might even be said that he came from heaven to reclaim all the inheritance lost by the first Adam in the garden.

Moreover, we must be careful not to dissociate the effect from the cause. Paul suggests that creation's restoration is somehow mysteriously, though at the same time vitally, connected to the revealing of the sons of God. Whatever is true of the latter is presumably also correct of the former, whether by crisis or by process. What do I mean by this? Quite simply that by whatever degree it may be said that the revelation—or, perhaps more accurately, the revealing—of the sons of God is to be instantaneous, then by that same degree shall be the restoration—or restoring—also of the lower created order. Similarly, to the extent that it may be accurately regarded as progressive for the one, so must it be for the other. Thus, nature's destiny is, and has always been, intrinsically linked to that of "the sons of God." Or, to put it another way, the fate of creation in the purpose of God cannot be separated from the faith of the pinnacle of creation, for they stand—or fall—together in that same purpose.

The tense used in the Greek word structure suggests that both are to be fully realized at a specifically appointed time, designated exclusively by the decree of Almighty God. Of course, imagery is used here also, Paul referring to creation in terms of a pregnant woman on the point of delivery. This imagery, however, implies that the final moments leading up to that day will be a season of progressive preparation. For, though in the midst of the pains of childbirth there comes a definite point of delivery, this being the consummation of the latter stages of labor, it is itself but the closing episode of the period of pregnancy. It heralds also the beginning of new life.

The truth is, of course, that it is equally appropriate to interpret the text in accordance with both time frames. The revelation of the sons of God has already begun and yet awaits completion. Dare we imagine the restoring of creation to be any less valid in both time frames? But note the word used. It is not that creation is hoping against all the evidence that a verdict might be given that will set it at liberty, nor merely anticipating that this could possibly be so. The Greek *apokarodokia* is translated "eager" (NIV) or "earnest expectation" (KJV). However, a more literal rendering would be "to watch attentively with outstretched head," which is as it is faithfully represented in the Weymouth New Testament. It is a noun used only here and in Paul's letter to the Philippians (Phil 1:20), though its appearance in classical literature may be familiar to some: it is that employed to describe the watchman awaiting a beacon of light to signal the capture of Troy in Aeschylus' *Agamemnon*.

Although this kind of personification of inanimate things continues to be a common literary device, not to mention one that has found an easy transition onto the silver screen, it would be inaccurate to label it as an example of prosopopoeia, *per se*. Rather, it sits more comfortably under the category of anthropomorphism. Whereas the former relates to the representation of an absent, dead, or imaginary person speaking, the latter invites us to reflect upon the perceived attribution of human characteristics or conduct to inanimate objects, the animal creation, or natural phenomena. Examples of prosopopoeia might include: "If my wife was here with me now, she would strongly advise me against buying this shirt, saying . . ." or "If Calvin was alive today, he would be appalled at what is being attributed to him. I can almost hear his words . . ." (though they would probably be words translated into English). The Bible is awash with examples of anthropomorphic qualities being assigned to God, the wind, the earth, etc. In popular culture, more familiar cases in point would include C. S. Lewis' Narnia series, Tolkien's Lord of the Rings trilogy, Walt Disney's *Looney Tunes* characters, the films *Teenage Ninja Mutant Turtles* and *Planet of the Apes*, and far too many other works of art to mention, though perhaps the soft sculptures of Claes Oldenburg would serve as a fitting token.

If the consummate restorative act for creation is to be the final unveiling of the redeemed as the sons of God, then it seems reasonable to presume that the progressive unfolding of that revelation will somehow be matched by a similarly sequential march toward restoration on the part of the created order. Grant Osborne's observation is of particular note here: "It is interesting that creation longs for the revelation of *the sons of God* here rather than its own, recognizing that the primary thrust is on the future glory of God's people."⁶⁴ Although it must readily be conceded that such a conclusion is not rendered impossible by the text, surely the wider context suggests that creation's intense yearning is more concerned with the former being the key that will unlock the latter.

Summary

To recognize Jesus only as a Suffering Servant is as odious as it is hideous. Moreover, it is to devalue the place with which Scripture affords him as the Conquering King. Whilst it is true that he died for our sins, he did so that he might thereby destroy the works of the evil one. And yet, this was but the final act in the defeat of Satan in which Jesus had been engaged since shortly after his baptism. Indeed, it might even be said that his whole life had been leading strategically and systematically toward his death from the crib to the cross. Yes, it was in Jesus' death that he is most clearly portrayed as an innocent Victim, but this is only part of the gospel message, vital though it is. Christ did not just overcome death by virtue of his resurrection, but rose from death because he had already triumphed over death in the grave. In other words, Christ the Victor demonstrated his victory in the power of his resurrection, a denial of which surely leaves humanity—and creation—still in fear of the oppressor and his hordes.

SUMMARY

After a recent walk around the surrounding countryside and grounds of a Roman Catholic high school in the north of England, my wife and I visited its tea rooms and gift shop. There were the usual sundry items for sale: pens sporting the college logo; an assortment of confectionary items, all bearing a photograph of the impressive buildings; potentially intoxicating beverages made on site; CDs of monks chanting in Gregorian fashion; and icons to suit every decor. As one might imagine, there were also crucifixes of almost every size and material imaginable, all with one common feature—Jesus was shown to be still hanging there.

Although I do not count myself among those who regard this in itself to be as problematic as do some of my peers, the utter lack of any gift showing an empty cross is perhaps symptomatic of an overemphasis of the death of Christ at the expense of giving due recognition to his having been raised from that death. Those of a more liberal approach to Scripture's revelation

---

64. Osborne, *Romans*, 211.

might well ask if it really matters. Well, it certainly mattered to the Apostle Paul, whose counsel to the Corinthian believers on this very issue was: "if Christ has not been raised, your faith is futile." Quite a stinging rebuke; but he doesn't end there. Not only does the resurrection of Christ add substance to our faith, but without it the atonement is robbed of its potency, for we "are still in [our] sins" (1 Cor 15:17).

Whilst it is extremely unlikely that this is what Paul would have had in mind when he spoke elsewhere of proclaiming "the whole counsel of God" (Acts 20:27—ASV), the principles governing such a responsibility are surely sufficiently applicable to embrace both the death of Christ *and* his resurrection within its auspices. Clearly, in the context of the reality of the atonement, one without the other is not the whole counsel of God, quite simply because it does not reflect the complete will of God in this regard. Jesus was, indeed, "delivered over to death for our sins," but our justification is dependent upon him thereafter being raised to life (Rom 4:25).

He was the perfect sacrifice, and he needed to be in order to avert the wrath of God, effect man's redemption, bring about the great exchange that took place in our justification and, thereby, reconcile us to the Father. But it was necessary that the work of Christ did not merely place us back into Adam's unfallen condition, lest we thereafter repeat his folly. The defeat of Satan, the overcoming of powers allied with him, and the defeat of the death principle not only removed such a possibility, but also gave renewed hope for the whole of the created order that it might, at last, fulfill its own potential. Thus, may we echo the words of the hymn writer:

> In him the tribes of Adam boast
> More blessings than their father lost.[65]

---

65. Isaac Watts, 1674–1748.

3

The Benefits of the Atonement

The subject of the chapter before us has proved to be not without doctrinal disparity, as we shall see. One would think, having arrived at a reasonably satisfactory agreement regarding man's need and that need having been met, that there would be little left upon which to differ. Nothing could be further from the truth. Each of the subdivisions of this chapter has given cause for some of the most animated examples of theological discord to hamper the Christian church. By tackling the issues head on, of course, I too run the risk of disenfranchising myself from those whose fervor might be offended by my own convictions. Some have remained silent for fear of upsetting the dogmatic apple-cart or, perhaps, in some misguided attempt to preserve "the unity of the Spirit" (Eph 4:3). In other words, the boast of such an apparently unified message is either the product of compromise or is born of the fact that we singularly fail to discuss our differences. I remain unconvinced that this is what the apostle had in mind.

The benefits of the atonement viewed from a purely eschatological milieu is an obvious minefield, especially when those advantages for some can only be regarded as such in the context of shortcomings for others. The idea that divine election might provide the basis for the dispensing of both is anathema to many, but should not for that reason alone be the grounds for our refusal to search the Scriptures that we might be thus enlightened. In my experience, those who steadfastly take such a position usually fall into one of three distinct categories, though there may be some overlapping between them:

- their denominationally conditioned constitutional allegiance dictates their quest for truth;
- their reputation amongst their peers is of more import to them than they might forcibly concede; or
- their interpretation of the Bible tends more toward supposition than substance.

For my part, I have no denominational allegiance that supersedes my commitment to the revelation of Scripture, no reputation to protect other than a diligent pursuit for the unveiling of its contents, and—I trust—a desire that my conclusions be based on the evidence I find there. This does not necessarily make the arguments I posit any less prone to error, but it should ensure that I am disinclined to be protective of those that are proven to be biblically invalid.

Thus, having established both the absolute necessity for the atonement, as the only possible means by which God and man could be effectively reconciled, and the reality of the atonement having actually taken place in history, we must now turn our attention toward the tangible benefits of the atonement.

APPLYING THE ACHIEVEMENTS OF THE ATONEMENT

Before we can consider how best to apply the achievements of Christ's atonement, we must first of all be clear in our understanding about what the atonement actually accomplished. In vague terms, of course, we might reasonably conclude that it attained everything that necessitated its reality. For example, we could settle for the fact that the death and resurrection of Jesus simply reversed the effects of Adam's fall. This is quite true, but it is a truth that requires further qualification lest its simplicity be taken advantage of by the possibility for error. Otherwise, we might be left to conclude that all the cross really achieved for fallen humanity was to give it a second chance where Adam failed, but with the same potential to repeat that failure. We have already seen that this is clearly not the case. But are there limitations? And if so, what are they, how can their apparent incompatibility with the biblical evidence that suggests otherwise be satisfactorily explained, and how may Christian believers be assured of their status within the confines of such boundaries, if they do exist?

The Extent of Christ's Atonement

Almost since the beginning of the Christian era, the question has been posed: "For whom did Christ die?" Although the centuries have produced many interesting theories, with detailed arguments allegedly to sustain each one, they essentially fall into one of two categories: universal or limited atonement. It must be noted that universal atonement refers to the scope of reconciliation's availability and must not be confused with universal salvation, which deals with its perceived application. Those who believe in limited atonement, however, maintain that Christ died for the elect alone.

Amongst those who generally defend a universal atonement are Roman Catholics, Eastern Orthodox, Lutherans, Arminians, and Amyraldians. Whilst the doctrine of limited atonement is commonly associated with Calvinism, it is not something that John Calvin actually taught, though the ethos of it can be clearly traced throughout his work. Indeed, it was Augustine, in an attempt to promote the sovereign grace of God, who proposed also that Christ died exclusively for those whom the Father had predestined to eternal life.

Champions of each persuasion resolutely point to Scripture in support of their respective views. Those who hold to the universality of the atonement refer their opponents to John 3:16, Romans 5:18 and 1 John 2:12, while those who vociferously lay claim to a limited atonement do so with the apparent endorsement of Matthew 1:21, 20:28 and John 17:9. It would seem that the main point of contention for each company is the desire to protect the integrity of Scripture from the potential excesses of the other.

Thus, the difficulty faced by those seeking to define the extent of Christ's atonement continues to be shrouded in confusion and misunderstanding, in spite of—or perhaps, because of—centuries of debate on the subject. Louis Berkhof makes the following attempt to bring some semblance of clarity to the issue:

> The question . . . is not a) whether the satisfaction rendered by Christ was in itself sufficient for the salvation of all men, since this is admitted by all; b) whether the saving benefits are actually applied to every man, for the great majority of those who teach a universal atonement do not believe that all are actually saved; c) whether the *bona fide* offer of salvation is made to all who hear the gospel, on the condition of repentance and faith, since the Reformed Church does not call this into question; nor d) whether any of the fruits of the death of Christ accrue to the benefit of the non-elect in virtue of their close association with the people of God, since this is explicitly taught by

many Reformed scholars. On the other hand, the question does relate to the design of the atonement. Did the Father in sending Christ, and did Christ in coming into the world to make atonement for sin, do this with the design or for the purpose of saving only the elect or all men?[1]

Berkhof's strong affirmation that the question relates solely to "the design of the atonement" is in many ways symptomatic of the unfortunate ambiguity with which Reformed theologians have often availed themselves. The object of the argument is surely not the purpose of God alone, but the reality of what actually took place in the context of that design. Of course, the theological implications of the issue demand that the conclusions of each will be identical (that is, what comes to be exists because God deems it so), but by focusing on the question thus, it becomes possible to clarify any potential misunderstanding by the manner in which it is answered.

The distinction has already been made between universal atonement and universal salvation. It cannot be denied, however, that historically many have failed to recognize this difference, teaching instead that the saving effect of the atonement is identical to the extent of the atonement in its universality. The logical conclusion of such an argument is that everyone will, therefore, be saved. On the other hand, those who promote the limited effects of the atonement demand that its extent must be similarly restricted, reasoning that were this not so then part of the atoning work of Christ is in vain, since some for whom he died will not be finally saved.

In effect, one's view of the extent of the atonement has become dependent upon and determined by the dogma held concerning what Scripture teaches about the nature of the atonement. Christ did die for all and yet he also died only for his people. The Bible speaks of both positions with similar frequency and with equal conviction, though the apparent paradox is not entirely beyond rational explanation.

When we say that "Christ died only for his people," it is accurate in the sense that they alone become the eternal beneficiaries of all that his death procured. The difficulty arises when it is assumed that this implies Christ's death makes the gospel available exclusively to those for whom he died in the sense thus described. Reformed theologians, despite their general soundness of doctrine, have not been particularly noted for their sensitivity in acknowledging the potential opacity and cause for offence in the declaration that Christ died for his own only. In a similar fashion, those of a non-Reformed persuasion are to be congratulated on their theology if the phrase "Christ died for all" is to be understood as meaning that his death makes

---

1. Berkhof, *Systematic Theology*, 393–94.

salvation available to everyone, for this too is in accord with the biblical revelation (see John 6:51; 1 Tim 2:6; 1 John 2:2). The real issue here is that a qualification must be offered that leaves no doubt as to the grounds of the atonement, so that it is not surmised that the gospel's offer of salvation to all implies that everyone will be saved, regardless of application.

Arguably the most significant word of the phrase: "For whom did Christ die?" is the preposition "for." What we mean by this one word will help us in our understanding, not only of the question posed, but also of the conclusion we thereby reach. The *Concise Oxford Dictionary* offers a somewhat lengthy list of more than twenty possibilities, including: in the interest or to the benefit of; in defense, support, or favor of; suitable or appropriate to; in respect of or with reference to; representing or in place of; in exchange against; as the price of; as the penalty of; in requital of; as a reward for; with a view to; corresponding to; in order to achieve; in the character of; because of; in spite of; considering or making due allowance in respect of; and in order to be.

Clearly, many of these can be dismissed almost without too much thought, while others could only possibly be considered in a purely metaphorical context. Of those that remain, the respective meanings contrived are potentially quite diverse. In relation to Christ's death, the original Greek is a little more helpful, the following verses serving as valid examples:

> "[Christ] died *for* us so that, whether we are awake or asleep, we may live together with him" (1 Thess 5:10).

> "For Christ died *for* your sins once for all, the righteous *for* the unrighteous, to bring you to God" (1 Pet 3:18a).

> "For Christ's love compels us, because we are convinced that one died *for* all, and therefore all died" (2 Cor 5:14).

In the first two cases cited above, the emboldened/italicized word translated "for" is the Greek *peri*, which in both contexts means "concerning," that is, "with regards to." As the subject of each (i.e., "us" and "your") is fellow Christian believers, our quest is somewhat unaided, though if anything it leans toward a limited view of Christ's atonement. In the last two quotations, the italicized only word "for" translates *huper*, meaning "on behalf of." As that used by Peter must be seen as a qualifying clause to the first part, the same conditions must apply: he is addressing fellow Christians. The Corinthian text does seem to suggest hope for those who promote a more universal approach. Such optimism begins to diminish, however, as we widen the scope of our gaze to consider the broader context, where the "all" (Greek *pantos*) could just as easily mean "all of us" as "all humans without exception."

The argument posited by those who favor a limited atonement in both design and application is often presented that to consider otherwise offends their imagination. To this I can only comment that the offense of our minds should not be the uppermost criterion by which we determine a doctrine—any doctrine—to be legitimate or unfounded. Moreover, it seems wholly unprofitable to invalidate certain Scriptures because they either seem to contradict other known biblical passages or the logical implications of them cause us discomfort. Might I suggest that the real cause for both avenues is the honor with which we esteem the human intellect? It seems unthinkable for us to concede that we simply do not know how such incidents could possibly be reconciled.

It is my opinion that the evidence of Scripture is not sufficiently conclusive to promote or dismiss the doctrine of limited atonement. However, I can also say that many of the so-called proofs used to endorse the idea are based largely on ignorance, misinformation, leaps of fallacy, and arguments that—if consistently applied—would cause more damage to the pursuit of truth than might otherwise be the case. One such is that if there is no tangible correlation between Christ's death and what it actually procured in real terms, then some—perhaps a large portion—of what was purchased was in vain. If this is so, then the same might be said of God's purpose in creation. Although it would be both wrong and hypocritical of me to dismiss reason as a legitimate tool in the armory of those who pursue truth, such reason must always be subject to Scripture's revelation, not *vice versa*. Where the two cannot be reconciled, reason must be laid aside until it has the capacity to grasp the infinite wisdom of God as he has unveiled it to us in his Word.

But let us consider the reasonable argument for a moment. The Canon(s) of Dort promote: "the belief that the satisfaction rendered by Christ on the cross was of infinite value and worth by virtue of Christ's incarnation but that its intended object was not sinners in general, or every individual, but rather those who God had elected from eternity." Mathematically speaking, only two values are beyond meaningful division: zero and infinity. Half of nothing is still nothing. Similarly, anything of infinite value cannot be altered by being made subject to either fraction or percentage. Thus, if the sacrifice of Christ is of infinite value, not only can it have no limit, but neither can its value be diminished by making only a portion of it applicable. I realize, of course, that such a position leaves me wide open for accusations of being no more than a four-point Calvinist. I'm not particularly troubled by this as it places me in quite good company, possibly even that of John Calvin himself. But I'm afraid it is as much as my conviction of Scripture's revelation will allow.

But remember, the overall heading of this section is "Applying the Achievements of the Atonement." It is one thing to suggest that he died for all, though not all will avail themselves of the opportunity to be saved, which is afforded by his death. So in what way(s) might it be said that those who fail in that regard are yet beneficiaries? Well, first of all they benefit insofar that they have the opportunity that it might be otherwise. And they are also recipients of the common grace that ensues from the atonement, including the shared blessing that comes about by virtue of the kingdom rule of God being expressed on earth in the present age.[2]

A Christian teacher, well known on the U.K. charismatic preaching circuit around twenty years ago, once told me that where there are issues of which we cannot be sure, it is always prudent to cling all the more to those things of which we can be certain. I do not have the capacity to satisfactorily resolve the apparent contradictions that logic might force me to grant in relation to the question before us here. My best guesses are just that. To my mind, those of a more dogmatic approach have similarly failed but perhaps without the strength of character required to concede as much. I am indebted to the writings of Jim Packer for many things, not least of which is the spark of light he shines on an otherwise gloomy picture:

> [W]hat sort of knowledge of God's action in Christ's death may we have? . . . it is a unique kind of knowledge which, though real, is not full; it is knowledge of what is discernible within a circle of light against the background of a larger darkness; it is, in short, knowledge of a mystery, the mystery of the living God at work . . . Now the atonement is a mystery in the defined sense, one aspect of the total mystery of God . . . What makes it a mystery is that creatures like ourselves can comprehend it only in part. To say this does not open the door to scepticism, for our knowledge of divine realities (like our knowledge of each other) is genuine knowledge expressed in notions which, as far as they go, are true. But it does close the door against rationalism, in the sense of theorizing that claims to explain with finality any aspect of God's way of existing and working. And with that, it alerts us to the fact that the presence in our theology of unsolved problems is not necessarily a reflection on the truth or adequacy of our thoughts.[3]

---

2. See Woodall, *Kingdom*, 150–76.
3. Packer, *The Saving Work of God*, 88–90.

For expressing similar thoughts—though by no means as eloquently put—I have been labeled a coward for opting to take the easy route, often described as a "cop out." It may well be a relatively less demanding course, if only by virtue of the fact that there has been less frequent cause to reverse out of unnecessarily engaged culs-de-sac.

Where the Bible is silent, it is wise not to speculate. Likewise, when infinite wisdom seems to be contradictory to finite reason, it is sensible to resist the temptation to reject part of that wisdom in order to more forcibly promote another aspect. The simplicity of Scripture's perspective on the matter before us can be stated thus: Christ died to extend the offer of salvation to all; not everyone will embrace the invitation to receive that offer. Anything that goes beyond this in either direction may well bring stimulation to the intellect, but must finally be bound within the parameters of pure hypothesis, which is essentially a technical term for "guesswork."

The Doctrine of Election

A valid point of reference with which to begin this subsection is a look at Anglican Article seventeen, dating from 1571 and entitled *Of Predestination and Election*:

> Predestination to Life is the everlasting purpose of God, whereby, before the foundations of the earth were laid, he hath constantly decreed by his counsel secret to us, to deliver from curse and damnation those whom he hath chosen in Christ out of mankind, and to bring them by Christ to everlasting salvation, as vessels made to honour. Wherefore, they which be endued with so excellent a benefit of God be called according to God's purpose by his Spirit working in due season; they through Grace obey the calling; they be justified freely; they be made sons of God by adoption; they be made like the image of his only-begotten Son Jesus Christ; they walk religiously in good works; and at length, by God's mercy, they attain to everlasting felicity.
>
> As the godly consideration of Predestination and our Election in Christ is full of sweet, pleasant and unspeakable comfort to godly persons, and such as feel in themselves the working of the Spirit of Christ, mortifying the works of the flesh and their earthly members, and drawing up their mind to high and heavenly things, as well as because it doth greatly establish and confirm their faith of eternal Salvation to be enjoyed through Christ, as because it doth fervently kindle their love towards God: So, for curious and carnal persons, lacking the Spirit of Christ, to

have continually before their eyes the sentence of God's predestination is a most dangerous downfall, whereby the Devil doth thrust them either into desperation or into wretchlessness of most unclean living no less perilous than desperation.

Furthermore, we must receive God's promises in such wise as they be generally set forth to us in holy Scripture; and, in our doings that will of God is to be followed which we have expressly declared unto us in the Word of God.[4]

The concept of election embraces two principal characteristics: promise and accountability. This was true of Israel under the old covenant and is no less so for the church in the present age. Election has been defined as "the act of choice whereby God picks an individual or group out of a larger company for a purpose or destiny of his own appointment."[5] The foundations of the doctrine of election can be clearly identified in the Old Testament with the choosing of certain people for specific tasks, such as Abraham, Isaac, Jacob, Moses, the tribe of Levi, the judges, the prophets, and the kings. Even the choice of Israel as a nation to represent Yahweh's name in all the earth was an act of divine election.

In the New Testament, the use of the word "election" may be summarized under three distinct categories, according to its various applications. The Messiah, in fulfillment of the Servant/Savior prophecies made about him, was declared by the Father to be his "Son, whom [he had] chosen" (Greek *ekklegmenos*, literally "picked out from"—Luke 9:35). Similarly, the early apostles are often referred to in terms of them being objects of Christ's arbitrary choice from amongst the disciples (6:13), as are church deacons and apostolic delegates (Acts 6:5; 15:22, 25). As vastly important as these considerations undoubtedly are in their own right, however, it is in the sense of divine election as a sovereign, gracious, eternal choice of individual sinners to become the recipients of God's salvation in and through Christ Jesus that concerns us here. It is perhaps significant that this emphasis is not fully developed until we reach the theological writings of Paul's epistles, where some key factors are worthy of our attention.

Although the theme of election can be traced throughout Paul's letters, by far the fullest treatment on the subject is provoked by his sense of urgency to bring comprehensive instruction to the church at Rome. Here he has the opportunity to describe God's sovereign right to choose, while at the same time highlighting the breadth of his forgiveness (Rom 11:28–32). Only the most imaginative of minds could reasonably argue in favor of the premise

---

4. Ibid., 149–50.
5. J. I. Packer, "Election," in Douglas, *New Bible Dictionary*, 314.

that election for eternal life assumes also some being chosen for everlasting damnation, based on the content of the letter to the Romans. The bias of Scripture in this regard is always positive and, where there is mention of the hardening of men's hearts (9:22), it is obviously in the context of there having been a deliberate and willful rejection of the gospel message, their deeds thereby placing them irrevocably outside of God's grace. It should also be noted that Paul's consistent starting point is the mercy of God, emphasizing the fact that his favor is essentially unmerited. No one, in fact, can rightfully lay claim to God's blessing. That he chooses to demonstrate his love thus is exclusively due to divine prerogative.

Election, then, is first of all presented as being a sovereign decision based on divine grace (Rom 11:5; 2 Tim 1:9). It is totally unearned, aroused solely by the intrinsic good pleasure of an Almighty God (Eph 1:5–9), man being utterly devoid of any capacity to have it conferred upon him as a reward for accomplishment. No amount of effort on our part could ever warrant such favor, for even mankind's seemingly worthwhile deeds are no more than soiled linen when compared to the inherent beauty, majesty, and righteousness of a holy Father (see Isa 64:6). Indeed, Scripture reveals plainly that God made his own choice known to us while we "were still powerless . . . still sinners . . . [and] God's enemies" (Rom 5:6–10), and worthy recipients of nothing but his indignation (1:18–32).

For this reason, it must be fully understood that God does not owe mercy to anyone—it is a gift. Those who receive such benevolence are to be eternally thankful, joyously giving praise in a manner befitting their newfound liberty; those who do not cannot claim to have been denied something they deserve. We can only concur with one commentator who succinctly observes: "The wonder is not that [God] withholds mercy from some, but that he should be gracious to any."[6] There can be no knowledge of the biblical revelation of election, therefore, unless there is a commensurate realization that it is essentially by grace.

Before we adopt a *che sarà, sarà* attitude to redemption, it is worth reminding ourselves that the Bible speaks as clearly on the subject of a gospel of global application as it does about election. Furthermore, it must again be stressed that human reason struggles to comprehend the divine initiative in its fulness. Does God's foreknowledge play a part, as suggested by Arminius? His view, in contrast to that of Calvin, was such that because God is omniscient, he is thereby able to see in advance those who will respond to Christ and continue to abide in him. Might I suggest that the alternative view only lacks appeal because we perceive it as some sort of fatalism. Both

---

6. Ibid., 316.

arguments depend upon a large helping of logic, but we are dealing with spiritual mysteries here.

When discussing the elect of God, divine favor and human obligation are not necessarily mutually irreconcilable. God's sovereignty and man's freedom to act within the parameters of such supremacy are incompatible only in the realm of our incapacity to consider them otherwise. If certain conditions pave the way for humanity to receive the blessing of God and we stubbornly refuse to follow these principles, then surely man's destiny is but a natural consequence of his own willful disobedience. Perhaps the words of Bernard of Clairvaux will help to shed some light: "Remove free will and there will be nothing left to save; remove grace and there will be nothing to save with."[7]

Similarly, the proof of election cannot be divorced from the purpose of election—it is restoration. As with all theology, if Jesus is not at its center, then it can hardly be described as biblical theology, for as the living Word is he not the fundamental subject of the revelation of the written Word? We are saved through Christ (Acts 4:12), chosen to bear his image (Rom 8:29) and, having had the stain of our guilt that sin inevitably brings removed, we are further called to display God's glory in all the earth (9:17).

Secondly, election is eternal, both in its counsel and in its realm. This is particularly evident from the fact that we were chosen in Christ "before the creation of the world to be holy and blameless in his sight. He predestined us to be adopted as his sons . . . in accordance with his pleasure and will—to the praise of his glorious grace" (Eph 1:4–6). In other words, God determined to exercise his love in such a way as to effect the salvation of those whom he knew according to a set purpose that will finally "bring all things in heaven and earth together under one head, even Christ" (v. 11). As such, the decision is unchangeable—the elect cannot be separated from the love of God (Rom 8:38–40), for it is founded on the basis of their union with Christ by faith.

Because election is used to describe the effect of God's grace in those who respond positively to the gospel message, and that such a choice is portrayed in Scripture as having taken place in the pre-creation counsels of the Godhead, there exists a certain unease among some scholars as to the actual grounds of election. That repentance and faith are vital to salvation is undeniable. That Jesus is the sole means by which redemption is made accessible to humanity is beyond question. Man's inability to attain anything resembling spiritual revelation without the convicting work of the Holy Spirit is seldom challenged. But does the fact that some are chosen to inherit eternal

---

7. Quoted in Hammond, *In Understanding*, 93.

life automatically presuppose that the rest are equally and deliberately set apart for everlasting separation?

Those who defend this "double predestination" do so chiefly on the grounds of the biblical witness as provided in Romans 9:10–23, maintaining that, whereas redemption is an expression of God's mercy, his innate sense of justice is displayed in reprobation. Implicit in the old covenant example of Israel as a people chosen by God to be his very own, it is argued, provides sufficient scriptural testimony to validate the idea of a double predestination. Where Israel was historically known as God's elect, so too it may be deduced were other nations rebuffed. Indeed, Israel's election was finally dependent upon them fulfilling specific covenantal conditions, failure to do so resulting in even their rejection (see Isa 5:24–26; Rom 11:15).

It is not for imperfect minds to attempt to reconcile truths that appear to be contradictory or to draw seemingly logical conclusions about spiritual matters where there is insufficient biblical evidence to support them. Likewise, we must seek to base our doctrinal positions on what the Bible actually teaches without denominational bias or constitutional favor. Thus, the following conclusions may be drawn:

- Scripture contains no emphatic record that can be used as the basis for a doctrine of double predestination, though it should also be acknowledged that there are isolated passages that may be presented as suggesting as much;
- Scripture clearly declares that salvation is grounded entirely in the elective will of God in Christ Jesus, emanating exclusively from God's sovereign choice. It is equally indisputable, however, that any mention of a specific decree of rejection is wholly absent;
- Scripture proclaims that, as well as the elect of God, there are also those who are not elect, their condition being described in terms of separation; and
- Scripture teaches the twofold destiny for mankind: that of the penitent and that of the reprobate.

The fate of the unsaved, therefore, seems to be predominantly governed by personal incredulity, willful disobedience, and intractable rejection on their part of the offer of salvation made available to them; it is not necessarily determined by divine decree (or, at least, not directly so). The arguments posited against election might have some credibility if those who were not found to be amongst the number of the elect had some biblical merit by which they could claim worthiness. They have not because none do. Election does not imply double predestination. By choosing some for salvation, on grounds that must ultimately remain a mystery to us, others are not *de facto* chosen for unbelief, but remain in precisely the same condition as before, once the divine choice is made. God's choice is always an expression of his sovereignty. In election, this is outworked in relation to two distinct groups: the elect and the non-elect. With one, his treatment reflects the way they deserve to be treated; toward the other, he sovereignly opts to express his dominion in mercy.

Although an admittedly imperfect example, when my wife and I decided to marry, she had a fairly vivid imaginary picture in her mind as to the kind of engagement ring she wanted to wear for the rest of her life. At first, this seemed like a good thing. Fifty-odd jewelers, hundreds of miles of travel, and several heated conversations later, the novelty had long passed the point of merely beginning to wane. When Barbara—finally—saw the one that most accurately reflected the mental image she had carried, there was no doubt whatsoever that this was *the* one. There were some very nice diamond rings on the same velvet display pad as that one; some were even less expensive, which had the bizarre effect of adding value in my estimation. Those not selected were not so much chosen to be rejected; they simply were not chosen.

Blessed Assurance

Our English word "assurance" is one of those nouns that requires no qualifying adjective, for it cannot be measured by degrees. We are either assured or we are not. To have an assurance is to be utterly devoid of doubt. The same is true of the Greek *plerophoria*, though it is often translated "full assurance" as if to emphasize the fact (see Heb 6:11; 10:22). Our difficulty to grasp the certainty with which the word "assurance" is inextricably linked is compounded by its misuse and abuse in the modern age. A verbal or written promise that is given with assurance should be sacrosanct, though it infrequently seems to be so.

Following my parents' divorce, I was raised by my maternal grandparents. I was five years old at the time and severely traumatized by the whole sorry episode. I have very little recollection of those years, but am informed by others that my recovery was a slow and painful process. I have also been told that a rather sudden and dramatic change took place when I was about ten that seemed to coincide with my discovery of and subsequent passion for association football (that is, soccer, for our American readers). Up until that point, I would spend my life moping about the place with a perennial "woe is me" expression on my face, an adequate reflection—I might add—of what little I do remember was going on inside me at the time. But then a spark ignited, possibly fuelled by Leeds United winning the then First Division Championship for the first time in their history (my grandfather was a season ticket holder, so I probably got carried away on the crest of his enthusiasm).

Thenceforth, every available waking moment would find me kicking a leather-encased pig's bladder around a school playground, village green, or back street, much to the annoyance of the neighbors. I would rush home from school, quickly change clothes, and dash out toward the "rec" (that is, recreation playing field) with ball under one arm and chomping through a buttered breadcake from the vacant hand. "Don't be late for your tea," commanded my grandmother. "I won't," I assured her. She may as well have not bothered. My assurances soon came to mean as little to her as her pleas meant to me.

I would like to say that this all changed spectacularly when I became a Christian at the age of sixteen. All I can say with any modicum of integrity is that it began slowly to engage with the transformation process in such a way that now, almost forty years later, my assurances more accurately reflect those of someone who is supposed to be a human representation of Christlikeness. The assurances of the Bible, however, are not subject to such change. They cannot become progressively more reliable, because they are inherently perfect. This is not because of some unknown, mystical trust that "the Scriptures" demand of us, but because those Scriptures are the words of God and both carry and convey his authority, and reflect his veracity. Thus, the assurance we have in such matters is guaranteed because it is grounded in God's immutable divine nature.

Thus, the assurance of salvation to those who believe is not based on their ability to exercise faith or necessarily to express faithfulness in the long term, but is exclusively dependent upon the sustaining integrity of God. Having taken the initiative, he has voluntarily bound himself to his covenant promise: "I will . . . be your God and you will be my people" (see Lev 26:11–12; Jer 32:28; Rev 21:3). It is significant that in each of the aforementioned references—and others with a similar directive—the corporeity of the blessing is emphatically stressed. Although conversion may well be a personal matter, there is no hint of a private walk thereafter, much less what has become known as "Christian anonymity."

Among the standard definitions of the word "assurance" as cited in the *Concise Oxford Dictionary* are "a positive declaration that a thing is true," "a solemn promise or guarantee," and "a certainty." It is never related to a "mind over matter" mentality whereby one becomes convinced of something irrespective of its validity, but it is always concerned with truth and/

or truthfulness. The blessed assurance that rightfully belongs to the child of God is that of salvation. It has become clear to me in the preparation of this work that there are many learned scholars, for whom I have the utmost regard and whose work is greatly appreciated, and yet they would often acknowledge seasons of uncertainty as to their standing before God. This is not a problem confined to the present day. Indeed, the very first generation of believers were so unsure of their salvation that the apostle John penned a whole epistle in the hope of addressing that very issue: "I write these things to you who believe in the name of the Son of God so that you may know that you have eternal life" (1 John 5:13). And how may we know? How is it possible for us to be assured that we have "received the Spirit of sonship"? Because it is "[t]he Spirit himself [who] testifies with our spirit that we are God's children" (Rom 8:15–16).

Note, however, that what is implied by Paul to the church at Rome is made explicit to the Galatian Christians: that the sonship of believers is ratified by the Holy Spirit, not inaugurated by him (see Gal 4:6; 2 Cor 5:5; Eph 1:13). In other words, this triune act of sovereignty consists in God (the Father) sending forth the (Holy) Spirit of his Son (Jesus Christ) into our hearts because we are sons, not in order to make us sons. Commenting on the above verse in the letter to the Galatians, William Hendriksen puts it this way: "because they are sons, God the Father, having adopted them as sons, has sent forth the Spirit into their hearts. They are sons; hence they receive the Holy Spirit. They receive the Holy Spirit; hence they become conscious of their sonship."[8]

Perhaps a more familiar term for "blessed assurance" is "eternal security." It is the premise upon which the "once saved, always saved" argument is based. The classic proof text almost invariably cited in support of the argument is taken directly from Jesus' lips: "My sheep listen to my voice; I know them and they follow me. I give them eternal life, and they shall never perish; no-one can snatch them out of my hand. My Father, who has given them to me, is greater than all; no-one can snatch them out of my Father's hand. I and the Father are one."[9]

I am also aware of those verses posited in defense of the counterargument, that genuine Christians can become subsequently lost, most notably:

> It is impossible for those who have once been enlightened, who have tasted the heavenly gift, who have shared in the Holy Spirit, who have tasted the goodness of the word of God and the powers of the coming age, if they fall away, to be brought back to

8. Hendriksen, *Galatians*, 160.
9. John 10:27–29.

repentance, because to their loss they are crucifying the Son of God all over again and subjecting him to public disgrace.[10]

Do these examples cancel each other out or are they to be viewed as contradictory? Is it one of those occasions that I mentioned earlier where the courses of action available to us are either to determine where the weight of evidence lies or to hold them both in tension until such a time that we have a more judicious understanding of the revelation?

Much has been made of the relationship between believing (Greek *pisteuo*) God the Father's declaration concerning his Son and having (*echo*) eternal life (see John 5:24). Henry Alford even goes so far as to suggest that they are commensurately interdependent conditions, the possession or remission of the one determining the tenure or forfeiture of the other.[11] The inference to be drawn is that salvation, once gained, can be subject to loss if the qualifying condition is not maintained. Such a conclusion would, indeed, be irrefutable if either it could be conclusively proven that the tense applicable to both the believing and the having are present continuous (or, at least, that the counterposition is sufficiently falsifiable as to cast reasonable doubt) or that the faith applied is its own object. Neither, of course, is true.

Personally, I do not consider that the words penned by the writer to the Hebrews conflicts with those spoken by Jesus at all. It could only be regarded as such if it could be proven that the traits described by the former were necessarily out of reach to all but genuine believers. Mere profession of faith does not save; the positive receiving of Christ by faith does. It is possible for an individual, even significant numbers of individuals in a local congregation, to receive a certain level of spiritual enlightenment, to have sampled the blessings poured out in a general sense on the congregation amongst whom they fellowship regularly, to give some form of enthusiastic recognition to the work of the Holy Spirit in their midst, engage with Scripture on a purely literary or intellectual level, and to marvel at the continuing demonstration of God's power in and through believers, yet still fall considerably short of personal saving faith. Indeed, I have often found that academic prowess and emotional negligence seem to go hand in hand. For those persons to subsequently turn to unbelief is to reject the opportunity for it to be otherwise. F. F. Bruce had this to say of it:

> God has pledged Himself to pardon all who truly repent, but Scripture and experience alike suggest that it is possible for

---

10. Heb 6:4–6.
11. Alford, *The New Testament*, 508.

human beings to arrive at a state of heart and life where they can no longer repent . . . To say that they cannot be brought to repentance so long as they persist in their renunciation of Christ would be a truism hardly worth putting into words.[12]

The wonderful security that being "in Christ" brings is that because salvation is so utterly dependent upon Christ's obedience as an established fact, those who by faith acknowledge this truth can never find themselves back "in Adam." Far from being tantamount to an invitation to sin, as many wrongly accused Paul of teaching, it is so liberating that its recipients are usually only too willing to express their gratitude as servants of righteousness. Those who do stumble can be confident that their sins are no longer regarded as the actions of a criminal in opposition to the law, but as those of a child who momentarily resists the love of the Father. As Denney wisely points out:

> It would be an imperfect view of the Pauline doctrine of reconciliation which did not emphasise its absoluteness or finality: "There is therefore now no condemnation to them that are in Christ Jesus." The man who believes absolutely in Christ is absolutely right with God. He has in Christ an assurance of God's love which triumphs over everything.[13]

In stark contrast to the twenty-fourth tenet of Arminianism, Reformed theology speaks of a *certitudo gratiae* or *certitudo salutis*, both terms referring to this personal assurance of salvation. Although Calvinistic thought relates eternal security to the perseverance of the saints, which might appear to remove it some distance from God's supremacy, it must also be noted that the capacity to maintain their walk with God on the part of believers also lies within the gift of God's sovereign power. Thus, we continue in him because he enables us to do so. Or to put it another way: we persevere in God because we are preserved by God.

Wayne Grudem suggests that "the use of the phrase *eternal security* can be quite misleading."[14] Whilst the reasons he cites draw a sympathetic response, they also point rather to the abuse by some of what it actually means to be saved in the first place. The practice of "baptizing" unbelievers, whether children or adults, simply transforms them from dry non-Christians into wet ones. Similarly, the raising of a hand at the end of an evangelistically presented message to indicate a decision to follow Christ

---

12. Bruce, *Hebrews*, 124.
13. Denney, *Reconciliation*, 168.
14. Grudem, *Systematic Theology*, 806.

can have as much to do with being fascinated by the preacher's oratory skills as it can a genuinely repentant disposition. The resultant false assurance could actually become a hindrance to what might otherwise be attainable. But none of this should obscure the clear biblical teaching that genuine assurance is annexed to legitimate conversion.

Now, I must concede that the word "eternal" can be taken to mean a qualitative trait and can also refer to the origin of that which it is used to qualify, as well as being employed to designate a sense of everlastingness. Can any of these three possibilities apply equally when used as an adjective to the noun "life"? Well, yes and no. None of them are automatically excluded in a general sense, but it does seem reasonable to suppose that when life and death are being contrasted and the word "eternal" is applied to both, then what it means for the one must also be true of the other. To suggest that "eternal death" refers to a quality of non-life or that it emanates from the eternal realm seems to be a stretch too far. Surely, "everlasting" death is the most likely understanding and, if that is so, then can "eternal life" be anything other, in essence, than that which is uninterrupted and beyond possible cessation? This is our hope; this is our security; this, indeed, is our blessed assurance.

Salvation, therefore, is God's irrevocable gift, undetermined by and independent of any works on man's part. Having found the church at Corinth as a whole to be almost completely devoid of moral uprightness, Paul never once questioned the genuineness of their profession of faith. Indeed, he took great pains to reassure them that they certainly were saved (velvet glove), while at the same time giving strong instruction regarding the dangers of violating the person of the Holy Spirit (iron fist). Of the biblical presentation on the doctrine of assurance, Jim Douglas offers the comment: "Assured faith in the New Testament has a double object: first, God's revealed truth, viewed comprehensively as a promise of salvation in Christ; second, the believer's own interest in that promise. In both uses, the assurance is correlative to and derived from divine testimony."[15]

And so, we might reasonably argue for a double assurance of our salvation and its continuing nature: the promise itself and the basis upon which that promise is guaranteed. Both, of course, are the Word of God. Are there any conditions upon or by which that promise, once received by faith in the atoning work of Christ Jesus, might be rescinded, suspended, or terminated? Put the question another way: Are there any conditions upon or by which God's promise can be imagined to have failed? I do not believe there are.

---

15. J. D. Douglas, "Assurance," in Douglas, *New Bible Dictionary*, 97.

Living in the Good of the Finished Work

As we have seen, the doctrine of election is a great comfort to the Christian. If there was the slightest possibility that we could lose our salvation, then such potential would indeed be the harbinger of anxiety, fear, and many sleepless nights. The assurance of God, however, remains upon us on account of what Christ has done; it is not determined in any way by what we may or may not do. The very notion of "once saved, may be lost" is, to my mind, a doctrine of the devil, designed to radically affect our relationship with God to such an extent that it finally frustrates the realization of his purpose in us. It may not cause us to deny the truth, but it will mar our worship, destroy our peace, and negate the promise of blessing in the here and now to those who believe.

Far from causing us to be lax, a sure knowledge of our election removes any hint of personal wrath. It is all of God, even the gift of faith required in order to receive salvation. Every blessing with which we are endowed flows abundantly and ungrudgingly from the electing grace of the Father. Such knowledge can and must end only in praise. It is not merely a subject for debate, but rather thanksgiving. The obvious conclusion to be drawn is that if election is, indeed, by grace, then all fear must be banished, for it is an expression of so perfect a love that it is far beyond man's comprehension. The grace of God is not a temporal attribute; it is eternal. If we could do nothing to earn it, how could we possibly lose it? Surely, nothing can cut us off from God's love in Christ. Such knowledge of election is not designed to promote moral negligence, but to incite us to humility, appreciation, worship, joy, and gratitude.

The basis of such a confident affirmation of eternal security is the belief in salvation by grace through faith (see Rom 1:17). Note that it is insufficient to champion a gospel of grace alone (*sola gratia*). Whilst it is true that works never enter the equation as a means to salvation, faith most certainly does. Grace still exists where faith does not, but it is a grace that fails to be fully effective because the gospel must be positively and purposefully taken hold of for grace to be transformed from a dormant state to one that is operational. Otherwise, the absence of faith causes the gift of salvation to be rejected (not ignored). As R. T. Kendall observes: "grace is offered to all men on the condition of faith, but no condition follows faith."[16] If this were not the case, then it would be salvation by grace through faith plus good deeds. But this is not the gospel.

---

16. Kendall, *Once Saved, Always Saved*, 42.

Of course, we would expect to see righteous acts as the fruit of repentance, though these must be perceived as an expression of the reality of salvation; they are not its condition. Christ's atoning work is sufficient; there is no shortfall to be topped up by the individual. A distinct lack of understanding concerning this truth was surely the root of the problem that beset the churches in Galatia. Having believed, they had somehow allowed the pure waters of their faith to become muddied by human effort (Gal 3:3). Justification could never come to us by observing the law, for it is by faith that the righteous shall proceed to live (v. 11).

The challenge for the Christian is to press on to adulthood. Having laid the foundations of repentance, faith, baptisms, *et al.* (Heb 6:1–4), it is imperative thereafter to build on such a base, brick upon brick. The alternative is spiritual adolescence, often displayed as either timidity or carnality. They are opposites but of the same coin: immaturity. Where the weak brother lives in fear, relying heavily on dead works, and without a proper understanding of the appropriation of grace, the carnal believer has a proclivity toward the cavalier, insensitivity, and boasting. Galatia and Corinth may well be their respective headquarters. Both are saved and will remain so, but neither has developed from infancy and quite possibly never will. One is doctrinally impoverished, the other emotionally sterile, the spiritual dignity of each being severely compromised. Although they have accepted God's gift, they have not done with it as they ought in order to receive very many rewards. The words of Dr. Martyn Lloyd-Jones serve as a warning to us all:

> The great and constant danger is that we should be content with something that is altogether less than that intended for us . . . In other words, certain people by nature are afraid of the supernatural, of the unusual, of disorder. You can be so afraid of disorder, so concerned about discipline and decorum and control, that you become guilty of what the Scripture calls "quenching the Spirit," and there is no question in my mind that there has been a great deal of this.[17]

We have already established that it is by faith in Jesus Christ that unrighteous man receives God's righteousness in exchange for his sin, that is, a new moral standing in union with the Father. This imputed probity then finds expression through intrinsic righteous acts, which conform to the will of God's law as written on our hearts by the Holy Spirit. Although the basic sense of sanctification is that of being set apart for a specific task, we have in mind here the process by which the Spirit of God transforms the life of the believer to mirror the pattern set by Jesus. Indeed, it is the power

---

17. Lloyd-Jones, *Joy Unspeakable*, 16, 18.

of his risen life that is reproduced in the Christian as he or she grows in grace. Whereas justification is essentially a critical, once for all experience, sanctification is progressive, culminating in our final destiny, that "we shall be like [Jesus], for we shall see him as he is" (1 John 3:2). The effects of such a radical change in the lives of ordinary people can have a globally positive influence. As Henry Turner has observed: "The watershed of the Resurrection led to the discovery by the Church of the continuing impact of the risen Lord, different in idiom but identical in impact with his fellowship with the disciples during his earthly life."[18]

Because Jesus has conquered Satan, his followers throughout the ages have also been released to overcome by virtue of new birth (1 John 5:4). Not that Christians are to reign by running away from pressure; we have been empowered by the Holy Spirit to face up to difficulties, rule over circumstance, and defeat the enemy in the midst of an environment that is largely unrighteous and diametrically opposed to God's kingdom rule. To enable us in this battle, believers have been granted access to what the Bible calls "spiritual armor," though the responsibility is clearly ours to ensure that we are at all times suitably attired (see Eph 6:10–17).

With the belt of truth in place, we develop an increasing knowledge of integrity and wholeness, which provides the basis for a more complete understanding of spiritual matters. The breastplate of Christ's righteousness protects us in our most vulnerable areas, where the heart might otherwise be overcome by improper emotion, leading to decisions that may well be ill advised. We are encouraged to be always ready to proclaim the gospel of peace, our feet fitted in eager anticipation. A practical application of the *rhema* word of Christ lifts the shield of faith into position as a defense mechanism against enemy assault (see also Rom 10:17). Potentially the greatest battlefield for the Christian engaged in spiritual warfare is the mind, so it is vital to ensure that only wholesome thoughts are allowed to permeate the helmet of salvation by constantly reminding ourselves that our security is to be found in Jesus alone. Finally, we must be confident in the Word of God, acknowledging its power by his Spirit to penetrate, divide, and discern (Heb 4:12).

The analogy Paul employs might at first glance suggest that only those at the forefront of the battle are to be dressed thus. After all, most earthly kingdoms have a representative body, either occupational or in reserve, which is expected to take on the duties of warfare should the occasion arise. Is it not the same concerning the kingdom of God? Well, again, yes and no. Yes, in the sense that only those within that kingdom and who are also

---

18. Turner, *Jesus, the Christ*, 109.

numbered amongst the enemies of Satan are included; and no because, on the basis of this qualifying clause, no Christian is exempt.

This being the case, the instruction to put on spiritual armor must not be regarded as advisory, but as an imperative. Indeed, those who fail to do so, whether by ignorance or willful disobedience, place themselves—wittingly or otherwise—in great danger. It is not that they thereby become targets for the enemy of their souls, for that is true of all believers at all times, but they do make themselves more prone to those attacks striking a blow that would thence render them less effective in their Christian walk than might otherwise be so. Just as the history of the Christian church reveals a tendency to focus on the latest—one might even conclude, fashionable—doctrine to have been long neglected to the detriment of other equally legitimate facets in what Paul describes as "the whole counsel of God" (Acts 20:27), so too here he commands that we are to put on "the whole armor of God" (Eph 6:11). The Greek is one word, *panoplia*, but it is a compound of *pas* ("all") and *hopion* ("a weapon") which, when used together in this way, signified "the complete equipment used by heavily armed infantry."[19]

Notice also that the command to fit oneself with this armor is not in the hope that it might be effective (or, at least, not the kind of hope that is normally associated with the word). Rather, its effectiveness is assured. Here, once again we see the interrelationship between divine grace and human responsibility, where the former is guaranteed by the latter. That notwithstanding, William Hendriksen is correct to draw our attention to the fact that the weapons/articles of clothing are identified as the "armor of God." That is: "It is *God* who has forged them. It is *God* who gives them. Not for one single moment is man able to employ them effectively except by *the power of God*."[20]

Although it should be obvious, whilst wearing the full armor of God repels the attacks of the enemy, it does not prevent their occasion. Jesus' cry on the cross that "It is finished!" was that of the triumphant, not one of triumphalism. Similarly, Paul's earnest directive to the believers at Ephesus bore testimony to his own experience as one who could elsewhere reassure the Christians at Corinth: "We are hard pressed on every side, but not crushed; perplexed, but not in despair; persecuted, but not abandoned; struck down, but not destroyed" (2 Cor 4:8–9). Though we are bereaved in heart, we are not bereft of hope.

This may not be the kind of teaching that many of us are accustomed to hearing in the milieu of living in the good of Christ's finished work, but it

---

19. Vine, *Expository Dictionary*, 67.
20. Hendriksen, *Ephesians*, 270.

is the more common biblical picture. Had Paul got it wrong? Definitely not! Was he writing in a different context? Well, a couple of verses earlier, he had been reminding his readers of the need to let "the light of the knowledge of the glory of God in the face of Christ" shine out in the darkness of the age (v. 6). Immediately afterwards, he goes on to say: "We always carry around in our [plural] body [singular] the death of Jesus, so that the life of Jesus may also be revealed in our body. For we who are alive are always being given over to death for Jesus' sake, so that his life may be revealed in our mortal body" (2 Cor 4:10–11).

Why should this be? If the work of Christ is truly finished and those who are to be found in him are to live their lives in the good of that finished work, then why should further trials befall them? Again, the wider context of Paul's teaching, both here and elsewhere, enables our fuller understanding:

- to prevent self-trust (2 Cor 1:9);
- to promote humility (12:7);
- to cause us to draw upon God's grace only (v. 9); and
- as a cog in the mechanism that leads ultimately to maturity (Rom 5:3–5).

It is significant that the overcoming of which Paul speaks (Rom 8:28–39) is not the blind, meaningless charade of mind-over-matter religiosity that seems to have gained access into many of the church pulpits and conference platforms of our day. Moreover, the biblical perspective on "reigning in life" is not one of God the Father navigating the Son's "body" through a painless, ethereal, trouble-free existence without cost, but that believers might learn to govern the situation in which they find themselves and not be dominated by it. Conquering, in military terms, may involve maintaining a certain *status quo*, either by holding one's ground or by simply recapturing lost territories through battle. Because Christians are called to be "more than conquerors," however, can we not reasonably anticipate in these days to possess domains hitherto locked to the gospel message? This is surely the inference behind Jesus' words to the disciples upon Peter's confession of his Messiahship that "the gates of Hades [would] not overcome [the church]" (Matt 16:16–19).

Much of our future inheritance remains a mystery, though Scripture does offer glimpses of what we may expect in the age to come, as we shall see. What is known, however, is that as believers we are encouraged to be diligent in our walk (Heb 11:6), to remain pure, faithful, and committed to the task before us (1 Tim 1:5), that we may "run in such a way as to get the prize" (1 Cor 9:24). We are to be recognized not so much for our achievements as in the wise stewardship of our talents (Matt 25:14–30). There is an inheritance awaiting the faithful, a crown that will last forever (Jas 1:12), and rewards to be distributed according to our perseverance (Luke 6:22–23), all of which are made possible only by the atoning work of Jesus.

The whole ethos of being reconciled to God must also include the idea of believers being reunited with his specific purpose for us, both as individuals and corporately. In this sense, reconciliation is far more than just a forensic term, for we are not truly in harmony of fellowship with the Father if we are at odds with the path he has chosen for us and, thereby, live in constant dread, animosity, resentment, despair, and despondency. The biblical concept of reconciliation embraces a radical new outlook on life. It first of all causes us to "be content whatever the circumstances" (Phil 4:11). In the face of adversity, we too can echo Paul's sentiments that "in all things we are more than conquerors through him who loved us" (Rom 8:37). To reduce the atonement to a mere stepping-stone between states is to rob it of its potency to change lives. Neither, on the other hand, must it be seen as a precursor to the power of positive thinking or a gateway to banal triumphalism. The biblical notion of living in the good of Christ's finished work is that we learn to rule in the midst of ordeal and affliction, not deny their existence.

Summary

Having considered the work of Christ as applied to sinful humanity, we have seen that, though his death has provided a means to salvation for all (*sufficiens*), it is only validated in the case of those comparatively few who avail themselves of the opportunity to repent and turn to him in faith (*efficiens*). Finite minds can never fully comprehend the eternal implications of the doctrine of election. All we must readily concede is that salvation is essentially and necessarily the work of God from beginning to end. As those who are in Christ, it is surely a great comfort to be reminded that we were chosen to be so before the foundations of the earth were laid. We might even say that we can rest secure, confident in the bizarrely unfathomable knowledge of what awaits us in eternity and, thus, find our lives wonderfully enriched in the here and now. This is just part of what Christ's atonement has achieved, but it is not all: there is far more.

WHAT ABOUT DEATH AND HELL?

There is one theme that is in some measure common to all religions, each with views as divergent as one might expect from such a subject. The quest for knowledge concerning man's existence after physical death has persisted down the ages. Speculation continues to abound as an integral part of every known philosophy and ideology throughout the world. So much so, in fact, that there has been no reason to amend the following words of James Thayer Addison in the eighty years since he penned them: "The belief that the soul of man survives his death is so nearly universal that we have no reliable record of a tribe or nation or religion in which it does not prevail."[21]

The question before us in this section deals with the nature of death from the perspective of the biblical revelation, especially in the context of the atonement of Christ. The implications associated with such a study are universal insofar that they concern both Christian and non-Christian alike. This is true irrespective of whether or not one chooses to believe in its veracity.

Beyond the Grave

To many, the topic of death as a conversation piece is as unsavory as its reality. Perhaps it is this fear that has dissuaded some otherwise eminent theologians from tackling the subject at all. When we speak of death in such general terms, of course, we have in mind the idea of nothing more than the absence of life as we know it in distinction from the rather more specialized sense of separation from God. It must be acknowledged, however, that for some the one inevitably includes the other. Physical death as such is universal (Heb 9:27). I have already established elsewhere that, for the redeemed, the termination of natural life is but the gateway to the fulness of eternal life with Christ Jesus. But is this union immediate? And, if so, in what state? And what of the unbeliever? These are the types of questions that we must endeavor to address in the light of Scripture's testimony.

One voice that has sought to bring some clarity to our understanding on the subject of death is that of Wolfhart Pannenberg, whose reasoned analytical style leads him to the following assessment:

> What does life after death mean? All the imaginable conceptions of it amount to expressing something inconceivable in the form of metaphor. However, what matters is whether or not such conceptions adequately express the motive that gave

---

21. Addison, *Life Beyond Death*, 3.

rise to them, that is, whether they appropriately formulate the destiny of human life that reaches out beyond death and that each individual seeks. In this sense, the diverse conceptions of a life beyond death can be subjected to an examination. They can be tested as to the extent to which they correspond to the anthropological roots that make such conceptions meaningful in the first place.[22]

The fact that death is associated with burial in most ancient Near Eastern religions as far back as the archaeological record allows is itself testimony to a perceived sense of material need beyond the grave. Thus, there is evidence of food, personal belongings, mementos of life, and even tools relating to the occupation of the deceased, all of which seem to be more in keeping with some primitive understanding of post-mortem existence than they are of any commemorative value. The custom of burying the body in the fetal position was also common practice as far back as the Paleolithic age, possibly indicating the hope in some form of reincarnation or birth into a different realm. Much of the expectations of these peoples are reflected in the art and literature of the period, especially those concerning Egyptian, Mesopotamian, and Canaanite cultures.

The Bible makes it clear that the universality of the death principle is exclusively due to the global reign of sin. Although not explicit, the creation of man in the *imago Dei* does seem strongly to indicate an original relationship between God and man in which the actual presence of death was entirely absent. This is not necessarily the same thing as saying that man was originally created as anything but mortal. It must be pointed out that, when considering the finer points of endless duration, God alone is immortal in the absolute sense of the word.

It does suggest, however, that Adam possessed the potential capacity to be granted eternal life as a reward for the successful completion of a season of probation. The very fact that this period was interrupted by failure in the form of wanton disobedience affords us no worthwhile opportunity to speculate on what otherwise might have been. What we do know is that death is now unavoidable because man is a sinner, not because he is a created being. The primary essence of death as it is revealed to us in Scripture seems to be exclusion from the presence of God (see Ps 88:3–5; Isa 38:9–20). This, too, presents a solemn reminder of the association of death with sin.

The Old Testament depicts the dead as being disembodied spirits in *Sheol*. But even this was subject to progressive development in the understanding of the Old Testament saints. That understanding can be both

---

22. Pannenberg, *What is Man?*, 45.

diminished and enhanced by the fact that the meaning of *Sheol* as used in the Hebrew Scriptures is not an entirely consistent one. It is spoken of in terms of punishment (Ps 49:13–14), judgment (Isa 5:14), darkness (Job 10:21), silence (Ps 94:17), and foreboding (88:12). In most cases, the use of metaphor abounds, thus making it increasingly difficult to draw much sense of what is being implied from a literal perspective with any conviction. What seems conclusive is that *Sheol* is unswervingly portrayed as a place where strength and joy are to be noted only for their absence. In his concluding remarks on the weight of evidence contained in the Psalms, George Eldon Ladd observes that:

> Such passages give us only glimpses of a hope of blessed existence after death. It is important to note that the hope is based in confidence in God's power over death, not on a view of something immortal in man. The Psalmists do not reflect . . . on the nature of the afterlife. There is merely confidence that even death cannot destroy the reality of fellowship with the living God. This is very different from the Greek view of immortality.[23]

During the intertestamental period, it seems that Judaism allowed for a wide variety of theories concerning the afterlife. The concept of *Sheol* also came in for some drastic rethinking at this time. Whereas it had previously been understood as a shadowy existence beyond death for everyone, by the time of Jesus' incarnation there was a growing belief in a bodily form of resurrection: the God-fearing to Paradise; the wicked to be cast into *Gehenna*. Indeed, there appears to be some grounds for basing Jesus' teaching on the parable of the rich man and Lazarus on this developing idea of *Sheol* in later Jewish literature. Certainly, the apparent divisions within *Sheol* for the righteous and the rebellious seem to justify such a premise (cf. Enoch 22:1–14; Luke 16:19–31).

The early church did not perceive these to be the final destinies of the good and the wicked respectively, but rather they were regarded as provisional locations, there being no direct passage between the two. Their temporary status was believed to be until God's judgment on the last day for the latter and the resurrection of Christ for the former, whenceforth the saints await only their resurrection bodies and rewards for things done in the old, earthly tent (see Matt 16:27; Rev 22:12).

Strangely, it was the *Hasidim*—that is, the spiritual forbears of the Pharisees—who were most responsible for cultivating the idea of the personal immortality of the soul (in the restricted sense, of course). Apocalyptic writers of this era certainly developed their eschatology along the lines

23. Ladd, *I Believe in the Resurrection*, 47.

of "God [fashioning] again the bones and the ashes of men . . . [raising] up mortals once more as they were before" (Sibylline Oracles 3, *Pseudepigrapha*). And again: "As many as with their whole heart make righteousness their first thought, these alone are able to master the weakness of the flesh, believing that unto God they do not die . . . but that they live unto God" (4 Maccabees 7:18).

Thus, the expression "intermediate state" refers to the condition of each individual person between death and resurrection. Concerning this period of intermediacy, there seems to be as much varied opinion as there is surrounding man's ultimate destiny. Some speak of "the sleep of the soul," while others prefer to think of a fully conscious, though disembodied, spirit awaiting the resurrection body with which to be clothed. More problematic to uphold is the view of some form of purgatorial discipline taking place to complete the work of sanctification in readiness for the spirit and the body to be united. There seems to have been what can only be described as an improbable exposition of 1 Corinthians 3:15 to accommodate such a position. Even more bizarre is the almost universalistic notion of the possibility of repentance beyond physical death, based largely on obscure interpretations of 1 Peter 3:18-20 and 4:6. Here, there is no hint of salvation ensuing from the declaration of the gospel, its hearers belonging essentially to the old covenant age.

Despite the hopes of many theologians of the Roman persuasion, the intermediate state offers the unsaved no further occasion to repent and embrace the gospel; neither does the Bible present it as a period of cleansing for unconfessed sin. For the believer, however, it is clearly implied that the intermediate state is to be a season during which his/her as yet bodiless spirit, in conscious communion with Christ, eagerly anticipates the acquiring of the resurrection body. In each instance, this state is both temporary and imperfect. Scripturally, then, there seems to be indisputable hope of a continued existence for the Christian of which he/she is appreciatively aware between the "putting off" of the temporal, earthly body and being clothed with a spiritual, heavenly body (see 1 Cor 15:53-54; 2 Cor 5:1-4).

The doctrine of psychopannychia, whereby the righteous spirit is thought to be asleep in Christ's presence, is also difficult to defend in the light of the biblical witness. Although the intermediate state possibly involves or includes a time of rest (see Heb 4:10; Rev 14:13), it is certainly one in which God's glory is to be expressed (Luke 20:38; 1 Pet 4:6). Arguably the most graphic New Testament evidence in this regard is the account of the manifestation before Jesus' most trusted disciples of Moses and Elijah on the Mount of Transfiguration (Mark 9:34). It is not within the remit of this work to discuss the significance of those Old Testament stalwarts' appearing. Suffice to say, however, that their presence clearly indicates a conscious existence between death and final glorification. Moreover, the implications of Jesus' teaching in the parable of the rich man and Lazarus, alluded to earlier, cannot easily be overlooked (Luke 16:19–31). Again, the Lord's promise to the penitent thief on the cross seems to suggest a measure of cognizance beyond death (23:43). And what are we to make of Paul's affirmation of a superior subsistence if not a fully perceptive awareness of "be[ing] with Christ" (Phil 1:22–24)?

This concept of a dormant spirit owes much to the Bible's use of the word "sleep" (e.g., 1 Cor 15:6). However, it is not necessarily at odds with a theology of consciousness, especially when we take account of typically Jewish idiom. As Hammond puts it: "'Some have fallen asleep' can as well mean that they have been removed from earthly life and activity as that they have been transferred to unconscious existence."[24] This being so, we can surely be as bold as the Apostle Paul in declaring that, for the Christian, "to die is gain," for to be "away from the body" is to be "at home with the Lord" (Phil 1:21; 2 Cor 5:8). The intermediate state, therefore, is not to be regarded as one of suspended animation, but of active interrelational communion with Jesus. This will be "far better," though as yet incomplete, for not until the resurrection are we to receive perfected, imperishable, powerful, immortal, spiritual, heavenly bodies in the likeness of Christ Jesus.

It is also important to stress that physical death should not be regarded as a punishment for personal sin as far as the Christian is concerned. It has often been asked—on the basis of apparently logical deduction—that if Christ has paid the penalty for sin for those who receive his offer of grace and if death is the wages of sin, then why do Christians still die? After all, Paul clearly affirms that "there is now no condemnation for those who are in Christ Jesus" (Rom 8:1). The fact remains, however, that Christians do still die (often in the most horrific of circumstances). Although the penal obligations of death have been fully met in Christ's death, death itself remains the last enemy yet to be destroyed (1 Cor 15:26). It is, in effect, the organic consequence of continuing to live in a fallen state, as are illness, disease, injury, the ageing process, and natural phenomena and disasters. Christians are not immune from any of these things, because God—for reasons known only to himself—has chosen to temporarily withhold some of the privileges of Christ's redemptive work. (Moreover, eternal life in its fullest expression is more suited to a better environment than presently exists on the earth.)

Even with the aid of divine revelation, then, the subject of death remains shrouded in some mystery. Of course, it must be acknowledged that

---

24. Hammond, *In Understanding*, 186.

the word "death" is not employed in exactly the same way throughout Scripture. Although physical death and eternal death ultimately amount to the same thing for those who are not "in Christ" (2 Cor 5:17), spiritual death is essentially a condition of separation from God during earthly existence (see Rom 8:6; Eph 2:1; 1 John 5:12). This is a position that may well lead to eternal death at the point of physical death, but it is one in which all are born "in Adam" and, therefore, have the potential in life to avail themselves of the opportunity of God's remedy, whereupon they may become spiritually awakened. For those who take hold of the cross of Christ, the end of this life is but a doorway into the fulness of eternal life. The end of the journey death may well be, yet it is but the beginning of the adventure.

A Universal Resurrection

As will be evident from the title of this subsection (that is, "What About Death and Hell?"), the main emphasis under consideration here is the fate of the unregenerate. Although the subject of resurrection is one of the primary motifs of the New Testament, its bias is irrefutably toward that of the redeemed. This is not to say, of course, that there is nothing from which we may gain some insight into the more extensive nature of resurrection. In his discussion on the New Testament treatment of the concept of resurrection, Loethar Coenen argues that:

> The general resurrection, which is inferred from that of Jesus, is . . . recorded . . . in the sense of the resurrection of the body; it is never a mere continuation of being or reawakening of the soul. As such, it was the real point of opposition to the proclamation of the gospel. It was rejected by the Sadducees, who held that only the Torah . . . was authoritative, and they claimed that the resurrection was not taught there. It was equally rejected by the Greeks, because the teaching was too materialistic for their thinking. Faith in a resurrection linked with judgment belongs to the fundamental elements of faith.[25]

Contrary to the objections raised by the Sadducees, the Apostle Paul defended his "hope . . . [in the] . . . resurrection of both the righteous and the wicked" as being in agreement with both the Law and the writings of the Prophets (Acts 24:14–15). The clear dynamic of Johannine theology, however, does seem to mark a noticeable distinction between "those who

---

25. L. Coenen, "Resurrection," in Brown, *Dictionary of New Testament Theology*, 3:277.

have done good [being raised] to live, and those who have done evil [being raised] to be condemned" (John 5:29). These, of course, were the words of Jesus who, because of his own imminent death, was ideally qualified (even in human terms) to speak on such matters. Although admittedly couched in apocalyptic phraseology, John again implies this twofold resurrection in his Revelation (20:4-6).

The "tree of life"—mentioned only in Genesis and Revelation—having been rendered inaccessible to fallen man, is to be made fully available once more, but only to those who have overcome (Rev 2:7), who have washed their robes (22:14), and who have remained faithful to the whole of the revelation of God's prophetic Word (v. 19). By implication, it would seem that the finally unrighteous are to be raised only in the sense of a divinely appointed reanimation, and for the sole purpose of appearing before the throne of Christ Jesus and acknowledging his sovereign right to rule in righteousness (Phil 2:9-11). This difference may be detected in Jesus' use of the phrase "resurrection from the dead" (Luke 20:35), the Greek *ek* giving a literal translation of "from among the dead ones" (see also Heb 6:2). The same terminology is employed by Paul in his letter to the Philippians (3:11). According to one commentator, the use of this particular expression:

> ... indicates the resurrection of the redeemed to life, as contrasted with the resurrection of the unsaved, which is practically no resurrection at all, as it is but the gateway to eternal death . . . In distinction from the resurrection to judgment of the spiritually dead, the resurrection to life of the redeemed is rightly called "the resurrection from among the dead ones."[26]

Because of the significance with which the New Testament presents the resurrection of believers, there has often been serious doubt cast as to whether there is to be a resurrection of the rebellious. The biblical perspective is plain enough. The clear evidence of Scripture is that all will rise, the godly and the ungodly, the regenerate and the reprobate. Although the soteriological aspect of the resurrection is foremost in the minds of the New Testament writers, there are nevertheless sufficient grounds to maintain the conviction of a universal resurrection. For the believer, though the works done in the flesh are to be judged, his/her personal destiny is inextricably linked to that of the risen Lord, Jesus Christ. The rebel, however, is faced with the prospect of being judged primarily for failing to respond favorably to the free offer of salvation.

I find myself rather unexpectedly having to qualify that, by using the term "universal resurrection," I do not mean to imply a commensurately

---

26. Geldenhuys, *Luke*, 513.

universal salvation. What has gone before should point the reader unequivocally away from such an idea. However, I have recently discovered that "universal resurrection" is a phrase employed by the Mormons to describe this very condition. To my mind, the only way they can do so is to betray arguably the most common principle of hermeneutics by interpreting a text out of context, thereby leaving no more than a pretext for a proof text. Perhaps "common resurrection" might avoid any such controversy, though I am tempted to think that some would find a way of distorting and/or abusing whatever terminology is being used.

Of course, the Mormons are not alone in their ignorance, for there are others who also lay aside the teaching of the Scriptures that, though all will "appear before the judgment seat of Christ" (2 Cor 5:10), "the wicked will not stand in the judgment" (Ps 1:5). In other words, the unrighteous will not be able to withstand God's wrath because they have not availed themselves of his provision whereby they might do so. The psalmist removes any doubt by adding for the sake of clarity: "For the Lord watches over the way of the righteous, but the way of the wicked shall perish" (v. 6). Thus, the destinations of each of the two paths and the destinies of those who choose to tread them are identical.

Although dispensationalists and pre-millennialists speak of a distinction between the resurrection of believers and that of unbelievers, thus effectively making them completely separate events, space does not allow me to make any worthy contribution to that particular argument either way. The point I wish to emphasize here is that the unbeliever will, indeed, be raised for judgment, not whether or not that event is to coincide with the resurrection of the elect of God. Likewise, the nature, extent, anatomical makeup, and physiological endurance capacities of the resurrection "bodies" of unbelievers is both beyond the revelation available to us and—we must, therefore, presume—unnecessary for us to know. We can guess that it must be recognizable as that belonging to the person associated with the former temporal body, but that is all realistically it can be: guesswork. What it most certainly will not possess is the potential for perfection or glorification. Emery Bancroft has this to say:

> The Scriptures state the fact and purpose of the resurrection of unbelievers but do not describe their bodies. It is strongly implied, however, that they will be mortal, corruptible bodies (Rev 20:12–13). The Scriptures are strangely silent on the subject of the resurrection of the unbeliever's body. The purpose and

result of their resurrection, namely, judgment and punishment, is about all that is given.[27]

Even in civil law courts, one would expect justice to include the non-prevailing of the wicked at the expense of the innocent and the separation of the former from the latter. Sadly, however, this does not always prove to be the case. Smart lawyers find loopholes, jury members are placed under increasing pressure to return a verdict that will not lead to them meeting with an untimely "accident," court officials may be offered financial incentives to ensure that a desired outcome is achieved, and witnesses suddenly and inexplicably withdraw their statements. Thus, law and order can sometimes be anything but lawful or orderly.

Not so on that day. How could it possibly be that way? When all are raised to appear before him, "[w]ill not the Judge of all the earth do right?" (Gen 18:25). God is a God of justice (Isa 30:18). His judgments are inextricably linked to his character, for they are righteous, just, and holy. The basis for such discrimination is man's response to the revealed will of God, which ultimately begs the question: "What have we done with Jesus?" Throughout the Old Testament, the concept of judgment consistently conveyed the idea of deliverance for the faithful. This was true of both the flood (Gen 6) and the exodus (Exod 12), each being types not only of baptism, but also of being liberated through judgment, their fulfillment being found in the cross of Christ. This one event in history enacted the totality of God's judgment, for it was here that Jesus was judged on man's behalf (Isa 53:6), the unregenerate were found guilty of rejecting him (John 12:31), Satan and his hordes were judged and effectively disarmed, rendering them powerless (Col 2:15; Heb 2:14–15), and sin itself was judged.

Although presented in parabolic form, the lessons to be gleaned from the story of the sheep and the goats should not be allowed to escape our attention in this context (see Matt 25:31–46). Once again, I find myself in agreement with Grudem, who refutes the dispensationalist rendering of this parable on the basis that its main object is not that of citizenship of the millennial kingdom of God on earth, but of eternal destinies.[28] The essential teaching of the parable of the sheep and the goats appears to be that the final and eternal destiny of men and women is not to be determined by any criterion other than what they have done or not done with Christ and those who belong to him.

Herein possibly lies a clue to the question of why such a resurrection might be deemed necessary. Those who deny its necessity might object on

---

27. Bancroft, *Christian Theology*, 318.
28. See Grudem, *Systematic Theology*, 1141–42.

the grounds that a person's eternal destiny is already known to God, so why do the unbelievers need to be raised in bodily form to announce something that by then will have long ceased to be a mystery? William Hendriksen suggests four possible reasons. Whilst not wishing to give the impression that I necessarily disagree with any of his findings in this matter, I would like especially to draw attention to two of them:

- The righteousness of God must be publicly displayed, that he may be glorified.
- The righteousness of Christ and the honor of his people must be publicly vindicated.[29]

Although it would be far too easy to use both of these statements as catalysts for their own in-depth study, or even find some pithy way of introducing a third that involved the righteousness of the Holy Spirit being publically acknowledged, it seems more apposite to make just a couple of observations. First of all, there is no need to artificially include the Holy Spirit when he shares naturally in the essence of the glory of the Father, the vindication of the Son, and the honor of the redeemed. Those who have rejected the salvation that could have been theirs, who have ridiculed and cajoled those who chose to serve him as subjects of the kingdom of God, oftentimes excusing their refutation and conduct on needing to see to believe, will belatedly have that opportunity, but to no avail.

Perhaps even more noteworthy, however, is this linking between righteousness with glorification and vindication. The annexing of righteousness and glory appears consistently throughout the Bible. This is especially—though by no means exclusively—so in the New Testament. Who could possibly forget the incident of Jesus praying that the Father would glorify him in his presence on account of him having brought glory to the Father by completing the work with which he had been entrusted (John 17:1–5)? And what formed the essence of that work? Remember, these words were uttered before the shame of Jesus' arrest, the ignominy of his trial, and the agony of the cross. In this context, was the completed work of which he spoke not to demonstrate the righteousness of the Father by adhering to his kingdom rule as a man? When we speak of glorifying the Father, I wonder if we do so with any clear sense of correlation between that and living righteously.

But the vindication of Christ is also associated with righteousness. There is a sense in which it would be correct to assert that Jesus' own resurrection demonstrated this. After all, it was primarily the fact of his righteousness, both intrinsic and experiential, that laid waste any claims the

---

29. Hendriksen, *Matthew*, 887.

grave might otherwise have had upon him. Included in that righteousness, we might cite the veracity of his words and the validity of his work.

It will probably come as no surprise that amongst those considered unrighteous will be many who in life had thought it possible to gain favor by any means other than the prescribed way. Good deeds alone will not meet that end. Faithful commitment to other religions will count for nothing. The prevailing tendency for humanistic endeavor will fail to have any influence beyond the current realm. Jesus alone is "the way and the truth and the life; no one [can enter the presence of] the Father [as a son] except through [him]" (John 14:6). His work of atonement will also be vindicated as righteous. Why righteous? Well, if it had been otherwise, can we possibly conceive that the Father would have deemed it acceptable?

Moreover, if we acknowledge all of this to be true, then lateral thinking forces us to concede that the opposite is equally so. If righteousness glorifies the Father, vindicates the Son, and honors the people of God, then unrighteousness can bring only shame, degradation, and disgrace. This, of course, is the lot of the rebellious and they may anticipate it, too, to be demonstrated fully on that day.

Eschatology is arguably the most difficult of subjects at which we may arrive at any satisfactory conclusions. The nature and content of the Bible's revelation is partly responsible for this; after all, not even the best of minds—so I'm told—find it easy to navigate their way through the composite symbolism of apocalyptic literature. Most of us have a tendency to imagine the future in the light of our perception of the present with, perhaps, a casual nod of deference to the past. Although this is especially so of the temporal realm, I have found it to be no less true when considering the eternal.

Similarly, our own preconceived ideas, the pressure to remain faithful to denominational confessions and constitutions, and the fact that just when we think we've got it all sewn up our closest friend says to us: "Yes, but what about . . . ?" all seem designed to add confusion rather than bring any clarity to the issues involved. Thankfully, the fact of a general resurrection is difficult to have too many opinions about, Wayne Grudem declaring in typically bold fashion that: "Scripture frequently affirms that there will be a great final judgment of believers and unbelievers. They will stand before the judgment seat of Christ in resurrected bodies and hear his proclamation of their eternal destiny."[30]

It is, therefore, amply and explicitly presented in Scripture that everyone is to be subject to a divine examination at the end of the age in respect of their standing in relation to Christ (see also John 3:36; Acts 10:42;

---

30. Grudem, *Systematic Theology*, 1140.

Rom 2:12–16; Rev 20:12–13). What is referred to with equal conviction and abundance is that two diverse resolutions will be passed: eternal life and conscious everlasting perdition. The idea of a universal judgment cannot reasonably be divorced from that of a universal resurrection, though Scripture does imply a markedly different sentence being passed to its participants. In the context of Jesus' teaching concerning those who are resurrected being no longer subject to death (Luke 20:35–36), it is clear that the criterion for continually enjoying the proximal presence of God is for "those who are considered worthy of taking part in that age" (v. 34).

The purpose and consequence of the unbeliever's resurrection rightly belongs to the remainder of this subsection. For now, however, suffice for me to leave you with the poignant words of Hank Hanegraaff:

> Do you believe in the resurrection of believers? I mean, do you really believe in the resurrection of believers? Or do you just say you believe? Are you absolutely certain that one day those who have died in Christ will be resurrected to eternal life in heaven? If you are, you can be just as certain that unbelievers will be resurrected to eternal torment in hell.[31]

A Day of Reckoning

According to the writer of the epistle to the Hebrews, a proper understanding of "eternal judgment" is a foundational truth for the Christian (Heb 6:2). This being the case, then it is vital that we grasp something of how the original readership would have comprehended the term. Because "eternity" is principally to do with quality, its use alongside "judgment" must be regarded as progressively dictating the level of kingdom rule in life from the acceptance of the finished work of the cross, through the character-building process of sanctification, to the consummation of all things at the end of the age. It is in this sense, therefore, that eternal judgment is to be seen as having past, present, and future applications for the flock of God.

The root meaning of the word "judgment" (Greek *krisis*) is that of separation. Its Hebrew counterpart, *seper*, refers to someone who dispenses justice, whether it is punitive in the case of the wrongdoer or as vindicating the righteous. The judgment such a one administers is proportional to a set measure or standard by which he or she is governed. It does not seem unreasonable to presume, therefore, that the biblical phrase "eternal judgment" represents God's capacity to differentiate in utter righteousness. Although at

---

31. Hanegraaff, *Resurrection*, 75–76.

first glance, the word "judgment" evokes images that are perhaps not best described in terms of blessing, it is to the child of God the most comforting of issues, as we shall see.

Comments attributed to the early church fathers regarding the last judgment are negligible, except for an acknowledgment of its inevitability. Their later counterparts, including Augustine, added little insight, though many asserted a figurative understanding of those Scriptures that speak of the end times. Debates concerned with annihilationism versus everlasting punishment, varying degrees of both torment and blessing, Roman Catholic views on purgatory, *limbus infantum* (that is, the alleged abode of unbaptized children), and *limbus patrum* (the intermediate resting place of the Old Testament saints) abounded down the centuries. Some still continue to this day. Relatively few, however, persist in the universalistic belief that eventually all, including the devil, will ultimately be saved.

As far as universal judgment is concerned, it seems difficult to imagine how Scripture could be perceived as anything less than unequivocal: "Man is destined to die once, and after that to face the judgment" (Heb 9:27). Although there have been examples of individuals facing death more than once (1 Kgs 17:17–25; 2 Kgs 4:32–37; Luke 8:41–56; Matt 27:51–53; Acts 9:36–42), the fact that such episodes stand out as unusual demonstrates that they are exceptions to the norm. The gist and context of the writer to the Hebrews is surely clear: all men may expect to die once. The emphasis is also weighted toward what they may then anticipate beyond that experience: judgment. Commenting on this verse, Alan Stibbs reminds us that:

> . . . this final settlement of eternal destiny by the decisive action of a single life and death in human history corresponds with, and is confirmed by, all that is revealed by God concerning the solemn responsible character and eternal consequences of all human life in this present world. For all men live and die once, and according to the deeds done in that one lifetime their eternal judgment is settled.[32]

Only the integrity of a righteous God could be considered appropriate for such a sober occasion. No earthly intellect can fully understand what severity of pain will reside in the heart of the Father over some of those upon whom he must pass judgment. No human mind can know in advance exactly who will finally be declared obedient or rebellious. What we can be absolutely certain of, however, is that there will be no miscarriage of justice, for "will not the Judge of all the earth do right?" (Gen 18:25).

---

32. A. M. Stibbs, "Hebrews," in Guthrie and Motyer, *New Bible Commentary*, 1207.

The Judge of all mankind is also the Savior of the world: Jesus (Acts 17:31). His judgment, unlike man's sense of justice, is inherently pure. There are no hidden agendas or unrighteous motives with the Son of Man, nor is there a shadow of turning with him. The sentences that are to be meted out will be final and unchangeable. There is no scriptural basis for a theology that embraces purgatorial discipline, for the atonement of Christ is exclusively and abundantly sufficient to both justify and sanctify. Any idea of some interim period of probation is to be similarly rejected. God's Word gives plentiful warning that it is only on this side of physical death that humanity is afforded the occasion to accept or reject his Messiah (see Matt 12:32; 2 Cor 5:10; Heb 2:1–3; 9:27).

If we are to understand the biblical perspective correctly, then it would appear that believers are to enter into the presence of God either immediately upon death or—in the case of those who remain alive—at the second coming of Jesus. Similarly, the finally ungodly will enter into separation from God at the point of physical death. Why then, it may be argued, does God see fit to decree a specific act of judgment at the end of the age? It could hardly be to accommodate any divine purpose, as if he does not already know the condition of men's hearts or the principle by which their earthly conduct has been determined. This forms no mystery to the divine Being; the day of reckoning offers no unveiling to the One who is omniscient. The words of Louis Berkhof are again valid on this point when he says that:

> It will serve the purpose rather of displaying before all rational creatures the declarative glory of God in a formal, forensic act, which magnifies on the one hand His holiness and righteousness, and on the other hand, His grace and mercy. Moreover, it should be borne in mind that the judgment at the last day will differ from that at the death of each individual in more than one respect. It will not be secret, but public; it will not pertain to the soul only, but also to the body; it will not have reference to a single individual, but to all men.[33]

Thus, a dictionary definition of the phrase "day of reckoning" could be something along the lines of: "a time when the effects of one's past mistakes or misdeeds catch up with him/her." This wholly negative emphasis is fairly commonplace. In an age where fiscal rectitude is often evaluated on the grounds of how much credit is made available, it is perhaps difficult to think positively in relation to such matters. However, a more general classification might be: "a time when all accounts are to be settled in full."

---

33. Berkhof, *Systematic Theology*, 731.

THE BENEFITS OF THE ATONEMENT 161

The last judgment is one to be faced by believers and unbelievers alike. Those who are found to be "in Adam" upon their death will face judgment for their rejection of Christ (see 2 Cor 5:10). They are to experience "the second death" reserved for the punishment of Satan and his followers (Matt 25:41; Heb 10:26–27; Jude 6–7). Those who are "in Christ" will not be judged in terms of redemption, that already having been assured, for it is through grace that we are saved (Eph 2:8–9), the seal of our adoption as sons being the Holy Spirit.

Christians have not so much evaded judgment by accepting Christ as they have endured it in him, in much the same way as the typological act of Noah and his companions in the ark. It is upon this basis alone that we find atonement. The price has been paid with nothing left owing, for where the fire of judgment has been it can burn no more. For the believer on the day of reckoning, the question of guilt for sin does not arise because it has already been removed by the atoning sacrifice of Jesus. This should not promote a lifestyle of antinomian behavior in the present age, a subject with which the Apostle Paul deals at length (see Rom 5:20–6:14), given that our fellowship with the Father is only maintained as we continue to walk in the realm of his judgment. May those of us who have accepted the provision of his Son never step outside such a sphere of authority, lest it be thus proved to be mere mental assent only.

Although the judging of our deeds does not determine the believer's destiny, the fire of testing will consume all that is of no eternal value, while that which is proved to be beneficial will earn great rewards. It is well worth reminding ourselves of Paul's testimony when he was provoked to encourage the Philippian believers to "press on towards the goal to win the prize for which God has called [us] heavenwards in Christ Jesus" (Phil 3:14). For the Christian, then, the day of reckoning is not one that we are to anticipate with trepidation, but we look forward to it with unparalleled excitement at the prospect of receiving rewards from the Judge of the universe.

The fact of a final judgment of all to take place at the end of the age is about the only thing agreed upon by pre-millennialist, post-millennialist, and a-millennialist alike. For the purposes of this study, it is both unnecessary and unhelpful to discuss the various vagaries of each position, all of which appeal to Scripture for support in positing their respective arguments. Suffice to say that—on this point, at least—I am forced to find agreement with Sergius Bulgakov, when he affirms that:

> Although our lot will be decided finally at the last judgment of Christ, already at the so-called preliminary judgment, which takes place after death for each person, the designation for glory

and a crown of holiness becomes clear. It glows on the brow of a godly person even in his lifetime, for the judgment is only an open confirmation of his real state. Life eternal in God begins here, in the flux of time; but on departure from this life it becomes the defining principle of existence.[34]

Hypotheses aimed at determining the precise date of the Day of Judgment, even if we are to allow for the possibility of it being identified within such temporal parameters, are as futile as they are fuelled by an ignorance of Scripture's warnings against being obsessively concerned by eschatological details. According to one radical "Christian" group, the "day" in question was due to begin on May 21, 2011 and would last for five months (that is, until October 21 of the same year). All I can say is that I'm grateful not to have cancelled my Christmas plans for that year on the strength of such misguided pseudo-prophecy. Am I being deliberately flippant? Maybe just a little. It is one of my many weaknesses. It should not be allowed to escape our notice, however, that the self-styled mouthpiece for this particular declaration, based on a perceived "gift" of being able to fathom such mysteries from the Bible "calendar" of events, has offered little by way of explanation since that somewhat less than fateful day passed without occasion.

Of course, such peculiar musings are neither uncommon nor infrequent. They are not even necessarily the most bizarre to surface in the history of Christendom. Only recently, I heard a fairly well-known so-called evangelical conference speaker proffer that, though it would be inappropriate to suggest that only Calvinists were Christians, he could not possibly conceive that anyone could be a true Christian without also being a five-point Calvinist. The congregation's response was a long silence, the kind that usually has the word "stunned" appendaged to it. I'm not sure whether he was attempting to be funny and failed or trying to demonstrate his intellect and instead served only to show off his ineptitude. Well, here's a flash: not only does such arrogance rule out sixteen centuries of believing saints, including the Apostle Paul, but in the terms employed by this particular preacher to define Calvinism, it probably also places John Calvin himself outside of salvation's province.

But that is not the subject of this section; apart from the fact that, for this guy, the day of reckoning promises to be a solemn occasion for unbeliever, Arminian, two-, three-, and four-point Calvinist alike. Moreover, to make our eternal destiny subject to affording mental assent to a set of doctrines, denominational allegiance, or constitutional statements of faith is

---

34. S. Bulgakov, "The Virgin and the Saints in Orthodoxy," in Clendenin, *Eastern Orthodox Theology*, 69.

itself tantamount to proffering a doctrine of salvation by works. Perhaps, in order to reflect this position, the great Reformed epithet should be amended to: *justificare sola fidei et corpus dogma Calvin et symbolum credo 1689*. The only works to so govern our eternal plight are those of Christ's atoning sacrifice and our individual response to it.

Paul did not shirk from preaching the fact of a coming day of judgment. It is a sobering message, but it is a vital one that the church can ill afford to neglect. If that was sufficiently true to earn apostolic concern two thousand years ago, then how much more so today? When debating with the philosophers of his age at Athens, Paul's call for repentance was on the basis that God "has set a day when he will judge the world with justice by the man he has appointed" for the task (Acts 17:31). Whether this means that the actual day is fixed and, therefore, known in the divine diary or not is uncertain. What is more clear is that there will come such a day.

By way of summary, the following points may be observed as factual according to the biblical presentation of events surrounding the Day of Judgment at the climax of world history:

- everyone who has ever existed (with the obvious exception of Jesus) will be judged (Acts 10:42; Rom 14:10–12);
- although believers are not to be judged by their works in terms of meritorial benefit, such works will themselves be judged as worthy fruit of repentance (see Matt 16:27; Rom 2:6; Rev 22:12);
- the final judgment is really an execution of the fate each individual has previously aligned himself or herself to by the personal choices they made in life (Matt 10:32–33; John 3:19–20; Rev 22:12); and
- relationship ultimately determines destiny: those who are found to be "in Christ" shall be "with Christ"; those who are outside of him shall not know the blessing of his presence in eternity (2 Thess 1:8–10).

Hell and Its Occupants

There is a certain proclivity in much current Christian thought to minimize the possibility of eternal punishment for the finally reprobate. If that itself sounds like a contradiction in terms, then it is intentionally so. After all, how can you possibly minimize something that is essentially eternal in nature without removing a little of its core essence so that it becomes something less entirely? That said, however, it would not be prudent of me to accuse such persons as lacking in wisdom, much less of heretical tendencies, as many are close friends whose genuineness of faith is—to me, at least—irrefutable.

But my understanding of the biblical narrative is such that it constrains me to affirm that the extent of the scriptural data concerning the fate of the unsaved (whether by direct reference or implied testimony) can only properly be interpreted in the light of a continued existence of separation from the blessed presence of God. Moreover, it is this that the Bible depicts as hell.

It becomes clear to the serious student that when Scripture speaks of the ultimate fate of the dead it employs an assortment of concepts. Often these are imported from secular influence, but at other times this has involved a significant change of characteristics. Although the Bible contains no single declaration that might be described as unequivocal or definitive— even in the writings of the Apostle Paul—the power of death can only correctly be seen in the light of the triumph of the cross of Christ.

Hades is presented as the temporary abode of the wicked deceased, to which they are justly banished. It is uncertain whether the word *katoteros* is used in the sense of the deep realms of the human world, the threat of death in the midst of life, or indeed the depths of the sphere of the dead itself. The two terms *abyssos* and *gehenna* come to us directly in their religious form from Judaism. *Abyssos* relates to a specific place of terror that is effectively the lair of demons, whereas *gehenna* is portrayed in Scripture as the end-time furnace of hell, to which the reprobate are to be eternally damned at the last judgment. According to Richard Bauckham: "The final destiny of the wicked is 'hell,' which translates Gk. 'Gehenna,' derived from the Heb. 'ge-hinnom,' 'the valley of Hinnom.' This originally denoted a valley outside Jerusalem, where child sacrifices were offered to Molech (2 Chr 28:3; 33:6). It became a symbol of judgment in Jer 7:31–33; 19:6ff, and in the intertestamental literature the term for the eschatological hell of fire."[35] At the time of writing, Dr. Bauckham was lecturing in the history of Christian thought at the University of Manchester. Whilst acknowledging his obvious scholarly expertise in the field, it would be remiss of me not to draw attention to the fact that nowhere does the Bible teach that hell was designed for fallen man as a place of punishment for his rebellion. It is spoken of as the destiny of demons (Matt 8:29), the beast and the false prophet (Rev 19:20), Satan (20:10), and death and Hades (v. 14). Hell only becomes the abode of the rebellious because they have chosen to align themselves with those for whom it was prepared rather than embrace that which could be theirs in Christ. Indeed, they perish essentially because they have "refused to love the truth and so be saved" (2 Thess 2:10). It is, therefore, into this context that Scripture's mention of hell must be placed: the offer of salvation through the gospel of Jesus on the basis of repentance and faith. The Bible sets before men their

---

35. R. J. Bauckham, "Eschatology," in Douglas, *New Bible Dictionary*, 346.

true purpose in Christ and they are solemnly charged with the magnitude of neglecting to avail themselves of that opportunity.

Of course, any teaching on the topic of hell is likely to be unpopular and liable to make its proponents the subjects of disapproval, ridicule, and derision. This is not an exclusively modern concept. Toward the end of the nineteenth century, and in the face of an increasing rejection of the orthodox doctrine of hell, Edward Meyrick Goulburn made the following profound and detailed proclamation:

> It is a dangerous thing to meddle with the theology of the Bible; because all its doctrines, though many of them sear far beyond us into the region of mystery, are yet so wonderfully coherent that to touch one is to imperil the rest. Scriptural theology resembles an arch, so constructed that all the great stones shall be key-stones. Displace any of these stones, and you will find that the whole fabric falls to pieces under your hands. Dislodge the doctrine of eternal punishment from the system of Scriptural theology, and you will find, if you employ against it similar objections, that the Atonement itself begins to give way; for if you are determined to reject the idea of a finite sin having an infinite penalty, you will find at least equally hard, or even more hard, to understand how a finite sin can demand an infinitely precious Sacrifice.[36]

It almost goes without saying that universalists will find such an idea preposterous. Their claim that all will ultimately be saved reduces hell to nothing more than a place of graphic imagery, devised to provoke moral integrity based on fear. If this were true, then the evidence of world history would seem to suggest that it has patently failed in its design. Commenting on the attraction of universalism in our day and its advocates finding alleged support in Scripture, Eryl Davies somewhat succinctly notes that:

> The texts to which they appeal, such as 1 Corinthians 15:51, Philippians 2:10 and 1 Timothy 2:4, do not . . . teach universalism. The first text—"We shall not all sleep, but we shall all be changed"—has reference to believers only. The words in Philippians—"That at the name of Jesus every knee should bow"—affirm that the ungodly will acknowledge Christ's Lordship; yet we know from other Scriptures that for them this will be done unwillingly and apart from salvation. The last reference that God "will have all men saved"—underlines the universality of salvation, but only in the sense that God purposes to save

---

36. Goulburn, *Everlasting Punishment*, 26.

people from different backgrounds of race, culture and status. In view, then, of Christ's clear teaching concerning the future punishment of sinners, universalism must be rejected.[37]

Just as there are to be rewards for the righteous acts of the saints, dependent upon the appropriation of individual abilities, so too are there to be commensurate degrees of torment for the unjust. Salvation is not the issue here, for that is a free gift dispensed according to God's sovereign pleasure and accessible only this side of physical death. Nevertheless, it was Jesus, the One in whom redemption was made possible, who warned that amongst those who declined the invitation would be some who "will be beaten with many blows," while others "will be beaten with few blows" (see Matt 11:22–24; Luke 12:46–48).

It would seem that the yardstick by which they will be judged is to be based upon the revelation received, though all hidden thoughts, each secret deed, and every careless word will be exposed to the light of God's righteous standard and dealt with accordingly (see Eccl 12:14; Matt 12:36; Luke 12:2–3; Rom 2:16). Allowing for the fact that such punishment is ascribed to be everlasting, we may only legitimately conclude that the difference is in terms of severity and not duration. The Christian can take no delight in the fate of the ungodly; their plight is not one to be mocked. Indeed, the doctrine of hell must surely provoke the recipients of Christ's favor to diligence and the urgent promotion of the gospel message. Under no more serious consideration has the saying been so apposite: "There but for the grace of God go I."

In a literary style that remains faithful to true apocalyptic imagery, the New Testament presents hell as a place to be shunned. It is dramatically and graphically portrayed as a location of blackest outer darkness (Matt 25:30; 2 Pet 2:17; Jude 13), unquenchable fire (Matt 18:8; Mark 9:43), undying worm (v. 48), where intense sorrow and remorse are expressed, represented by weeping and gnashing of teeth (Matt 8:12; 25:30), a fiery lake of burning sulfur (Rev 19:20; 20:10; 21:8), and the bodies and spirits of the unrighteous are to be destroyed by the second death (2:11; 20:14). There is little evidence to suggest that this is to be understood as annihilation, especially given that elsewhere in Scripture destruction refers to the irrevocable giving over of something (or someone) to the Lord's displeasure.

Whilst it must be acknowledged that the genre contains a strong element of composite symbolism in the language it employs, the clear implications are of the horror and irreversibility of such a fate and that the text is representative of a condition far worse than the natural mind could

---

37. Davies, *The Wrath of God*, 42.

otherwise comprehend. Moreover, we know from other passages in Scripture that hell is essentially a place of exclusion from the presence of God (see Matt 7:23; 2 Thess 1:9).

The nature of duration is a tricky one to grasp, much less explain, concerning the occupancy of hell's inhabitants. A good friend of mine denies the everlastingness of those who find themselves so destined after the last judgment. Along with others who support the idea of annihilationism, he cannot make room for something so imperfect in what will surely then be the perfect kingdom of God. My immediate response to this was that hell represents a graphic example of God's just judgment, and is truly perfect in so doing. Maybe a little glib, I know, but no less true for all that. But there is a more considered argument.

Again, we must revisit what we understand by the time/space continuum, especially in respect of God's relation to it. That he voluntarily subjected himself to its temporal limitations in the incarnation as its Redeemer is not in question. That he necessarily stands outside those same limitations as its Creator is similarly beyond the doubt of most believers. But is there any way in which time and space may be correctly described as infinite, which would *ipso facto* alter that relationship? Scientists would have us believe there is. I would offer that to attribute infinite quality to an essentially finite concept is a contradiction in terms and, therefore, both invalid and unsustainable. Moreover, in its absolute sense, infinity can only properly be ascribed to God.

And so, we are led to consider the presence of God. Indeed, we must contemplate what we mean by the presence of God, for to acknowledge his omnipresence must surely also negate the possibility of his absence any where and at any time, or even in any sense beyond location and/or duration. To minds that grapple even with the extent of such natural boundaries, how much more inexplicable do we find it to imagine beyond those limitations? And does hell itself lie not only beyond such extremities, but also outside our capacity to imagine God's presence there? To put it in the form of an intentional conundrum: is it possible for God to be present in that most God-forsaken of places?

Perhaps the most logical way to answer that question is to turn it completely around: is it conceivable that the only Being to which the term "infinite" can plausibly be applied should be absent from that which—by deduced definition—is thereby finite? By almost the same token, if we were to allow that it might be so, then would not his absence therewith militate against what we perceive of his omnipresence? But how far does revelation permit us to exercise lateral thinking in order to arrive at—what are, after all—conclusions bordering on the speculative? Well, Scripture provides us with more support for such an idea than we might always be willing to concede. David's albeit veiled testimony was: "Where can I go from your Spirit? Where can I flee from your presence? If I go up to the heavens, you are there; if I make my bed in the depths [that is, *Sheol*], you are there" (Ps 139:7–8).

But doesn't such an idea both contradict and contravene what we understand by eternal death being effectively separation from God? Possibly. Or perhaps we simply need to re-examine what Scripture actually means by separation from God in the light of his essential omnipresence. Or more to the point, what do we mean by God's presence? Preachers of a certain persuasion are often guilty of conditioning our minds by speaking of us entering into God's presence, drawing closer to it, or bathing in the pure joy now that we find ourselves there. And therein, I believe, lies the key. God is no more present when the church comes together on a Sunday morning than he is at my place of work on a Friday afternoon, though my awareness—or sense—of it may be dramatically heightened (hopefully) in the former setting. Similarly, there is a prevailing mindset that equates God's presence exclusively with blessing (unless your names happen to be Ananias and Sapphira, of course—see Acts 5:1–10). Despite the silence of the pulpits, however, the Bible often testifies to God being present both to sustain (Heb 1:3) and to punish (Amos 9:2). I must conclude, therefore, that though hell is not to be considered as a place of the blessed presence of God, this should not be understood to necessarily imply his absolute absence thence.

The doctrine of hell as the final and unchangeable destiny of the unregenerate should not be one that fills believers with personal dread. But neither should our demeanor be anything but a mournful one for the plight of those so destined. I can think of no more fitting way to articulate how it makes me feel than that so eloquently expressed by Wayne Grudem:

> It is hard—and it should be hard—for us to think of this doctrine today. If our hearts are never moved with deep sorrow when we contemplate this doctrine, then there is a serious deficiency in our spiritual and emotional sensibilities . . . The reason it is hard for us to think of the doctrine of hell is because God has put in our hearts a portion of his own love for people created in his image, even his love for sinners who rebel against him. As long as we are in this life, and as long as we see and think about others who need to hear the gospel and trust in Christ for salvation, it should cause us great distress and agony of spirit to think about eternal punishment.[38]

---

38. Grudem, *Systematic Theology*, 1151–52.

As Grudem rightly points out, however uncomfortable and discomfiting such a proposition may make us feel, we do those no favors for whom hell currently appears to await by burying our heads in the sand, wishing it were not so. From our present perspective, those who seem to have no eternal future but hell's occupancy are heaven's opportunity. When it is too late for them to respond favorably to that opportunity, they will not be able to claim that the sentence carried out against them is a miscarriage of justice or the conveyance of an unrighteous decree. God's judgments reflect his character, for they are as true and just as he (see Rev 19:1).

And so, though we should be careful to acknowledge that many of the biblical texts to which we may look for support concerning the end times are presented to us in the form of complex imagery, we must also concede that such evidence as there is speaks of hell as a location rather than a condition. Moreover, it will be a place wherein shall reside, in continual conscious torment, those who have refused to love the truth and so be spared that agony (see Matt 24:5; 25:30, 46; Luke 16:19–31). There is little more detail than that of which we can be certain.

Summary

The Bible describes the nature of death as a return to the dust, falling asleep, and the absence of life. For the finally unrepentant, death is also couched in terms akin to destruction. For believers, however, dying is but the prelude to a personal resurrection, whence they will awake from the sleep of death into Christ's blessed presence. At the return of Jesus, of course, the resurrection will apply to the wicked as well as the redeemed. At that time—if, indeed, the concept of a chronological succession of moments is still applicable—the latter will receive their glorious resurrection bodies, while the former will be consigned to eternal torment in the fire of hell (that is, *gehenna*). It somehow seems only natural to hope that this might not be the case, especially for those who are in bereavement over the loss of a loved one who demonstrated no authentic signs of Christian allegiance. However, we do neither them nor ourselves any favors in pretending it to be otherwise.

THE AGE TO COME

We now come to the final section in this work, in which we will consider the prospects for the believer in the age to come. If these could be collated together and summarized in just one word, then perhaps that word would be "life." In this regard, it is surely not without significance that Jesus is described as "the Word of life" (1 John 1:1). Earlier, the same author spoke of Jesus in terms of him being One "in [whom] was life" (John 1:4), and that he had "authority over all people that he might give life" (17:2). Having already discussed both the reality and consequences of what this communication of life means for us in the present (see also Col 3:4), all that remains is that we should view the implications of that impartation in relation to our future hope (1:27). This is not quite so straightforward a consideration as might be imagined, as we shall see.

Eternal Life and Its Rewards

The phrase *zoe aionios* is one that is used throughout the New Testament, though it is not so restricted in its use as to refer only to believers' existence in the presence of God in the age to come. It is also employed in the sense of the quality of life in the present as a foretaste of that which awaits us. It is perhaps for this reason that Stephen Travis has spoken of the significance of eternal life in the following terms:

> . . . because Christ's first coming has already inaugurated his kingdom, eternal life is experienced by the believer during the present life (Jn 3:36; 5:24; 1 Jn 5:13; 2 Cor 4:7–18). Since eternal life means "the life of the age to come," it implies . . . a quality of life derived from relationship with Christ (Rom 6:23; Jn 17:3). Thus the perfect life of God's ultimate kingdom is the consummation of life "in Christ" experienced now (Col 3:1–4; Jn 6:54). Although death marks a discontinuity between this life and the next, eternal life guarantees a continuity of relationship to Christ even through death.[39]

The interrelationship between life in this world and the one to follow is a common thread in the New Testament, hinted at under the old covenant, and becoming more fully developed in the intertestamental literature. So commonly understood was it by the time of Christ that often the idea of a glorious future was spoken of simply as *zoe* without any qualifying reference point. Perhaps the most graphic use, certainly by Jesus, is presented in the parable of the sheep and the goats (Matt 25:31–46), where the contrast could not be put more vividly: "Then [the unrighteous] will go away to eternal punishment, but the righteous to eternal life" (v. 46).

---

39. S. H. Travis, "Eschatology," in Ferguson and Wright, *New Dictionary of Theology*, 230.

In his—at times controversial—anthropologically based study, Wolfhart Pannenberg reminds us that:

> Only from a standpoint within the events itself is time divided into past, future and present. Seen from beyond the flow of time, all events coincide in an eternal present. We already experience that in an initial way in our own consciousness of the present. The unity of our life in the eternal concurrence of events can ... enter into our life only after death, with the resurrection of the dead. However, eternity means judgment, because in the eternal concurrence our life must perish because of its contradictions and especially because of the basic contradiction between the self and its infinite destiny. Only for the person who is in community with Jesus does the resurrection mean eternal life as well as judgment.[40]

Arguably one of the most neglected aspects in modern theology relating to the age to come for believers is the distribution of post-judicial rewards. And yet the New Testament treatment of the subject simply cannot be swept aside. Jesus spoke of it on many occasions, encouraging his hearers that at his coming, every individual shall be rewarded in accordance with his or her deeds (Matt 16:27). Whether through false humility, embarrassment, or pretence at some form of pseudo-spiritual maturity, the idea of a prize, crown, or reward seems particularly alien to much current Christian thought. What, then, are we to make of Christ's words, or Paul's excited tones (1 Cor 9:17–25; Phil 3:14; 2 Tim 4:8), or James's motivation (Jas 1:12), or Peter's provocation (1 Pet 5:4)? Let us consider the biblical evidence.

Before we look at the scriptural data that encourages us to seek rewards, it is important to lay hold of the Bible's teaching with regard to retribution. In his first recorded letter to the church at Corinth, the Apostle Paul speaks of the distinct possibility that Christians may suffer loss on the last day (see 1 Cor 3:11–15). It is not without significance that the analogy used in the passage observes many varying materials, all of which have building potential, and this seems to be a matter of personal choice. The foundation, however, is mandatory: it can be none other than Jesus (v. 11). The test, of course, lies not in their apparent capabilities to produce a building, for they all share this quality. But how will each be affected by fire? That is the challenge.

Paul was fully aware of the potentially disastrous consequences of adopting a *che sarà, sarà* approach to his ministry. Not for him the sitting back and just being "glad to be saved" mentality. So rigorous was Paul in

---

40. Pannenberg, *What is Man?*, 81.

his self-examination that he would often speak in such graphic terms as making his body a slave to righteousness so that, having preached to others, he himself would not be disqualified for the prize (1 Cor 9:27). John also charged his readers to be diligent, lest they should miss out on their full rewards (2 John 8).

We are also assured in Scripture as to recompense, a sort of divine reimbursement against any incurred spiritual expenditure, and with interest rates that are quite literally out of this world! Christ himself promised that "great is [our] reward in heaven" on account of those who insult, reject, and malign us "because of the Son of Man" (Luke 6:22–23). Paul echoed something of the same sentiment when he advised the Corinthian believers that temporal difficulties are minimal when compared to the glory they are to attain in eternity (2 Cor 4:17). Restoration always seems to carry with it an in-built multiplication factor. Nowhere is this more evident than in Jesus' pledge that all who suffer loss for his sake "will receive a hundred times as much" in addition to eternal life (Matt 19:29). The context makes it clear that this will take place "at the renewal of all things" (v. 28).

The Greek noun *misthos* and its related verb form *apodedemi* both convey the idea of a payment having been distributed or received for work carried out. One commentator remarks that: "Any reward depends for its significance upon the character of its bestower, and God's rewards . . . are inseparable from the covenant to which his commands are annexed."[41] With this in mind, Jesus' teaching on—and, indeed, his encouragement to actively pursue—divine rewards is always inextricably linked to a living faith (see John 6:28; Jas 2:14–16).

When contemplating heavenly rewards of this kind, we must be careful not to confuse them with our spiritual inheritance. This is the promise of God to every person who receives the provision of his Son as the coming sacrifice for his or her sins from the moment they believe. It is far above any human qualification, made possible entirely and exclusively by Christ's mediatorial work upon the cross and in relation to the new covenant in his blood (see Heb 9:15). As such, Christians can look forward to receiving their inheritance, come what may. Indeed, we too may exercise the same assurance as the apostle Peter that not only is it beyond loss, but it is also housed in heaven, even now awaiting our rightful claim upon it (1 Pet 1:3–4). There are, however, additional bonuses that we are each in a position to receive, which Scripture refers to as crowns and prizes.

Two Greek words are translated "crown" in the New Testament. *Diadema* usually refers to a symbol of royalty or honor, but the most commonly

---

41. M. R. W. Farrer, "Reward," in Douglas, *New Bible Dictionary*, 1029.

used is *stephanos*, which denotes a circlet, as in the crown of thorns enforcedly worn by Jesus at the crucifixion (Matt 27:29). While *stephanos* occasionally relates to regal headgear, it is more frequently associated with a victor's laurel wreath, and it is this image that Paul most often seeks to convey. The outstanding differences between that which was awarded to the Olympic champion of canonical metaphor and what believers may expect to receive is that the latter is to be "a crown that will last forever" (1 Cor 9:25), a "crown of life" (Jas 1:12), and "the crown of righteousness" (2 Tim 4:8).

No one can ever logically or logistically calculate the size of an individual's reward. However, it is possible to be dogmatic about one thing: "we must all appear before the judgment [Greek *bema*] seat of Christ, that each one may receive what is due to him [or her] for the things done while in the body, whether good or bad" (2 Cor 5:10). Of course, the context suggests that this was originally given as a warning against illicit conduct, but may it not serve also as an encouragement that believers might be spurred on to an even greater reward? It may well be sufficient for some to "be saved . . . as those escaping through flames" (1 Cor 3:15), but if there exists in the heart of God a purpose for those who belong to him to obtain much more than this, then surely it is incumbent upon them to desire it also. Paul knew of the possibility of a reward to accompany salvation and was neither ashamed nor too proud to vehemently pursue it. John, too, beheld the Son of Man speaking so distinctly: "I am coming soon! My reward is with me, and I will give to everyone according to what he has done" (Rev 22:12).

To our finite understanding, we might logically conclude from the fact of degrees of rewards in eternity that those with fewer might in some way be incomplete or imperfect, as if they were to be lacking by the measure to which they fall short of others more amply honored. In other words, there will exist an inequality of experience amongst believers in eternity. Perhaps this says more about the extent to which our minds are conditioned by temporal matters, where possessions dictate our level of happiness. True bliss exists in the presence of God. That alone will suffice. Moreover, the knowledge that the apportioning of rewards will have been made in accordance with the Almighty's perfect decree should not be cause for regret, but for rejoicing. Or, to put it another way: inequality does not necessarily equate with injustice.

There are many issues relating to the afterlife that must remain outside of the realm of dogma. The best we can claim is an opinion based upon where we consider the weight of evidence to fall. In the course of time, that opinion may alter as does our understanding of the testimony before us. One thing that I feel I can say with some reasonable conviction is that eternal life and eternal rewards are not synonymous terms. The reason I believe

I can be so forthright is that the former, even in its temporal manifestation, is nowhere described in Scripture as anything but a gift. It cannot be earned, as if to some it might be a wage. Eternal life is related exclusively to faith; eternal rewards are annexed especially to faithfulness on the part of the one so rewarded. Salvation is conditioned only by belief; rewards are determined by behavior.

But I also find it impossible at the present time to perceive of the quality of life intrinsic to that gift as subject to change or fluctuation, barring of course the restrictions that inhibit it this side of the resurrection. If rewards can add to that perfection, does such potential not render the gift somewhat less than perfect? To rational minds, such a conclusion seems not only reasonable, but also the only one to be truly justifiable. And yet, we cannot for that reason alone dismiss or disregard the emphasis placed upon eternal rewards and the godly pursuit thereof by Christian believers. We must either search more diligently for the truth of the matter or else acknowledge that such truth is presently beyond us, without it necessarily negating its own veracity.

However, it must also be noted that to deny the legitimacy of those passages that seem to speak of rewards as actually referring to salvation *per se* poses more questions than it solves. Most notable amongst them is that it would seem to call into question—in his own mind at least—the security of the Apostle Paul's salvation. No doubt this would be music to the ears of those who belong to the "once saved, may be lost" brigade. But, as we have seen, the assurance of salvation is a recurring theme of the New Testament. To cast any doubt upon it does not merely thereby call for a radical reevaluation of those texts that seem to support it, but actually makes a nonsense of them, there being no other plausible interpretation.

For example, if the correct interpretation of Paul's analogy of running the race "in such a way as to get the prize" (1 Cor 9:24) is, indeed, ultimate salvation, then that would appear to introduce not only some disharmony to the New Testament Scriptures in general, but also sharp contradiction to the Pauline writings in particular. Elsewhere, the apostle intimates that salvation is absolutely free to the recipient (Rom 3:24; 4:3–8; Eph 2:9). Earlier in this very same letter to the believers at Corinth, he had contrasted eternal rewards and salvation, surely leaving us in no doubt that, though justification is by faith, there yet awaits a judgment of one's faithfulness (see 1 Cor 3:14–15). The latter will have no bearing on the former, for it is built on a more sure foundation than mere human diligence.

For some, it seems that the difficulty lies not so much in the concept of rewards as in the inference that they can be earned, as if our faithfulness somehow places us in God's debt. It is a reasonable concern. However, when properly understood—and qualified as such—the terminology used is no more of a threat than it is to speak of eternal life as our inheritance. That is our right on account of Christ's finished work; eternal rewards are ours to be "earned" in respect of God's promise toward us on account of our "work" of faithfulness. Thus, redemption is effected exclusively by the work of Christ Jesus in obedience to the Father's will for humanity; rewards are affected solely by the works of the individual in obeisance to the Father's revealed purpose for them in that same Christ Jesus. One is related to imputed righteousness; the other is to do with outworked righteousness.

A Bodily Resurrection

Although the mystery of what Scripture refers to as "the end of the age" (Matt 13:40–49), or "the last days" (Mic 4:1; Isa 2:2; John 11:24), continues to be partially veiled, there is sufficient biblical data to be able to deduce that at the second coming of Jesus, those who have died "in Christ" will be raised (see 1 Cor 15:23; 1 Thess 4:16), and those who remain alive at his parousia will be changed into a form of post-resurrection existence without having to pass through death (1 Cor 15:52; 1 Thess 4:17). Whilst there was a limited acknowledgment of some form of resurrection during the Old Testament period (see Isa 25:8; Dan 12:2), which became more prevalent during the intertestamental years, it is to the pages of the New Testament that we must turn for a more fully developed theological understanding of eschatological resurrection.

In many ways, the resurrection of Jesus Christ is God's surety of the promises he had made to effect man's redemption. The Apostle Paul clearly viewed it from this perspective. The whole basis of his gospel message was laid on the foundation of the assurance of salvation through Christ's resurrection. For him, there could be no compromise. If Jesus was raised—not only from the dead, but also from the power of death itself—then the way was thence made clear for humanity to be free from sin and the bondage of its decay. If not, then the possibility of release was merely a façade, conversion to Christianity being just another religious experience among so many others. This very sentiment was addressed by Paul to the church at Corinth when he penned the following: "If Christ has not been raised, our preaching is useless and so is your faith . . . And if Christ has not been raised, your faith is futile; you are still in your sins . . . If only for this life we have hope in Christ, we are to be pitied more than all men" (1 Cor 15:14–19).

The impact of the resurrection of Jesus was not simply in his being raised to life from death. As supernatural as that indubitably was, there had previously been recorded instances of that having taken place, most notably in the ministry of Jesus himself (see Mark 5:41–42; John 11:43–44). The significance of Christ's resurrection, however, is that it opened the door to eternal life for a fallen human race. From that point in history, Christians are guaranteed the unimaginable benefits of sharing in his resurrection life, both in this present age (Rom 8:11; Eph 2:5–10; Col 2:12), and in the age to come (John 11:26; 2 Cor 1:22; 5:4–10).

During the period of the early church fathers, the prevailing view was one of belief in the resurrection of the body.[42] Whilst Clement of Alexandria implied the identity of the future body with that of the present, however, Origen portrayed the resurrection body as one that was essentially spirit and, therefore, not subject to its previous temporal limitations. Far from being alone in his deductions, Origen did nevertheless represent the minority view. Most of his contemporaries held that the future body would be an exact replica of that formed in the current age.

Generally speaking, the view of the church in the East assumed a more spiritual dimension to that in the West, with Gregory of Nyssa and Gregory of Nazianzus, along with John Chrysostom, following the sentiments as expressed by Origen. Thomas Aquinas speculated on the notion that the resurrection body will substantially be that which existed immediately prior to death, yet impulsively obedient to the directives of the spirit, subject to neither growth nor decay, and capable of fleeting, almost effortless, motion. The consensus of opinion at the Reformation was to identify the resurrection body with the present temporal frame. With the advent of progressive modern science and the development of medical understanding, many have felt the need to deny the literalism of those Scriptures that speak of the resurrection, either consigning them to the realm of poetic fancy or else interpreting them as merely analogous references to the continued existence of personality after death.

The biblical presentation of the climax to the redemptive work of Christ, however, is that of the believer's glorification. This is when the physical body is to undergo such a radical transformation as to render it perfect, incorruptible, spiritual in essence, and totally suited to its renewed environment, having been completely and irrevocably released from the consequences of Adam's rebellion. Where there was previously frustration, there will be fulfillment; where hitherto the body had known only death and decay, there is to be nothing but life and vitality; where history had been bringing us agonizingly to that point in God that is presently cloaked in mystery and enigma, the receipt of our resurrection bodies will leave no

---

42. See Berkhof, *Systematic Theology*, 720.

question unanswered or unanswerable. So much so, in fact, that Wayne Grudem has offered the following definition of glorification:

> [It] is the final step in the application of redemption. It will happen when Christ returns and raises from the dead the bodies of all believers for all time who have died, and reunites them with their souls, and changes the bodies of all believers who remain alive, thereby giving all believers at the same time perfect resurrection bodies like his own.[43]

Amongst George Eldon Ladd's observations concerning Paul's comments in 1 Corinthians 15 (based on the conclusion that the apostle's encounter with Jesus was not merely a vision, but a personal encounter with the risen Christ), he affirms that "the resurrection body of Jesus was of the same order as the resurrection bodies of the saints at the end of the age." He further notes that: "it was Paul's familiarity with the theology of glory, and his experience of meeting Jesus in his glorified state, that led Paul to his theology of glorified bodies in the eschatological resurrection."[44]

Any relationship that persists between the physical body and the spiritual body is clearly not one of substance, but of personality. According to Paul's understanding of it, that which is raised only relates to that which is sown as does a harvest to the seed wherein it is contained (see 1 Cor 15:35–54). There is, however, to be a progression of identity, a discernible continuity whereby each persona represented in the resurrection body will bear some semblance to that which was sown, effecting recognition by those with whom we were most familiar. The following table, derived from 1 Corinthians 15, amply demonstrates this principle of sowing and reaping:

that which was sown . . .	(1 Cor 15)	is raised . . .
. . . as perishable	(v. 42)	. . . imperishable
. . . in dishonor	(v. 43a)	. . . in glory
. . . in weakness	(v. 43b)	. . . in power
. . . a natural body	(v. 44)	. . . a spiritual body

Paul's teaching on this matter is well known to many of us. But I wonder if its finer points might be obscured to us by such familiarity. A farmer sows, the seed figuratively dies, and after a period of nurturing and nutrient supply, hey presto: up pops a plant. It is so obvious that there is no need to look any further for the lesson Paul affords—or is there? Well, what may not be so glaringly apparent is that it is not even the material substance of the seed

---

43. Grudem, *Systematic Theology*, 828.
44. Ladd, *I Believe in the Resurrection*, 123–25.

that provides for its own continuity, but the life contained therein. It is this (eternal) life that allows for the persistence of type, despite the discontinuity of (temporal) substance.[45] The resurrection body, therefore, is fully compatible with the New Testament emphasis on restoration; not so with any religious ideal of reincarnation or reconstitution.

We must, thus, banish from our thinking any notion that the resurrection body of the righteous will merely be a resuscitated corpse. As we have seen, Paul seemed to address such concerns amongst the Corinthian believers by reminding them first of all of Christ's own resurrection and, secondly, of their invitation to partake in it. The natural body is subject to decay, mortality, limitation, and bondage because it is ours by virtue of our sharing in Adam's guilt. The spiritual body, on the other hand, is not similarly conditioned, as it represents the ideal vehicle with which to clothe the redeemed (that is, atoned for) child of God.

Moreover, those who argue against the physicality of the resurrection body on the grounds that Paul speaks of it as essentially a spiritual body have failed to understand the direction taken by Greek adjectives ending in *-kos*, in this case *pneumatikos*. Some English translations have been particularly unhelpful by cloaking the true distinction being made by Paul in this regard, most notably the annotated versions (e.g., RSV, NRSV). Far from describing the substance out of which this resurrection body is to be made, Paul is, in fact, drawing our attention to that which animates the object. The difference is akin to that between saying: "I traveled to the venue on an electric-powered train as opposed to a steam-driven one"; whether the carriages were made of aluminum, wood, sheet metal, or fiberglass is not the issue.

Even that with which this "spiritual" body is contrasted is something of a mistranslation in some versions. To speak of the current state as physical suggests that it will become non-physical, which is utterly inaccurate. Such thinking has given rise to the ghostlike form that is often conjured in the minds of those who give credence to such nonsense. If it alludes to anything, then it is psychical, but again only in the sense of that which gives it animation (that is, the sin-tainted soul), with no reference at all to its essential substance.

Of course, there is a very good doctrinal reason why the subject of the resurrection body of the righteous is so important. Although some have dismissed it as almost an unnecessary appendage to primary belief in the atoning work of Christ, Scripture is far less indifferent. Indeed, the whole thrust of Paul's argument is that the implications of there being no resurrection for

---

45. See Harris, *From Grave to Glory*, 411–12.

believers is that it throws into question Jesus' own resurrection and, thereby, also our justification (see 1 Cor 15:13–19; Rom 4:25). Notice the words Paul uses to describe man's plight if this were not so: "useless," "false," "futile," and "lost." How grim! "But," he goes on, "Christ has indeed been raised from the dead" (v. 20), thus assuring not only our justification from sin(s), but also our own resurrection, and that with bodies fit for the purpose (vv. 35–54).

As implied earlier under the heading "The Constitution of Man," the dualistic perception of man in certain anthropological circles owes more to Greek philosophy than to the biblical revelation. In the Bible, the human body is spoken of as the product of a creative act of God, upon which he pronounced a verdict of "very good" (Gen 1:31). Man, therefore, is not perceived of as a soul imprisoned within a shell of evil matter, from which the inner self frustratingly yearns release. Rather, he is a whole person, body and spirit, and for the believer the redemptive process involves his complete self being progressively restored, the final act of transformation to be climaxed with the resurrection body. In this regard, and with particular reference to Jesus' declaration that, though he was dead, he is now alive for ever and ever, and in possession of "the keys of death and Hades" (Rev 1:18), William Hendriksen poses the question: "Does not the Son of Man reveal that He has the keys of death whenever He welcomes the soul of a believer into heaven? And does He not prove that He has the keys of Hades when at His coming He reunites the soul and body of the believer, a body now gloriously transformed?"[46]

An erroneous theological understanding of the human body historically has given rise to asceticism. In alleged recognition of Paul's exhortation to treat the body harshly (Col 2:21–23), many have been guilty of actually mistreating the body. Some have even viewed the body as an evil tent in which the immaterial spirit is enslaved. This misconception patently contradicts the biblical theme of the atonement, which is concerned with the redemption of the whole man, including the physical body (see Rom 8:23). As the "firstfruits of those who have fallen asleep" (1 Cor 15:3), Jesus took his glorified body with him. This was not a replacement shell, much less a patched-up version of the old one; it was a radically transformed resurrection body.

What cannot be ignored, of course, is that while we remain in our mortal bodies on this earth, we and all around us are subject to the process of decay, which for the vast majority will culminate in physical death. For the believer, however, death is not the end. Although we are being transformed in life to Christ's glorious image, the completion of that process awaits us at

---

46. Hendriksen, *More Than Conquerors*, 57.

the resurrection when that which is perishable, dishonorable, and weak will become imperishable, glorious, and powerful (1 Cor 15:42–44). Christians are not destined to spend eternity as disembodied spirits, but each one is to be vitally and marvelously changed into his or her spiritual body (v. 44) by the Spirit of their risen Lord, Jesus Christ. (NB: the use of gender terminology here is not intended to imply post-resurrection reproductive capabilities—see Matt 22:30.)

By way of summary, I am once again indebted to the findings of Hammond:

> After comparing Scripture with Scripture, the most we can assert concerning the resurrection body is that:
>
> i. It will have human likeness, with the possibility that the facial expression may be recognised by those known on earth.
> ii. It will possess new powers unknown to man in his present state.
> iii. It will be "spiritual," "imperishable," and "immortal."
> iv. It will be "like" unto our Lord's glorified body.
> v. It will have a definite relation to the present mortal body.[47]

Heaven's Inhabitants

In agreement with what we know of ancient Hebrew idiom, both the Old and New Testaments speak of heaven in the plural (Heb. *shamayim*; Gk. *ouranos*). A minimal amount of scholarly research in this area would reward the student with the understanding that the word "heaven" is generally used in one of three ways in Scripture. The immediate heavens are simply the skies or atmosphere, the realm of meteorological phenomena (see Gen 8:2; Ps 147:8), and the air space of winged creatures (Hos 2:18). Beyond this there is the domain of the stars, where sun, moon, and planetary bodies are located (Gen 1:14, 17)—the heaven of outer space. Finally, and of primary concern to us in the present context, is the sanctuary of God, his dwelling place (Isa 63:15; Matt 6:9).

God, of course, is omnipresent, and in no way restricted to any temporal/spatial locality. Indeed, he fills both heaven and earth (Jer 23:24). Paradoxically, however, there is yet a sense in which it might be said that God abides in heaven (25:30). This apparent contradiction is nowhere more dialectically brought together for us than at the completion of the temple in Israel, when Solomon prayed: "The heavens, even the highest heavens,

---

47. Hammond, *In Understanding*, 189.

cannot contain you. How much less this temple that I have built . . . Now arise, O Lord God, and come to your resting place" (2 Chr 6:18, 41). The key to our understanding is surely to be found in the words of God himself who, speaking through the prophet Isaiah, declared that: "Heaven is my throne, and the earth is my footstool" (Isa 66:1). Although heaven cannot contain God, it is nevertheless described as the seat of his government, the place wherein he has chosen to be enthroned (see Ps 2:4; Heb 8:1; Rev 4:1-2).

Heaven is also the place where Jesus is. At the incarnation, the Christ came from heaven to accomplish the redemptive purpose of the Father (see John 3:13; 1 Cor 15:47; Phil 2:8). In this respect, he compared himself to God's miraculous provision of manna for Israel in the wilderness (John 6:33). But he also returned to heaven that he might resume his place in the counsel of the Godhead (Mark 6:19), not only as High Priest (Heb 9:24), but also as conquering King (1 Pet 3:21-22). Moreover, it is from heaven that Jesus will return to earth (Phil 3:20; 1 Thess 4:16), that we may thereafter be eternally with him (John 14:1-3; 1 Thess 4:17). But where will this be?

The traditional belief within Christendom has always been that heaven is the final destiny of the righteous, though this is not as explicit in Scripture as many assume. According to the book of Revelation, the eventual abode of the saints is to be within the sphere of "a new heaven and a new earth" (Rev 21:1). Whether this is to be a completely new realm altogether or a renewal of the present creation continues to arouse debate, particularly amongst Lutheran and Reformed scholars. Both parties appeal to Scripture as providing evidence for their respective claims. The weight of biblical testimony does seem to favor a renewal climax, those passages that imply annihilation of the old order possibly referring graphically to the cessation of the earth's existence in its current form. The apocalyptic nature of the genre certainly allows for this kind of literary device to be employed.

There is an admitted difficulty in how we are to understand John's citation of this new heaven and new earth. The milieu in which it finds itself somewhat compounds the obscurity. Much of Revelation is presented in the form of composite symbolism, the key to its interpretation residing in an appreciation of that fact. But are we to comprehend this new heaven and new earth in anything but a literal sense? It is a widely acknowledged hermeneutical principle that we must deviate from the literal only out of necessity. Despite the propensity of imagery in John's apocalypse, there are no other reasons to afford a non-literal interpretation to our understanding of this end-time new heaven and new earth. It is not necessary to do so. Indeed, this fact alone makes it more necessary that we should not do so.

When attempting to arrive at a more reasoned understanding of Scripture, it is a wise policy to ask questions of the text: "What does this mean?" "What would its original readership have understood by it?" "What are the potential implications of such an understanding?" "How might this challenge any preconceived ideas I may have about other related issues?" "Do I need to adjust my doctrinal position in any way to accommodate this freshly acquired revelation?" This is not to be equated with being blown about by every wind of doctrine (Eph 4:14). But neither should we drive ourselves so far down a theological cul-de-sac that it proves more difficult to back out (or down) than it needs to be.

One example of this can be observed in those who maintain that the new earth will be one that precisely replicates the old earth's pre-fallen paradisiacal condition. Whilst I can in some ways understand the logic behind such a position, I do not believe those who hold to it have sufficiently thought matters through. I say this on two counts. First of all, if the condition of the new earth is merely one that imitates the original condition of the old, then it remains subject to the same potential to become tainted by sin. Now, I realize that it only succumbed to such potential by the failure of Adam in the first instance, which is no longer possible because of the restored image of God in man through Christ Jesus. But surely that is the point. The new earth must be one that is a fitting environment not only for unfallen man, but man without the capacity to fall. Arguing in support of the "renewed" creation position, Wayne Grudem concludes that:

> A strong consideration in favor of this viewpoint is the fact that God made the original physical creation "very good" (Gen 1:31). There is therefore nothing inherently sinful or evil or 'unspiritual' about the physical world that God made or the creatures that he put in it, or about the physical bodies that he gave us at creation. Though all of these things have been marred and distorted by sin, God will not completely destroy the physical world (which would be an acknowledgment that sin had frustrated and defeated God's purposes), but rather he will perfect the entire creation and bring it into harmony with the purposes for which he originally created it. Therefore we can expect that in the new heavens and new earth there will be a fully perfect earth that is once again "very good."[48]

Secondly (though not entirely unrelated), the original newly created earth contained within it the seed-form of everything it might have become in the fulness of time had Adam not fallen. It was the true *genesis*. The indications given by John's Revelation are such that this new earth will be the fulfillment—or the coming to fruition—of that seed. In other words, the

---

48. Grudem, *Systematic Theology*, 1161.

new earth will present the original intention in God's heart for his created order.

Moreover, because the curse contingent upon the fall will have been removed (both in principle and in fact), the inhabitants of this new earth will not find its soil so reluctant to give of its yield. This is good news for gardeners and farmers alike. It is possibly enough for the most heathen of them to turn to Christ. Perhaps we should even incorporate this into our mission strategy in rural areas. If the gospel message fails to convince them of their plight, dangle this carrot before their eyes: no more briars, thorns, or weeds in the hereafter. Although work will be involved (for that is not a product of the fall), it will not be toilsome or burdensome. No more sweating of the brow in these fields.

Agriculturalist/horticulturalists aside, what kind of people will inhabit this new earth? Let us briefly consider the following verses:

> . . . in keeping with [God's] promise we are looking forward to a new heaven and a new earth, the home of righteousness.[49]

> After this I looked and there was a great multitude that no one could count, from every nation, tribe, people and language, standing before the throne and in front of the Lamb. They were wearing white robes and were holding palm branches in their hands.[50]

> Then I saw a new heaven and a new earth, for the first heaven and the first earth had passed away, and there was no longer any sea. I saw the Holy City, the new Jerusalem, coming down out of heaven from God, prepared as a bride beautifully dressed for her husband. And I heard a loud voice from the throne saying, "Now the dwelling of God is with men, and he will live with them. They will be his people, and God himself will be with them and be their God."[51]

From these and similar verses, we can deduce that they who find themselves inhabiting the new earth will be:

- those whose disposition is not at variance with their righteous surroundings;

---

49. 2 Pet 3:13.
50. Rev 7:9.
51. Rev 21:1–3.

- representative of every possible cultural stream from their previous habitation;
- those whose primary objective is to please Christ;
- those who have undergone divine preparation in order to ensure their compatibility with their new home; and
- those with whom their covenant God is pleased to dwell.

There is also a certain degree of vagueness concerning the exact nature of where God's people go immediately upon death having taken place. Many theologians maintain that believers go straight to heaven to be with Christ as disembodied spirits, awaiting only the occasion when they are to receive their resurrection bodies. Others defend the position that the righteous soul enters a period of prolonged sleep during the intermediate state, known as psychopannychia. Both the Roman Catholic and some of the Greek Orthodox persuasion hold that, for those who die at peace with the church but with unconfessed venial sins, there is to be a season of purgatorial cleansing to endure. (There seems to be no legitimate biblical evidence to support such a view.) What all of these theories fail to take into account is that when Scripture speaks of a post-death existence, it does so in terms of the finite boundaries of our experience of the time/space continuum. At death, we shall no longer be subject to such temporal/spatial limitations. Thus, it is not beyond the realm of theological possibility to propose that when we die we do so to awake immediately on the day of resurrection, even though many years may have passed by earth's time.

I have often heard it preached that there will be three things that will surprise us when finally we take our place in the eternal realm: to find some there we did not expect, to find some missing who we considered to be nailed-on certainties, and to find ourselves among the number of the former. Despite the projected humility of this last point, the believer's assurance of which Scripture amply testifies prevents me from identifying with it. I trust that will not come across as an arrogant gesture; it is definitely not intended to be. Rather, it is a statement of my confidence that he who has begun a good work in me will ultimately bring it to completion (Phil 1:6). Moreover, we can be assured that none will be there who should not be, nor any who are unjustly absent. "Will not the God of all the earth do right?" (Gen 18:25).

The Wedding Supper of the Lamb

From the time of the prophet Isaiah, there has been the anticipation within Judaism of an inaugural function to mark Messiah's eschatological rule. The tone of his prophetic declaration leaves no room for ambiguity:

> . . . the Lord Almighty will prepare a feast of rich food for all peoples, a banquet of aged wine . . . the best meats and the finest of wines. On this mountain he will destroy the shroud that enfolds all peoples, the sheet that covers all nations; he will swallow up death for ever. The Sovereign Lord will wipe away the tears from all faces; he will remove the disgrace of his people from all the earth. The Lord has spoken.[52]

By the time of Jesus' public ministry on earth, the concept of heavenly festivity had become so ingrained in the Hebrew culture that it was often conveyed as part of an informal greeting: "Blessed is the man who will eat at the feast in the kingdom of God" (Luke 14:15). Indeed, much of the way in which Jesus related his message of the kingdom took place during meals, furnishing the ideal setting for him to affirm the basics of his gospel: provision, covenant, and messianic expectation. Having begun his work at a wedding feast in Cana of Galilee (John 2:1–11), he drew it to a close at the final supper with his closest friends (Matt 26:17–30). It was here, of course, that he instituted the communion as a solemn declaration and vital reminder of the believer's covenant relationship to "the Lord's death until he comes" (1 Cor 11:26).

I have written elsewhere that the primary emphasis of what we variously refer to as the Lord's/Last Supper, the Eucharist, Holy Communion, and the Covenant meal is that we remember Christ as we partake of it.[53] It is both a solemn and a joyous occasion. We are not encouraged only to remember Christ's death, as prominent a feature though that most certainly is. Nor should we focus solely on his resurrection, without which there would be no justification. Rather, it is the person of Christ that warrants our attention. Of course, we must always remain mindful of what he has done, but the weight of evidence in Scripture concerning his praiseworthiness relates more to who he is. And yet, somewhat bizarrely, it is only those who acknowledge what he has done who will also have their eyes opened to recognize who he is.

But there is also the sense in which we look forward as we eat the bread (or water biscuit) and drink the wine (or diluted blackcurrant juice). This is

---

52. Isa 25:6–8.
53. See Woodall, *Covenant*, 126–32.

not so much a remembrance, except perhaps in that we remind ourselves of Jesus' earlier promises concerning what will take place. In this respect, the Lord's Supper may be seen as a foretaste, even a type, of the wedding supper of the Lamb. Indeed, it is highly likely that this is what Jesus intended to convey when he said that he would "not eat [of] it again until it finds fulfillment in the kingdom of God" (Luke 22:16; see also vv. 18, 29–30). As Ralph Martin suggests, there are "eschatological overtones" to the Lord's Supper;[54] it is to our detriment that we ignore or neglect them. Thus, the occasion of Jesus sharing the emblems with his closest disciples in that upper room may only be described as the Last Supper in a restricted sense. It most certainly was not the final time he would ever do so.

All of these instances, along with many other parabolic illustrations, prefigure "the supper of the Lamb" (Rev 19:9). Scripture presents this as an occasion for great merriment, where the risen Christ will freely distribute fruit from the tree of life to those who are invited, and lead his people in triumphant procession to the springs of living water (see also 2:17; 7:16–17). Whether or not these are to be taken as literal forthcoming events is not the issue. (Those who point to the rational incompatibility of resurrection bodies taking food, however, must be reminded of the post-resurrection, pre-ascension Jesus doing just that.) The significance should be seen in the constant emphasis that the eternal kingdom is to be one of abundant sufficiency and where joy, satisfaction, and exuberant celebration are the hallmarks of believers continually experiencing the unlimited resources of their God.

The fact that there is to be a wedding supper naturally presupposes that a marriage has taken place. The bridegroom and his bride are the Lamb and the church: Jesus and the redeemed community, of which he is the head. As individual members of that committed body, believers are to be adorned in garments that they have previously prepared for themselves (Rev 19:7–8). Even in the Old Testament, natural Israel was spoken of as being joined to God in matrimonial terms (see Isa 62:4; Jer 2:2). Having broken covenant by indulging in spiritual adultery, it was left to the prophet Hosea to speak as God's mouthpiece concerning the fulfillment of his purpose through a new covenant: "I will betroth you to me for ever; I will betroth you in righteousness and justice, in love and compassion. I will betroth you in faithfulness, and you will acknowledge the Lord" (Hos 2:19–20).

There is arguably no more powerful imagery in Scripture than this, because there is no more potent intimacy of relationship than the joining of two people in the union of marriage. It is one that the Apostle Paul takes up

---

54. R. P. Martin, "Lord's Supper," in Douglas, *New Bible Dictionary*, 709.

when he compares the Bible's initial reference to marriage with the ultimate fulfillment of that union, Christ and his church (Eph 5:31–32). Indeed, Paul saw it as part of his apostolic commission to prepare those under his charge for the day when they would be presented "as a pure virgin" to Christ, their husband (2 Cor 11:2).

There has been some debate concerning the identity of the guests who are to be invited to the wedding supper (or marriage feast, if you prefer). The question arises because of a surmised contrast between the guests and the bride (see Rev 19:6–9). The fact that the two appear to be represented thus in such close proximity seems only to fuel the speculation. Are they the Jewish people and the Gentiles? Are some unbelievers to be allowed a glimpse of the blessed proceedings as a testimony against their unbelief thitherto? Are the guests simply the angelic host and, if so, why would they require special invitation?

Of course, we may never know until it actually happens, by which time we may well have far more glorious things to ponder. It is my opinion, however, that there is no contrast at all, but that the guests of verse 9 and the (corporate) bride of verse 7 are identical. The different terminology used to describe what I believe to be the redeemed community in both instances reflects not different subject matters but a differing relation to the object in each case. There seems to be a definite parenthetical pause between the end of verse eight and the beginning of verse nine.

I am not suggesting that such a break is indicative of missing text; just that the emphasis changes ever so slightly and, for that reason, we are dealing with two completely separate incidents. Or, rather, they each speak of essentially the same incident, but presented within two differing contextual frameworks. In the first, the church is the bride, for she is presented as one who has made herself ready for the groom, the Lamb. But the Lamb is not the object of the second reference; it is the One who gives the invitation: the Father, God.

But consider the inference to be drawn from this "beatitude." Although the attendance at the feast of those so called will be a joyous one, it would appear that the blessing invoked here relates even to the invitation: "Blessed are those who are invited . . ." (Rev 19:9). The KJV seems to present a more accurate translation here by identifying the blessing with being "called," where the Greek *keklemenoi* (*kaleo* together with the passive participle becomes an intensive perfect) carries with it the sense of having been chosen by way of privilege in accordance with the divine prerogative. Whilst not a wholly adequate synonym, perhaps the verb "summon" is at least a little closer in meaning than "invite." George Eldon Ladd illuminates us further:

Men cannot find access to the marriage feast on their own merits; they must receive a divine invitation. The initiative to salvation is always the call of God. The angel says to John, "These are the true words of God." In the face of all the evil that the church experiences on earth, the angel adds a solemn assurance that this promise of blessing in the messianic feast is the unfailing word of God.[55]

Notice also that the "invitation" on this occasion does not in and of itself necessarily negate the doctrine of election, as if there is the possibility of declination. Now, I am aware that this will arouse a certain amount of controversy, especially when this passage is set alongside the parable of the wedding banquet, told by Jesus (Matt 22:1–14). The argument continues apace in the opposite direction when we realize that the very same Greek compound *keklemenoi* appears. Should we not expect it, then, to convey the same meaning in both passages, especially when they share so much common detail otherwise? They are remarkably similar. But I believe the key to their one major difference lies in Jesus' concluding remark in the Matthean gospel account: "For many are invited, but few are called" (v. 14). The context suggests that this is not an inappropriate conclusion to make to the parable. Might I proffer that the same could not be said of John's vision of the end time for the simple reason that those invited are also called.

At the risk of stating the obvious, it is fitting that we remind ourselves of the nature of the marriage supper of the Lamb. The clue is found in the analogous title: it is to be a love feast. Anyone who has experienced a wedding ceremony—and especially the meal that follows—will know that it is a time for a party atmosphere. Any petty family squabbles are usually laid to one side in recognition of the fact that the day's events belong essentially to two people: the bride and the groom. The guests may include work colleagues, old school friends, and those who belong to shared institutions, such as gyms, sports clubs, or church social groups. Amongst the family members will be those who represent varying degrees of closeness, ranging from grandparents, parents, and siblings to uncles, aunts, and second cousins three times removed, who we last met when we shared a common interest in developing our speaking capabilities from "Gug, gug" to "Dadda!" But the day is not about them; it is about the bride and the groom.

For those who are in attendance on such an occasion, the awareness of certain details is vital. Where will it take place? On what date? By what time are we expected to arrive? Are there any food allergies of which the caterers need to be made aware? Is there to be provision for gifts to be presented to

---

55. Ladd, *Revelation*, 250.

the happy couple? And a host of other minutiae that someone who has only ever had the simple task of being the groom could not possibly be expected to know or even care too much about. That we are not made aware of such information in this case suggests that it is not incumbent upon us to know. Again, one of the most helpful pieces of advice I was given at college many years ago was this: "Where Scripture is silent, it is sagacious not to speculate." We do well to take that on board at all times, but perhaps especially so in relation to the contents of the book of Revelation.

What seems to be beyond the realm of conjecture is that the wedding supper of the Lamb can be identified with neither the wedding itself, nor the marriage that follows, and yet it is clearly related to both. It is a celebration of acknowledgment that the former has taken place and a joyous anticipation of the latter.

If we may be allowed to develop the imagery just a little further, the position of the church might now be considered to be in its betrothal phase. We are engaged to Christ by virtue of a dowry having been paid by the Father of the groom, which in this case consisted of the shed blood of his Son on behalf of the bride to be (see Matt 1:18; Luke 2:5). We now await the arrival of the groom, whereupon he will take us to be with him (Matt 25:1–13), perhaps the only "marriage" of which it can be said is truly made in heaven.

Although the wedding supper of the Lamb is rightly to be seen as a celebratory feast of the joining of bride and groom, church and Christ, it is but the beginning of the perfect marriage relationship. Just as human marriage was always intended to be an exclusive relationship of growing intimacy and developing recognition between two people, so eternity will be an occasion for the increase of his government (Isa 9:7) and an ever-growing sense of appreciation in respect of his faithfulness, power, and love. The age to come will not be one of static admiration, but of . . .

. . . Continued Service

Speculation abounds concerning the finer details of what happens "when we all get to heaven." Much of what currently passes for Christian theology on the subject seems to owe more to either an amalgamation of popular expectation or a complete misrepresentation of Scripture, rather than any reliance upon what the Bible actually teaches. Whilst many look forward to a never-ending era of utopian self-indulgence, others anticipate a form of existence in the magical world of curse-free pleasure. The thought of spending endless days drifting on a cloud, while strumming nineteenth-century hymn tunes on a solid gold harp is equally absurd.

These are just some of the idle notions that are often promoted with all seriousness as being synonymous with the concept of eternal life. But the biblical evidence suggests a restoration of all that was lost in Adam, not only in fact but also in terms of potential. And so, we can expect the removal of the curse, the reversal of the prohibitions placed upon man following original sin, the right of access being opened up once more to the tree of life, and the continual reign of the saints as servants of the Lamb (see Rev 22:3–5).

What there will not be is the absence of work. The work ethic introduced in Eden (Gen 2:15) was not in itself part of the curse for Adam, any more than childbirth was for Eve. Although pain and sweat may well be associated with the fall, work is a valid expression of how man reflects the creative image of the Father. Eden, in its pre-fallen state of relative perfection, was very much a place of industrious activity. There is no legitimate reason to believe that Paradise restored will be any less so: a place of praise and work, worship and service, in keeping with the biblical perspective of our "royal priesthood" (1 Pet 2:9).

What this is likely to mean in terms of the age to come I have already discussed in some detail elsewhere.[56] Whilst not wishing to offer anyone the excuse to refrain from purchasing a copy for themselves, the gist of my argument there is worth summarizing in this context. On the basis of the biblical evidence, particularly in the Old Testament, I noted that, although the priestly function was essentially one derived from consecration for service (see Isa 61:6), the basis for such a designation was to be identified in the candidates' being set apart by God and for him. Thus, we may concur with Alec Motyer's observation that: "The substantial truth . . . of the 'priesthood of all believers' in both the Old and New Testaments is freedom of access into the holy presence."[57] In this context, Hywel Jones is correct to assert that the assignation "kingdom of priests" is fundamentally "a kingdom whose citizens are all priests, each having right of access, worship and devotion to God."[58]

Just as the advantage of natural Israel over her contemporaries may be summarized in terms of her right of entry to the divine throne (in an albeit restricted temporal sense, of course), so too the priesthood of all believers—both temporally and eternally—consists in us having that same right of entry into God's presence. Does such priesthood consist only in that?

---

56. See Woodall, *Kingdom*, 186–93.
57. Motyer, *Bible Speaks Today*, 199.
58. H. R. Jones, "Exodus," in Guthrie and Motyer, *New Bible Commentary*, 131.

Well, yes and no. Certainly, if there was no more benefit than merely to be in God's presence, then surely that would suffice. But is it really conceivable that anyone could possibly find themselves before the presence of the Almighty and only stand there? Granted, the immediate sense of awe would probably render any other thought, idea, expression, emotion, or response temporarily obsolete. Without any concrete biblical evidence to support the theory, I imagine Adam's first moment of awareness of his Creator would have been quite similar. But as we, like he, begin to feel progressively more comfortable in God's presence, as awe gives way to wonder, wonder yields to worship, and worship succumbs to praise, we must surely then begin to consider how we might best serve this personal object of our devotion.

But what kind of service (or ministry, if you prefer) can be identified with the function of the saints in the age to come? Indeed, is it even appropriate to speak of post-resurrection sainthood in terms also of servanthood? John's apocalyptic vision of the song of the twenty-four elders suggests as much: "with your blood you purchased men for God from every tribe and language and people and nation. You have made them to be a kingdom and priests to serve our God, and they will reign on the earth" (Rev 5:9b–10). Of course, the argument may be made that, although the apostle is here given a glimpse of eternity, the phrase relating to the redeemed might apply only to their temporal status. And it would be a plausible one were it not for the present continuous tense of the word "be," which gives it the meaning "to be being." Admittedly, the word "serve" does not appear in the original and the KJV is correct on these grounds to omit it. But it is strongly implied by "priesthood" (Greek *hierateuma*), of which Vine reminds us consists in "offering spiritual sacrifices" (see 1 Pet 2:5) and "with the royal dignity of shewing forth the Lord's excellencies" (v. 9).[59]

Whenever I have broached the subject of post-resurrection Christian service, either publically or privately, I have tended to find general agreement regarding the principle, but—somewhat disturbingly, perhaps—a distinct lack of clear biblical basis for such a preposition. This, coupled with a similarly deficient clarity concerning the practical outworking of the concept suggests not so much a *mis*understanding as a belief utterly devoid of understanding. Maybe it's time to set the record straight.

As identified earlier, much of the information we have relating to the eschatological age is to be found in the final book of the Bible, John's Revelation. Tip-toeing through the minefield of composite symbolism to be found there can be as hazardous as instructive, especially if we do so with denominational sandals or the latest-fad spectacles about our person. Even

---

59. See Vine, *Expository Dictionary*, 884.

if this is not the case, there is admittedly little to inform us about how we might occupy the ceaseless moments of eternity. However, I do think there are sufficient clues both here and elsewhere.

The first such hint is easily missed. It is to be found in the twelfth verse of Revelation 22. Here's how some versions translate it:

> Behold, I am coming soon! My reward is with me, and I will give to everyone according to what he has done.[60]

> And, behold, I come quickly; and my reward is with me, to give every man according as his work shall be.[61]

> Behold, I am coming quickly, and My reward is with Me, to render to every man according to what he has done.[62]

> Behold, I am coming soon, bringing my recompense, to repay every one for what he has done.[63]

> Behold, I am coming soon, and I shall bring My wages and rewards with Me, to repay and render to each one just what his own actions and his own work merit.[64]

Not unusually, in my opinion, Eugene Peterson's Message serves only to compound any obscurity there might be:

> Yes, I'm on my way! I'll be there soon! I'm bringing my payroll with me. I'll pay all people in full for their life's work.

Indeed, of those English versions currently available to me, the New Living Translation, the New Century Version, the Good News Bible, the Holman Christian Standard Bible, and even Mounce's Reverse Interlinear New Testament could all be added to the list of those that fail to do justice to the original text. Only Darby—on this occasion, at least—follows the King James Version in reflecting something of the original by suggesting that the reward is as much related to works still to be done as it is to those already completed. Perhaps the use of the Greek *misthos* (translated "reward") is responsible for this overtly one-sided view. It is, after all, most commonly

---

60. New International Version.
61. King James Version.
62. New American Standard Bible.
63. Revised Standard Version.
64. Amplified Bible.

employed in connection with the paying of due wages to a hired hand.[65] However, a literal translation of the qualifying clause is more accurately: "to render to each man as the work is of him." A little vague, I know, but the possibility of future tasks in the age to come should not be ruled out solely on the basis of such ambiguity.

But is there nothing more substantial than this upon which to base such a theory? Well, yes there is, actually. Let us briefly consider two of Jesus' complementary parables of the kingdom, those of the talents (Matt 25:14–30) and the ten minas (Luke 19:11–27) respectively. Though some commentators argue that they may relate to the same incident, their dissimilarities make this difficult to maintain. In both, however, the climactic build-up to the judgment of the "wicked/lazy servant" (Matt 25:26; Luke 19:22) should not be allowed to divert our attention from the Master's appraisal of the faithful servants. Neither should the warning attached to the former's impiety detract from the lessons to be learned from the latter's integrity.

Although the finer details of each of these parables differ, the theme they present is a constant one: the acknowledgment, adherence to, and administration of responsibility in the here and now will be rewarded in the there and then. At face value, this seems to comply with the arguments of those who translate Revelation 22:12 exclusively in terms of the reward being associated with faithfulness for past deeds. But integral to that reward is the opportunity to further express those traits that earned it in the first instance in the context of eternity: "Well done . . . faithful servant . . . take charge . . . " (see Matt 25:21, 23; Luke 19:17, 19). In each case, the reward is pronounced in the present imperative, the sense of which is: "have and keep on having the authority your faithfulness has merited."

And so, we see that stewardship and servanthood are closely linked. Moreover, proven reliability effects increased responsibility. How must this relate to the age to come? Well, disciples still follow, worshippers persist in their worship, rulers carry on ruling, and servants continue to serve. In the words of William Hendriksen: "Though, in the light of their meaning for eternity, our responsibilities here and now are very important, they will be surpassed by those in the life hereafter."[66]

Thus, as we are to relate to both the throne of God and the temple of God, we will find that the tent of God is to be our covering (Rev 7:14–15). This is a beautiful picture of our role, drawn from the Old Testament imagery of the priestly ministry. For natural Israel, that was but a shadow of the

---

65. See Vine, *Expository Dictionary*, 966, 1205.
66. Hendriksen, *Matthew*, 885.

reality that is to come, where countless multitudes will engage in worshipful service, ministering in praise and prayer before the King of kings on his throne, the Great High Priest in his temple (5:8–14; 15:1–4; 19:1–8). However, he is also the True Prophet, and our acts of worship are not to be restricted to the inner courts, but we are similarly to serve him "in the city" (22:3). As citizens of that city, members of the redeemed community, and administrators of his rule, it is the Lord's servants who will exercise his government in the age to come (see Heb 2:5).

The wonderful union of Groom and bride, Head and body, is not to be the end of the adventure; it is merely the beginning. The wedding supper of the Lamb must finally make way for the marriage to begin, for intimacy and understanding to be developed, for mysteries to be unveiled, for saints to take charge of cities with no hindrance to spoil, no obstacle to mar, and that for all of eternity.

Preparation Begins in this Life

Much of the New Testament is concerned with equipping the saints for eternity, whether that be in Christ's teaching as recorded for us in the gospel accounts, Paul's apostolic instruction to those first-century churches, or the other general epistles. Phrases like "laying up treasure" and "running the race" are commonly known (and, it would seem, almost as frequently misunderstood). In terms of how "kingdom now" might be seen as an ideal preparation for "kingdom then" we can surely do no better than to look at the life of Jesus and seek to replicate the principles he adhered to. Thus, we will now turn our attention to consider Christ's perseverance, his obedience, and his commitment.

Christ's Perseverance

One of the tenets of Calvinism is the perseverance of the saints. It forms the last letter of the T-U-L-I-P acronym. It is also a much-maligned dogma by those who are not of a Calvinistic persuasion, sometimes without even daring to consider the biblical evidence or the implications of its denial. Wayne Grudem rather helpfully defines perseverance of the saints as the doctrine whereby "all those who are truly born again will be kept by God's power and will persevere as Christians until the end of their lives, and that only those who persevere until the end have been truly born again."[67] Put this way, I'm not sure what it is that detractors find so objectionable.

Of the words offered as reliable synonyms, "endurance" would sit most comfortably, though perhaps "determination" would not, as this might imply dogged confidence in one's self-will rather than dependence upon the power of God to sustain. And, I suspect, herein lies the hub of discontentment among those who are opposed to the doctrine, often vehemently so. But I have yet to encounter anyone who supports the doctrine to understand it in terms other than that such perseverance is only possible in view of a consistent appropriation of God's power. To be even more specific, believers persevere (or endure) by precisely the same means that they come to rest: "in Christ."

Consider Jesus' words: "My sheep listen to my voice; I know them and they follow me. I give them eternal life, and they shall never perish; no one can snatch them out of my hand" (John 10:27–28). First of all, note that he said: "I give them life" (present continuous, again), not "I will give them eternal life if they prove themselves ultimately worthy." The Galatian believers seemed to have understood it thus and swiftly received an apostolic rebuke as those who had thereby "fallen away from grace" (Gal 5:4).

Most significantly, however, is the phrase "they shall never perish." In the context of the topic before us, we might paraphrase: "they shall persevere/endure." As if to reinforce the emphatic construct of his words, Jesus adds: "no one can snatch them out of my hand." Now, I cannot recall hearing any expositor that I have heard over the course of the past thirty-odd years, preach in any vein other than to imply that the "no one" refers specifically to the devil. But I struggle to understand—if this is the case—why Jesus allowed for such ambiguity, when he could easily have uttered the arguably less enigmatic: "the devil cannot snatch them out of my hand." Could it be that "no one" actually means no one, including the individual him/herself? It would certainly be difficult to argue otherwise from the text.

Moreover, not only is it the case that the saints persevere inasmuch and insofar that they remain in Christ, nor even that such endurance is guaranteed by the promise of Christ's words, but that the assurance of our resolve rests in Christ's own perseverance to the end. That notwithstanding, there are also lessons we can learn by observing some of the traits that characterized those episodes where others less steadfast might have capitulated.

In many ways, Jesus' whole life was one ceaseless catalogue of events wherein he was required to demonstrate his perseverance. The failure of his own people to recognize who he was, the fickle behavior of his disciples,

---

67. Grudem, *Systematic Theology*, 788.

often governed—as it was—by how popular he seemed to be at any given time, the frenzied doggedness of the religious leaders to have him executed as a blasphemer, and the apparent futility of the coming cross all called for a steely determination to persevere. Another word that immediately springs to mind is "patience." Interestingly, alternative renderings of the Greek verb *hupomeno* include "to abide under" and "to bear up courageously."[68]

Perseverance denotes a responsive action. One endures in the face of personal hostility or circumstantial opposition. Rather helpfully, William Hendriksen lists the following examples where Paul cites such occasions on the part of Christ and/or his disciples:

> Rom 5:3–4: endurance in the midst of tribulation;
>
> Rom 15:4–5: endurance in the midst of reproach (cf. verse 3);
>
> 2 Cor 1:6: endurance in the midst of suffering;
>
> 2 Cor 6:4: endurance in the midst of affliction;
>
> 2 Cor 12:12: endurance in the midst of persecution, distress;
>
> 2 Thess 1:4: endurance in the midst of persecution;
>
> 1 Tim 6:11: endurance in the midst of "the good fight of faith" (see verse 12);
>
> 2 Tim 3:10: endurance in the midst of persecution, suffering (see verse 11).[69]

Christ's Obedience

How often we fool ourselves into believing that we are being obedient simply because we follow through on a given command when, in truth, to do so complies with our own wishes anyway! We also have a tendency to willfully misinterpret instructions to fit in with our own agenda. My sister loves to tell the tale of an incident that happened when we were both pre-school age. As a family, we had been out one early Friday evening to do our weekly shopping. On returning home, Kathryn and I were enlisted to help store the smaller items in their appropriate place in the kitchen. As the last of the bags was emptied, all that remained was a packet of famous brand chocolate digestive biscuits (or cookies, for our American readers). Almost fifty

---

68. Vine, *Expository Dictionary*, 359.
69. Hendriksen, *1 & 2 Thessalonians*, 198.

years on, I can still hear my mother's words: "Here, please put these away in the pantry; you know where they go." There was no reason for my sister to accompany me. I was quite capable of following this request on my own, thank you very much. But accompany me she did. We were well aware of where they were supposed to go and, boy, did we put them away: every last crumb. Of course, that was not what my mother had meant at all, and we both knew it.

But sometimes, even when we pat ourselves on the back for getting it right as per instruction, there is seldom an element of personal sacrifice involved. However, the test of how obedient we really are surely arrives when we are asked to do something (or not, as the case may be) that would otherwise be furthest from our minds. Are there any biblical examples from which we might learn? Well, think of Noah, for whom the immediate reward of his obedience seemed to be only ridicule and scorn from his peers. Consider Abraham who, having received the promised son, was asked to demonstrate whether the gift had replaced the Giver in his affections. Or what about Moses? Arguably the most potent testimony in Scripture concerning the mighty deliverer was that: "He chose to be ill-treated along with the people of God rather than to enjoy the pleasures of sin for a short time. He regarded disgrace for the sake of Christ as of greater value than the treasures of Egypt, because he was looking ahead to his reward" (Heb 11:25–26).

But what of Christ's obedience? What! That same Christ Jesus:

> Who, being in very nature God, did not consider equality with God something to be grasped, but made himself nothing, taking the very nature of a servant, being made in human likeness. And being found in appearance as a man, he humbled himself and became obedient to death—even death on a cross![70]

In connection with the gospel account of James and John desiring to be seated at either side of Jesus in his glory (Mark 10:35–45), many commentators focus on their untrained hearts being full of pride. Jesus' reply, however, unveils something of strategic importance. First of all, he asks them: "Can you drink the cup I drink or be baptized with the baptism I am baptized with?" (v. 38). On affirming that they can, Jesus goes on to say: "to sit at my right or left is not for me to grant. These places belong to those for whom they have been prepared" (v. 40). This teaches us two significant truths: our function (not our place) in eternity is determined by our faithfulness in the present; and no one will know what that is until after this age has passed.

---

70. Phil 2:6–8.

The "cup" Jesus drank and the "baptism" with which he was baptized refer primarily to his sufferings and death in obedience to the Father's will. When he "drank the cup" in the garden of Gethsemane, he effectively laid down his life, thereby accepting fully the will of God inwardly. His baptism by John in the Jordan was, of course, the pivotal declaration of his outward submission to that same will of God. Only such perfect obedience could bring its reward of his subsequent exaltation. In other words, it was because Jesus "became obedient to death—even death on a cross . . . [that] . . . God exalted him to the highest place and gave him the name that is above every name." Gordon Fee has this to say:

> The obedience that characterized his entire human life found its expression in [Jesus'] *death on a cross*. The emphasis on *obedient to death* points to his readiness, as one of us, to choose the path that led to a death "destined for our glory before time began" (1 Cor 2:7). Which is quite in keeping with him who, as God, impoverished himself by taking on the role of a slave.[71]

Christ's Commitment

"Commitment" is another of those words that is often subject to abuse or misrepresentation. Many husbands and wives claim to be committed to their marriage until a younger, richer, healthier, more bronzed alternative begins to pay them some attention. Businessmen galore wax lyrical about being committed to their latest venture when the forecast promises much in their favor, but are swift to retract their comments when there is a sharp downturn in the market economy. In the U.K., the number of sports fans pledging their commitment to the support of Chelsea Football Club has increased dramatically since a certain Russian oligarch took ownership and showed that he has the resources to pay millions in transfer fees and players' salaries.

A dictionary definition of the word "commitment" is "an engagement or obligation that restricts freedom of action"; to "pledge, involve, or bind (oneself) to a certain course or policy." This being so, to speak of wholehearted commitment is something of a tautology, as any engagement that is less than wholehearted can hardly be described as commitment at all. As the time of Jesus' pending death drew ever nearer, it is recorded of him that he: "resolutely set out for Jerusalem" (Luke 9:51). The Greek word used

---

71. Fee, *Philippians*, 97.

here is *sterizo*, which means to fix or establish with no conceivable room for maneuver or negotiation.[72]

If commitment can be graded at all, then this was the measure of Christ's commitment. He was fully determined to fulfill the task appointed to him, whatever the cost. In a prophetic context, Isaiah predicted this centuries before it unfolded in reality:

> The Sovereign Lord has given me an instructed tongue,
>   to know the word that sustains the weary.
> He wakens me morning by morning,
>   wakens my ear to listen like one being taught.
> The Sovereign Lord has opened my ears,
>   and I have not been rebellious;
> I have not drawn back.
> I offered my back to those who beat me,
>   my cheeks to those who pulled out my beard;
> I did not hide my face from mocking and spitting.
> Because the Sovereign Lord helps me,
>   I will not be disgraced.
> Therefore have I set my face like flint,
>   and I know I will not be put to shame.[73]

I trust I will not be guilty of reading too much into the text when I infer that to set one's face as flint toward one thing includes expressing that same steely determination against all other potential distractions, even those that may appear to be creditworthy on the surface. For Jesus at this time, his options were reduced to one: it was Jerusalem only. There was no: "I'll just carry on here for a while, healing the sick and preaching to the spiritually hungry. After all, they seem so receptive just now. Perhaps I got it wrong. Maybe the Father said, 'Endure here a while, Son.'"

People of purpose don't look for ships sailing in the opposite direction and then try to spiritualize the fact that there just happens to be one spare ticket left (Jonah 1:1–3); they follow through on their commitment. Moreover, it is insufficient to merely "break the tape"; we must have raced "according to the rules" (see 2 Tim 2:5). These are not ritualistic observances initiated by man, but righteous principles instituted by God to help us in our journey toward maturity. Paul puts it this way: "run in such a way as to get the prize" (1 Cor 9:24). Sadly, much of what passes for modern Christianity seems to be little more than a purposeless meandering through life in the vain hope that we can somehow skip past the enemy's minefield toward

---

72. See Vine, *Expository Dictionary*, 371, 1024.
73. Isa 50:4–7.

eternity. No ground is won because no clear objectives are set and, therefore, no strategy is devised to enable us to achieve any goal. The biblical concept of running the race, however, calls for true commitment (vv. 25–27), tangible aspirations (Phil 3:13–14) and, above all else, a faith that is resolute against all that would seek to undermine it (Col 2:16–19).

Although I have separated these three traits in Christ, it must be conceded that they can only be treated thus for the purpose of meaningful analysis. In so doing, the relationship between them must not be dismissed or ignored. Jesus' obedience to the Father's will was inextricably linked to his commitment toward that will which, in turn, caused him to persevere in the pursuit of that will regardless of the cost. May the lessons afforded not be lost on us.

Summary

The incarnation of Jesus was the historic focal point that unleashed the kingdom age upon society, for it is "in these last days [that God] has spoken to us by his Son" (Heb 1:2). In other words, we are they upon "whom the fulfillment of the ages has come" (1 Cor 10:11). It must be duly noted, however, that the doctrine of any given subject should not be regarded as only the conveyance of theological information without practical application. So, too, with eschatology, we do well to avoid merely an intellectual grasp of what we may expect to unfold in the future, for its hope is always demonstrated biblically as being relevant to Christian life in the present. Thus, any anticipation of Christ's coming must promote vigilance in the here and now, a desire to be found pure then should provoke the pursuit of righteousness in the meantime, and a longing to be presented perfect before the Father will prevent dabbling in wickedness before the world's gaze.

SUMMARY

John's apocalyptic vision suggests that heaven will be filled with Christians of a certain kind (Rev 12:11). They will be overcomers, but not those who have done so by singing "we shall overcome" endlessly in the hope that such repetition will bore their enemies into surrender, nor those who have overcome by identifying isolated Scripture verses that might give the impression of justifying their unrighteous conduct when taken out of context. Neither do they overcome by feeding their habitual appetite for grand living, celebrity-style recognition, or their disciples' plaudits being directed toward their diamond-encrusted Perspex pulpits. They overcome by the blood of the Lamb. Oh, for an end to bloodless sermons on the lips of those who claim to have overcome by any other means! A bloodless Christianity is a crossless Christianity and a crossless Christianity is a Christless Christianity. Remove Christ from Christianity and all that remains is just another religion devoid of power both to effect change in the human condition and to transform lives.

Whatever the mechanics may be concerning the similarity between the present creation and the one that is to come, their points of contrast are even more striking. The world in which we live is subject to decay, tainted by sin, and temporal; the realm we anticipate is perfect, beyond the influence of corruption, and eternal. In these facts alone there is surely ample incentive to conduct ourselves now in such a way as to "store up for [ourselves] treasures in heaven," if that truly is where our passions lie (see Matt 6:19–21). The benefits of the atonement in their fullest measure still await us. In some ways, both the identity and extent of many of them remains a mystery until that time. The kingdom is, indeed, coming. But it has already broken in upon us and so, too, the blessings associated with it.

Whilst I do not condone the attitude of those who perceive of the consummation of this age as some final salvage attempt from heaven to rescue believers from the mess they find themselves in, there is surely some comfort in Jesus' promise that he will return. To the individual, struggling to make sense of the horrors of the age, Jesus says: "I am coming soon." To those churches that find it ever more difficult to remain true to their convictions of righteous conduct, when others seem blatantly to disregard their behavioral responsibilities, Jesus says: "I am coming soon." To those who have reduced the name of the Son to little more than an expression of anger and frustration, who have denied his existence as nothing other than the fabrication of the inept and unstable, and who have sought to substitute the one true God with gods of their own making, Jesus says: "I am coming soon."

"Amen. Come, Lord Jesus."

Conclusion

The proposed aim of this work has been to present the biblical evidence as it relates to the atonement as being necessary to effect reconciliation between God and man, as being real in that its conditions were fully met in the only way possible, and being beneficial to those for whom the privileges were both intended and divinely appointed. On this basis, it has been crucial to keep the following objectives in mind:

i) to determine from Scripture precisely why the atonement became so necessary and what the potential implications of that necessity might be;

ii) to arrive at a greater understanding concerning the reality of the atonement having taken place as a matter of historical fact; and

iii) to examine the full extent of the benefits of the atonement for those who are prepared to avail themselves of the opportunity to receive them.

In chapter 1, we looked at the rise and fall of the human race in Adam. Effectively, everything we can know biblically about the creation is contained in just a few early chapters of the book of Genesis. We cannot be certain of how long ago it is since this took place. Despite the alleged conclusiveness of their techniques and apparatus, scientists are not agreed on when they think the earth began. Similarly, there is no definitive consensus amongst Christians as to how they might interpret the frankly scant evidence that Scripture affords regarding when our first parents roamed the earth. What we may say on the basis of that evidence is that their introduction was timed to coincide with an environment that flawlessly matched their requirements. Moreover, Adam and Eve were impeccably suited to the conditions in which they found themselves.

How swiftly did that first pair become dissatisfied with perfection! Not only does their act of rebellion defy description, but it also challenges our comprehension. And yet, the lessons to be learned are many and striking. Was the pursuit of autonomy a reaching out on the part of Adam to more fully express his humanity? If so, it was both misguided and ill-placed. The only way to be truly human is to embrace the fact that we are incomplete without a recognition of our innate need for the divine. Moreover, the delusion of adequacy outside of God is guaranteed to end in failure, whereas the perception of one's own shortcomings can lead only to those expectations being exceeded.

If there was a Venn diagram showing the entire human race and those of it who were without sin, only one name would occupy the common sector: Jesus. This is not just a statement of fact, but it is necessarily so, as we discovered in chapter 2. Having established that necessity, the reality of the atonement can never be separated from that which precipitated it. But neither should our previous condition in Adam dominate the focus of our attention and effectively, thereby, rob us of the joy of our salvation. It was not so that we should remain bound that Christ has made provision for believers to be free, but for freedom (Gal 5:1).

Such freedom is not a license to indulge the sinful nature, but to conduct ourselves within the parameters of godly behavior. True freedom can only be found where it is governed by righteousness. A friend of mine recently divorced when his wife (also a good friend) exercised her right to cite him on the grounds of his infidelity. Since the decree absolute came through, both parties are now legally free to remarry, if they so desire. As Christians, however, that freedom does not consist in the capacity to do entirely as they please; there are restrictions. Or, at least, if either or both of them implement the freedom that the law allows to the full extent beyond the confines of a pure conscience, then there will be consequences that may prove irrevocable. Biblical freedom has limits, though they are designed for our ultimate benefit.

Whilst it is true that much of chapter 3 dealt with the blessings of the atonement from a predominantly eschatological perspective, it must be understood that this is not exclusively so. Perhaps there has been a tendency for Christians to so concern ourselves with the qualitative nature of eternal life that we almost ignore that to which it is attached: life. Jesus came because it was necessary for him to do so, he lived in accordance with the demands of the law because only he could, he died that we might be rid of the burden and penalty of sin, he rose again for our justification, and he will come again so that we might be with him for ever. All weighty doctrines expressing valid truths. But see how Jesus himself spoke of the purpose of his ministry: "I have come that [you] may have life, and have it to the full" (John 10:10). Other translations refer to this life—to which we now have access—as being one of abundance (e.g., NASB, KJV). It is a life of exceeding measure, one that places Christians at a distinct advantage when compared to those who choose not to access such riches. It is life enjoyed fully, as originally intended.

But we must be careful not to imagine that such life is dependent upon material affluence for its gratification. Rather, it is a life that has learned the secret of contentment (Phil 4:12) and can follow the ethos of the advice Paul gave to Timothy: "Command those who are rich in this present world not to be arrogant nor to put their hope in wealth, which is so uncertain, but to put their hope in God, who richly provides us with everything for our enjoyment . . . [thus] lay[ing] up treasure for themselves as a firm foundation for the coming age, so that they may take hold of life that is truly life" (1 Tim 6:17–19).

Having to consider the eternal benefits of our salvation has been a fitting topic upon which to end our discussion of the atonement. That it follows naturally from the reality of the atonement is as awesome as it is obvious. The correlation that exists between the fact of the atonement and the fall that necessitated it leaves us similarly overwhelmed at God's provision and providence. But we must be careful how far we extend this lest we find ourselves sailing too close to the stormy waters of the supra-/infralapsarian debate. In the context of restoration, however, is there anything more certain than that the blessings that await the redeemed are at least equal (if not superior) to the original intention in God's heart for the pinnacle of his creation?

Bibliography

Addison, James T. *Life Beyond Death in the Beliefs of Mankind*. Boston: Houghton Mifflin, 1932.
Alford, Henry. *The New Testament for English Readers*. Chicago: Moody, 1960.
Bancroft, Emery H. *Christian Theology (Systematic and Biblical)*. Grand Rapids: Zondervan, 1970.
Banks, Robert J., ed. *Reconciliation and Hope*. Exeter, UK: Paternoster, 1974.
Barth, Karl. *Church Dogmatics, IV.1: The Doctrine of Reconciliation*. London: T. & T. Clark, 1957.
Bavinck, Herman. *The Doctrine of God*. Translated by William Hendriksen. Grand Rapids: Eerdmans, 1955.
Berkhof, Louis. *The History of Christian Doctrines*. Edinburgh: Banner of Truth, 1997.
———. *Systematic Theology*. Edinburgh: Banner of Truth, 1973.
Bonhoeffer, Dietrich. *Creation and Temptation: A Theological Exposition of Genesis 1–3*. Translated by John C. Fletcher. London: SCM, 1966.
Brown, Colin, ed. *Dictionary of New Testament Theology*. 4 vols. Carlisle, UK: Paternoster, 1986.
Bruce, Frederick F. *The Epistle to the Hebrews*. Grand Rapids: Eerdmans, 1964.
Brunner, Emil. *Man in Revolt: A Christian Anthropology*. Translated by Olive Wyon. London: Lutterworth, 1957.
———. *The Mediator: A Study of the Central Doctrine of the Christian Faith*. Translated by Olive Wyon. London: Lutterworth, 1952.
Butler, Basil C. *An Approach to Christianity*. London: Fount, 1981.
Calvin, John. *Geneva Series of Commentaries: Genesis*. Translated by John King. Edinburgh: Banner of Truth, 1992.
———. *Institutes of the Christian Religion*. Translated by Henry Beveridge. Grand Rapids: Eerdmans, 1970.
Clendenin, Daniel B., ed. *Eastern Orthodox Theology: A Contemporary Reader*. Grand Rapids: Baker Academic, 2003.
Dabney, Robert L. *Systematic Theology*. Edinburgh: Banner of Truth, 1985.
Davies, Eryl. *The Wrath of God*. Bridgend, UK: Evangelical Press of Wales, 1984.
Denney, James. *The Christian Doctrine of Reconciliation*. London: Hodder & Stoughton, 1917.
Dodd, C. H. *The Epistle of Paul to the Romans*. London: Hodder & Stoughton, 1942.
Douglas, J. D., ed. *New Bible Dictionary*. Leicester, UK: InterVarsity, 1992.

Fee, Gordon D. *New Testament Commentary Series: Philippians*. Leicester, UK: InterVarsity, 1999.
Ferguson, Sinclair, B., and David F. Wright, eds. *New Dictionary of Theology*. Leicester, UK: InterVarsity, 1993.
Finney, Charles G. *Lectures on Systematic Theology*. South Gate, CA: Colporter Kemp, 1944.
Geldenhuys, J. Norval. *Commentary on the Gospel of Luke*. Grand Rapids: Eerdmans, 1951.
Goulburn, Edward Meyrick. *Everlasting Punishment*. London: Rivington, 1881.
Grudem, Wayne A. *Systematic Theology: An Introduction to Biblical Doctrine*. Leicester, UK: InterVarsity, 1994.
Guthrie, Donald, and J. Alec Motyer, eds. *New Bible Commentary*. 3rd ed. Leicester, UK: InterVarsity, 1992.
Hammond, Thomas C. *In Understanding Be Men: A Handbook of Christian Doctrine*. Leicester, UK: InterVarsity, 1968.
Hanegraaff, Hank. *Resurrection: The Capstone in the Arch of Christianity*. Nashville: Thomas Nelson, 2000.
Hanson, Anthony Tyrrell. *The Wrath of the Lamb*. London: SPCK, 1959.
Harris, Murray J. *From Grave to Glory: Resurrection in the New Testament*. Grand Rapids: Zondervan, 1990.
Hendriksen, William. *More Than Conquerors: An Interpretation of the Book of Revelation*. Grand Rapids: Baker, 1998.
———. *New Testament Commentary: Ephesians*. Edinburgh: Banner of Truth, 1990.
———. *New Testament Commentary: 1 & 2 Thessalonians*. Edinburgh: Banner of Truth, 1991.
———. *New Testament Commentary: Galatians*. Edinburgh: Banner of Truth, 1979.
———. *New Testament Commentary: Matthew*. Edinburgh: Banner of Truth, 1989.
———. *New Testament Commentary: Romans*. Edinburgh: Banner of Truth, 1980.
Henry, Carl F. H., ed. *Basic Christian Doctrines*. Grand Rapids: Baker, 1979.
Hodge, Archibald Alexander. *The Atonement*. Darlington, UK: Evangelical, 1974.
———. *Outlines of Theology*. Edinburgh: Banner of Truth, 1972.
Kendall, R. T. *Once Saved, Always Saved*. London: Hodder & Stoughton, 1984.
Ladd, George Eldon. *A Commentary on the Revelation of John*. Grand Rapids: Eerdmans, 1972.
———. *I Believe in the Resurrection of Jesus*. London: Hodder & Stoughton, 1987.
Lidgett, John S. *The Spiritual Principle of the Atonement: As a Satisfaction Made to God for the Sins of the World*. London: C. H. Kelly, 1898.
Livingstone, E. A. "Original Righteousness." In *The Concise Oxford Dictionary of the Christian Church*. N.p. 2000. Online: http:www.encyclopedia.com/doc/1095-OriginalRighteousness.html.
Lloyd-Jones, D. Martyn. *Ephesians 2:1–22: God's Way of Reconciliation*. Edinburgh: Banner of Truth, 1981.
———. *Joy Unspeakable*. Eastbourne, UK: Kingsway, 1984.
———. *Romans 3:20—4:25: Atonement and Justification*. London: Banner of Truth, 1978.
———. *Romans 8:17–39: The Perseverance of the Saints*. Edinburgh: Banner of Truth, 1998.

Luther, Martin. *A Commentary on St. Paul's Epistle to the Galatians.* Grand Rapids: Baker, 1979.

———. *Works 37: Word and Sacrament III.* Philadelphia: Fortress, 1989.

MacLeod, George F. *The Whole Earth Shall Cry Glory.* Argyll, UK: Wild Goose, 1985.

Morris, Leon L. *The Cross in the New Testament.* Carlisle, UK: Paternoster, 1965.

Motyer, J. Alec. *The Bible Speaks Today: The Message of Exodus.* Leicester, UK: InterVarsity, 2005.

Moule, Charles F. D. *The Phenomenon of the New Testament: An Inquiry into the Implications of Certain Features of the New Testament.* London: SCM, 1967.

Osborne, Grant R. *New Testament Commentary Series: Romans.* Leicester, UK: InterVarsity, 2004.

Packer, James I. *Celebrating the Saving Work of God.* Vol. 1 of *Collected Shorter Writings of J. I. Packer.* Carlisle, UK: Paternoster, 2000.

———. *Concise Theology.* Leicester, UK: InterVarsity, 1993.

Pannenberg, Wolfhart. *What is Man?* Translated by Duane A. Priebe. Philadelphia: Fortress, 1977.

Penn-Lewis, Jessie. *The Warfare with Satan.* London: Marshall, 1908.

Pink, Arthur W. *Divine Covenants.* Grand Rapids: Baker, 1973.

Robertson, O. Palmer. *The Christ of the Covenants.* Phillipsburg, NJ: Presbyterian & Reformed, 1980.

Schleiermacher, Friedrich D. E. *The Christian Faith.* Translated by Donald Macpherson Baillie. London: Harper & Row, 1963.

Smith, David. *The Atonement in the Light of History and the Modern Spirit.* London: Hodder & Stoughton, 1919.

Smith, Ronald G. *The Doctrine of God.* London: Collins, 1970.

Sproul, R. C. *Chosen by God.* Wheaton, IL: Tyndale, 1994.

Stedman, Ray C. *New Testament Commentary Series: Hebrews.* Leicester, UK: InterVarsity, 1992.

Stott, John R. W. *The Cross of Christ.* Leicester, UK: InterVarsity, 2006.

Strong, Augustus H. *Systematic Theology.* London: Pickering & Inglis, 1970.

Tasker, Randolph V. G. *The Biblical Doctrine of the Wrath of God.* Lowestoft, UK: Tyndale, 1951.

Taylor, Vincent. *The Atonement in New Testament Teaching.* London: Epworth, 1958.

Turner, Henry E. W. *Jesus, the Christ.* London: Mowbray, 1976.

Vine, William E. *Expository Dictionary of New Testament Words.* Iowa Falls, IA: Riverside, 1975.

Wagner, C. Peter. *Confronting the Powers.* Ventura, CA: Regal, 1996.

Watson, David. *In Search of God.* Eastbourne, UK: Kingsway, 1985.

Woodall, Chris. *Covenant: The Basis of God's Self-Disclosure.* Eugene, OR: Wipf & Stock, 2011.

———. *Kingdom: The Expression of God's Rule.* Eugene, OR: Wipf & Stock, 2012.

www.ingramcontent.com/pod-product-compliance
Lightning Source LLC
Chambersburg PA
CBHW070321230426
43663CB00011B/2185